ADOLESCENTS AND PARENTAL DIVORCE

Helping Teens Thrive When Families Divide

JOANNE E. CARLSON, MSW
Author, *The Parent Effect*

Edited by Kimberly Lausten
Layout by Kathryn Galán, Wynnpix Productions
Cover by Pixel Studios
Cover photo by Istock
Independently Published

Print ISBN: 978-0-5783 5917-5
Ebook ISBN: 978-0-5783 5918 2
Library of Congress Control Number: 2022900803

Disclaimer: This publication is designed to provide up-to-date and accurate information on the impact of divorce. It is not intended as a substitute for psychological or legal advice from a licensed professional. Families struggling with the issues related to divorce are encouraged to seek the help of a licensed psychotherapist or family law attorney. Case examples throughout this publication are based on actual clients or stories from social conversations. Many examples are composites of client experiences. All identifying information has been altered to protect the privacy of these individuals and families.

For Pat

My husband, my friend
There are soulmates in this world
and you are mine

Contents

Introduction

Divorce and remarriage have become commonplace in America. There is no longer a stigma associated with these decisions, though stories of ongoing custody battles between celebrity couples can still make the news. Despite societal acceptance, divorce is often challenging and transformative for all involved. Children in the family are inexorably brought into the process and experience a wide range of emotional and behavioral responses. In addressing the issues children face, many books, articles, and websites lump all ages together, though children and teenagers process parental divorce and remarriage differently. Adolescence is a distinct developmental stage and, as such, deserves to be addressed in depth.

The changes of adolescence allow teens to be intellectually aware of the issues inherent in the divorce process but this awareness does not protect them from the emotional repercussions. *Adolescents and Parental Divorce* strives to provide a comprehensive, balanced look at parental and teen responses to the life changes divorce brings. It is my hope that this work will give adolescents a voice, provide parents with a better understanding of the impact of divorce, and increase therapists' and other professionals' knowledge about divorce's role in teen emotions and behaviors.

My research into recent scientific studies and my professional experience have shown that while parental divorce can be challenging, teens can adapt and thrive. Short-term reactions are inevitable but can be overcome with time. Long-term effects are typically associated with divorces that are drawn out and conflict laden. Breaking up a family is a decision that should be made with careful thought and emotional sensitivity to the possible responses of all family members. Necessary changes should be made without anger or impulsively. Do not confuse teenage bravado with healthy coping. Divorce changes a family's structure and dynamics, but the love and sense of connection should continue. Ex-spouses are still parents who maintain the responsibility of raising and loving their mutual children.

Adolescents naturally undergo a number of significant cognitive, social, and physical changes. Parental divorce can make the developmental tasks of adolescence more complicated and can even interfere with some of the steps that need to take place. There are shifts in family relationships, economic adjustments, new household rules and responsibilities to adapt to, and possibly a change in school or neighborhood. A parent's divorce alters the way a teen perceives their parent, authority, marriage, and relationships. Many teens lose the ability to venture out into the world with a stable home as a safety net. Others forgo their own developmental needs to take care of their distressed parent. Many assume more responsibility in the home and for younger siblings. Teen reactions may include anger at parents for their perceived failures, changes in academic functioning, and increased vulnerability to peer pressure. Some teens find relief from a conflicted home life. Others find ways to adapt and even to develop their inner strengths.

Most teens ultimately adjust to the changes in their family situation in a healthy manner. However, some effects can be evident into adulthood. These might be seen in peer interactions, conflict styles, and family relationships. Adult children of divorce often experience repercussions in their own intimate relationships, interactions with co-workers, work ethics, and career choices.

Adolescents and Parental Divorce focuses on the emotions and behavior of parents and their adolescents. Chapter one explores the reactions of parents to their separation and divorce. Divorce is not a single event but a series of phases that occur over the course of several years. Its impact is felt by every family member but it is the adult reactions that set the stage. Parental responses offer a powerful guideline for the teen's adjustment.

The inevitable family changes and the possible custodial arrangements are presented in chapter two. Single parents, non-residential parents, and absentee parents create special issues for the emotional well-being of teenagers. Single mothers and fathers face a number of stresses and often have difficulty providing adequate supervision. Non-custodial parents should maintain a connection with their teenagers to optimize a teen's healthy adjustment. Parent-teen relationships can shift during divorce; research has shown that the bond with both parents plays an important role in the emotional well-being of adolescents. Most parents strive to maintain closeness with and provide supervision of their teens even as they struggle with their own reactions.

Parenting style can shift during divorce with the reestablishment of a family system. Some parents become disengaged while others increase their control. Permissive parenting often develops from a parent feeling overwhelmed or needing to have their teen's approval. Parenting styles often readjust once the family stabilizes.

Chapter three explores the various adolescent behavioral and emotional reactions to parental separation. Resilient adolescents may adapt quite well, while others may experience fear, anger, grief, or anxiety. Teen responses may result in academic decline or various forms of acting out. A parent's actions, the stage of the divorce process, and the amount of parental conflict will impact the teen's responses.

Chapter four addresses a number of specific situations that arise when families are dealing with divorce. Interparental conflict, parental alienation, and parentification are all reviewed in depth. Intense arguments and disrespect between adults in the family have widespread impact on everyone's development and emotional health. Interparental conflict has been shown to be the most destructive aspect of divorce.

A parent's remarriage creates another significant life transition for teenagers and is explored in chapter five. Divorce is difficult and life becomes even more complicated when one or both parents remarry or choose to cohabitate. Teens and stepparents rarely transition to a family relationship quickly or easily. For many teenagers, the creation of a stepfamily feels more like a loss rather than a gain. A new stepparent may change the teen's relationship with his or her biological parent. However, functional stepfamilies can be a source of emotional strength. They can re-establish relationships with a parent, provide a model of a happy marriage, and free the teen from feeling responsible for their parents' emotional well-being. Happy stepfamilies are not a myth, just a project that requires awareness, patience, and a sense of humor.

Chapter six focuses on common sense recommendations to help parents and teens adjust to the issues that develop during a divorce. Parents need to be aware that the emotions they express and the actions they take can make the transition easier or more traumatic for their teens. Suggestions are provided to help families cope and even thrive with the many issues that divorce and remarriage creates. Divorce will always be a significant life event but the journey does not have to be quite so difficult. Parents and teens benefit from advice that encourages healthy coping strategies.

Chapter seven explores how divorce during childhood or adolescence directly affects the development of personality characteristics such as attitudes toward love and marriage, conflict styles, and intimacy issues. Adult children of divorce often feel that they carry the lessons and emotions associated with the divorce into their adult life

As a psychotherapist who has worked with adolescents and families for over forty years, I have had the unique opportunity to be privy to the thoughts and feelings of numerous adolescents and parents who are separated, divorced, or remarried. Some of my most poignant and distressing cases involved these families and their struggles. Just the mention of divorce results in memories and stories for so many individuals. Therefore, I decided to share my interest and knowledge in the form of this book.

I have always had a love of research and writing and previously published my first book, *The Parent Effect,* in which I shared my awareness of the various parenting styles that impact adolescent behavior and subsequent adult characteristics. The impact of divorce was a common thread in many cases I encountered during my career. I researched hundreds of journal articles, books, and websites to assure a balanced presentation of the information. Further, my discussions with colleagues and family law attorneys have provided real life information on the impact of divorce.

Many of the stories from my years as a therapist and conversations with friends and neighbors are incorporated in the examples in this book. The examples are meant as illustrations of the information presented and in no way represent any particular family or individual. Their stories and identities have been altered to protect the confidentiality of my previous clients. Many of the examples are composites of clients I worked with over the years. To all of these incredible people who trusted me with their stories, their pain, and their emotional growth, I thank you. To all the families who find help in these pages, my hope is that this book will make a difference in your lives during the complicated experience of divorce.

1.

I Hate You – Don't Leave Me!

Divorce and Adult Reactions

She had learned through passage that transition is a part of life, that it is not an ending, it is a beginning.

—Flavia, ***To Take Away the Hurt***[1]

Love, specifically romantic love, is the emotion that most people credit with their choice to marry or move in together. Other reasons include sexual attraction, fear of loneliness, financial security, desire for a family, or a culturally arranged marriage. Most enter this relationship with hope and a belief in happily ever after. Adding children to this relationship can strengthen the bond and creates an interdependency of individuals in the family unit. The decision to leave is never easy. The associated feelings are numerous and intense. The process by which this uncoupling occurs is called separation or divorce. Separation is usually the initial stage in which couples cease living together as a statement of the unhappiness between the partners. Separation, and in some states legal separation, provides a means by which the couple divides their life collections and move forward independently. Divorce is the legal dissolution of a marriage. Divorce and separation are the emotional, physical, social, and financial ending of a marriage. For the purpose of this work, the terms divorce and separation are applicable to couples that are legally wed, common-law, or living together and are going through the steps to discontinue their relationship. For many of those who once professed to "love one another till death do they part," the experience of divorce becomes more of a Grimm's fairy tale than a Disney happily-ever-after story.

Divorce impacts all members of the family. Divorce is the legal termination of the marriage, but the family continues in altered form. When the children in the family undergoing divorce are teenagers, the issues pertaining to the parents' divorce are entwined in the developmental tasks of adolescence. The teenager's reactions are unique and powerful. To understand the teenager's experience, it is important to be aware of the parents' emotional and behavioral reactions during the process. The parents' actions coupled with the teen's developmental stage become the blueprints for the teen's responses.

Phases of Divorce

Divorce is a process rather than a single action or legal document. The process involves a number of phases that unfold over time. People mistakenly associate the legal time frame with the process of divorce, but the changes and adjustments occur over several years. These phases (as I have conceptualized them) can be defined as Unhappiness, Decision, Implementation, Struggle and Transition, and Adjustment. Each phase will vary in terms of time and emotional stress. Let us briefly explore each of these phases.

Unhappiness

Couples begin their lives together with hope and a willingness to make adjustments for the new relationship. As this work examines the impact on families with teenagers, the assumption is that the marriage functioned reasonably well for a number of years. The early years may well have been ones of satisfaction and connection; the couple built a life and had children together. However, at some point something significant and tangible changed in the relationship. Unhappiness crept in. Key to this stage is the awareness by one or both partners that they are not happy and are seriously considering getting out of the relationship.

Perhaps the change occurred slowly with the couple growing apart. Too often the feeling of unhappiness was minimized or ignored for a number of years. One spouse may have been content in the relationship while the other was slowly becoming dissatisfied. In many homes one partner has been emotionally pulling away but the other partner chose not to acknowledge this reality. Other couples were contentious early on and this conflict became intolerable over the years. Some issues may arise more suddenly, such as the discovery of an affair. In homes in which there were divergent parenting styles, parents may have become more contentious when the developmental changes characteristic of adolescence created additional stress and highlighted the couple's differences.

Awareness of the marital problems and the possibility of divorce may lead to renewed efforts toward improving the relationship. Some couples try marriage counseling. Others may decide to tolerate the unhappiness a little longer for the sake of the children. For many, these efforts do not result in sufficient change or satisfaction to keep the marriage alive.

In homes where there is a considerable amount of conflict, the children, especially adolescents, are increasingly aware and may even be drawn into the fray. When the dissatisfaction is quieter and more hidden, the teen may not be aware of the depth of unhappiness in the marriage. Teenagers typically stay out of their parent's marital problems unless they are directly drawn in or there is a degree of conflict or violence that cannot be ignored.

Decision

Eventually, in an unhappy or dysfunctional relationship one or both partners come to realize that they want out of the marriage. This decision is rarely mutual. This conclusion is almost always made with a considerable amount of thought and anguish. While some decisions are impulsive, perhaps in the case of infidelity, most are a response to years of dissatisfaction. Even with a history of conflict or incapability, most partners are ambivalent about taking the actual steps necessary to dissolve the marriage. Denial, fear, and guilt predominate this phase.

Families with teenagers usually have been together for years and had many satisfying experiences together. Choosing to leave when children are still in the home often indicates that either the decision came after a particularly distressing situation or the parent has rationalized that their teens are able to handle the changes that will take place. Most parents do not wish to make life difficult for their adolescents and they grapple with their decision to divorce. In some cases, the teen has encouraged the separation, especially when the conflict is excessive or if spousal abuse is occurring.

Gail is 37 and has been married for 17 years, with a 12-year-old son and 15-year-old daughter. Her husband, Glen, 42, is a software developer in a high-level position and she is a stay-at-home mom. Gail reports years of discontent as her husband is a workaholic, and is controlling, critical, and emotionally distant with her and their children. Conflicts with their teens were escalating and the atmosphere in the home was becoming intolerable.

Gail came into therapy seeking support for her decision to leave. She stated that her husband's control and lack of emotional connection was becoming unbearable. Gail admitted having wanted to leave for many years and was angry with herself for allowing Glen to be so domineering. She felt resentful toward her spouse for his treatment of her and the children. Understandably, Gail acknowledged being afraid of her husband's reaction to her request for a divorce. As a stay-at-home mother, she also worried about her possible change in lifestyle. Gail was particularly concerned about the effect divorce would have on her children and struggled with guilt over breaking up her family. However, it was her children's expressions of unhappiness that led her to finally consider separating. During the course of treatment, she was able to identify her own insecurities and to gain the strength to ask her husband to move out.

The partner who decides to bring up the topic of divorce may be either ambivalent or resolute in their choice. Often, they rehearse what they will say. Many have developed a litany of grievances that help them justify their decision. Some try to create an atmosphere that appears more conducive to the option of divorce. Allowing an infidelity to be discovered can lead to separation. One mother had accrued a significant amount of family debt and hoped that revealing that information would so anger her husband that he would demand a divorce, making him the initiator.

Some preliminary preparations are usually included in the decision phase. Many adults seek legal advice and start making plans financially. Some search for alternative housing options. Stay-at-home parents may go back to school or look for employment. In discussing her decision, a woman writes the following:

> I started to put things into motion strategically. I faced reality, built up my self-esteem, learned to love myself, put the past behind me, read self-help books, started thinking positive thoughts about my future, walked, exercised, prayed, and took as much me time as I needed to heal. ... When I was strong enough and ready in every aspect, I filed for divorce. (p. 18)[2]

When there is concern about the spouse's reaction becoming violent, preparations for a safe escape may be made. Most adults plan some of their post-separation actions prior to announcing their decision.

Often this decision evolves into a series of discussions between the couple. Many of these conversations become heated. Acceptance of the decision is rarely immediate or straightforward. Accusations of betrayal and pleas for reconciliation are common. While some of these discussions are kept private, it is naive to believe that a teenager in the home does not overhear or pick up on the tension. Parents often avoid sharing the decision with the children until they are ready to make significant steps toward separation. Sharing separation plans with the teen may be a way to prepare the teen for what is coming or to seek the teen's support. Conflict escalation between a parent and teen may be the impetus for a parent's decision. In cases of parental substance abuse or criminal activity, the other spouse may choose to leave for the well-being of the teen. For whatever reason, the decision to dissolve the marriage is one that causes considerable anguish and contemplation for parents.

After the decision has been made, both spouses must act to start the process of separation. At this point, the adolescents become participants in the process. Teens will certainly have opinions about changes taking place in the family. One client informed her 17-year-old son that she was thinking of leaving his alcoholic father after an intense argument over his drinking. The son asked his mother to wait until he finished high school so that he would not have to struggle with custody and visitation issues. Following his graduation, he told his mom to go for it.

Implementation

This phase is probably the most difficult one for all involved. Change begins to occur on all levels. Everyone feels vulnerable. Implementation of the decision means that the issue is no longer kept secret or just another conversation between parents; concrete actions are taken. During this phase, a number of activities take place including consulting attorneys, making decisions about living arrangements, and sharing this information with the children. The order of these actions differs for each family.

Disclosing to a teen that the family is going to undergo a divorce is somewhat different than sharing the information with younger children. Teens will often want an explanation as to why the separation is taking place, even if they don't ask outright. For most adolescents, the salient issues are how it will affect their lives. Teens want to remain in their home, attend their current schools, and be with their friends. Continuing to stay with their friends is of utmost importance to most adolescents. During the initial conversation, the teen should be informed about the decision, which parent is moving out, and what type of contact the teenager will have with the non-residential parent.

As the divorce begins to unfold, other family members may become involved in the process, including grandparents, aunts and uncles, and close family friends. Teens may actively seek information from extended family when they feel that their parents are not being forthcoming. Extended family should ideally function as a support for the family and not rush to judgment or take sides.

The who, when, where, and what of divorce are decisions that should take time and consideration. In *The Good Divorce* (1994), Psychologist C. Ahrons states that, "One key to a good divorce is becoming able to see how decisions made early in the process affect the emotional adjustment of the whole family" (p. 108).[3] The initial choices and actions made by the parents are critical to how well a family manages the divorce process. Once decisions are made, changes can occur immediately, irrationally, or more slowly and deliberately over a period of time. Actions that occur abruptly increase the likelihood that conflict will arise and the transitions will be traumatic.

There may be a disagreement between the adults as to who is leaving the family home and how the financial arrangement will work. In some cases, a judge will decide who stays by issuing a temporary court order. The implementation of the decision should not be impulsive, poorly thought out, or borne out of anger, as this will cause a considerable amount of stress for all family members. Most people will remember the day that one of the parents moved out as it signifies the reality of the family disruption. Over the years, I have heard distressing tales of parents storming out of the house, parents packing up belongings while the child was at school, and even parents suddenly disappearing for extended periods of time. These memories are usually a source of lifelong pain. Some families may function as close to normal as possible while other families walk around on eggshells, avoiding the issues. Boundaries between the couple should be clear and respectful, although this is rarely the case during the implementation phase.

When one parent moves out, teens begin dealing with their parents living in two different locations. In the majority of families, it is the father who moves to an apartment, in with other family members, or even in with friends. If the couple is able to be civil with each other, the division of furniture and other household items is made with the needs of all family members considered. Most parents initially take just enough with them to provide for temporary housing. In more conflicted situations, one parent leaves with only his or her personal belongings or takes as much as possible as an act of revenge. One man's ex-wife even took all the bathroom tissue and towels in the house.

During the transition it is often helpful to ask teens for their input in either selecting the parent's new apartment or, at the very least, helping them move. It is also beneficial to have teens participate in making a space for themselves at the non-custodial parent's new home. As most teenagers will have opinions about visitation, many parents, especially with older teenagers, may allow the teen to make some of their own decisions about how visitation is handled. Others fight bitterly over this issue. Most eventually adopt their state's standard visitation policy.

Considerable emotional issues occur during this phase as it is the stage of greatest transition. Parents feel scared about solo parenting, finances, and facing their social group. Sadness and loneliness are almost universal. Many feel relieved, especially when the decision phase was very tumultuous. This phase sets the stage for the unfolding of the transition and adjustment phases.

Struggle and Transition

This is the longest phase in the divorce process in which the couple separates and starts the legal process of divorce. Initial decisions are often made when the parents are in a state of shock, fear, or even anger. For most families, temporary orders are set either by parental agreement or court order, but these are simply a stopgap until the final decisions are made. Temporary orders usually delineate who has custody of the children, establish visitation schedules, set the child support amount, and place restrictions on each partner's access to and use of family finances and belongings. Specifics of these orders may vary depending on the particular statues of the state resided in. Complications may occur if the couple files in different states.

The transition from being a couple to being single involves a great deal of internal struggle individually and between the couple. For many, their identity is tied up in being married and letting this go is life-altering. In this phase everything is at stake: child custody, household belongings, plans for the family dog, finances, social connections, and even social and personal identity. A tremendous sense of loss permeates this stage. This is also the period of heightened conflict, as anger and a desire for retaliation may surface.

It is extremely difficult for parents to avoid dragging their teenagers into the situation when emotions are so raw. Often parents are not fully aware of what they are saying to their teen, or of what the teen is overhearing. In some cases, parents may send angry, negative messages through the teenager during periods of visitation. During this time teenagers are often acutely aware of the stress in the family. Some may try to avoid dealing with the parental conflict while others become overly focused on their parents' marital interactions. Too many arguments, especially ones that become mean and nasty, can seriously disrupt a teen's emotional functioning. The absence of conflict can confuse the teen and lead to the mistaken hope that the parents will reunite. This phase begins and ends with a family but the structure changes and the impact is experienced by everyone.

Adjustment

In this phase there is a settling down of individuals, situations, and emotions. This can take two to three years but may last much longer in some families and for some adolescents. What matters most at this stage is the ability of the divorced couple to move on with their lives, let go of the anger or grief, and create a workable co-parenting relationship. When conflict between the couple continues, and when new or unresolved issues arise, the adjustment may be tenuous.

Adjustment occurs when the adults have established separate and functional lives. Each parent has a home base, financial stability (or at least separated finances), and is functioning day-to-day. New or reestablished social lives exist. In these families, teens have been able to accept the divorce and have worked out visitation with the non-residential parent. For some teens there is a loss of regular visitation with one parent due to a parental move or choice. This can make the adjustment more difficult. Teens may benefit by some distance from a controlling, contentious, or abusive parent. Teens can be quite resilient and will work through most situations and continue with their development. When a parent chooses to remarry or cohabitate, there can be a return to earlier phases of functioning for the teen or parents.

The phases discussed here are experienced differently by parents and teens, depending on individual characteristics and family dynamics. Outside sources, including extended family, friends, neighbors, and professionals such as attorneys and therapists can also impact the experience. Importantly, parents set the stage for how adolescents cope, as they are the primary decision makers and their reactions establish the atmosphere in the family. Conflict between parents that continues unchecked can result in the phases being prolonged and more problematic for the teen.

Reactions of Divorcing Adults

Adults navigating the journey of divorce find themselves experiencing a wide range of roller-coaster emotions. Responses to the changing family situation may be extreme and uncharacteristic of the individual. Most people go through what I refer to as the "divorce crazies." The feelings evoked as the couple breaks apart are numerous and diverse. Many of the emotions are common to the experience, but individual personality influences the type, choice, and intensity of the feelings expressed.

Divorce transitions create a reactive pattern of emotional responses. An action or expression of a feeling by one spouse will result in a reaction from the other spouse that, in turn, precipitates additional reactions. For example, once a spouse admits that they are unhappy and considering a divorce the other spouse feels rejected and responds by emptying the bank account. Adults must keep in mind that these expressions of emotion and behaviors are being observed by the teens in the family. In most homes, the adolescents have a front-row seat to the drama unfolding as the family shifts, changes, and sometimes falls apart completely.

Divorce often brings these adults into therapy to help navigate the surprising intensity of emotions. Some come in early on seeking help with making the decision of their life. The implementation phase often brings one or both partners into counseling to assist with the specifics of separating and to have their feelings acknowledged by their spouse or at least by the therapist. Some spouses agree to couples counseling, if only to validate their decision and appease the one being left. The transition stage encompasses the most change and brings out the most core emotions surrounding the divorce. Many adults will need support during the transition period. Family and friends offer concern and advice but may be biased and only act to aggravate the situation between the couple.

Denial and Guilt

Denial is an unwillingness or inability to accept what is being said or happening. In divorce, there is usually one partner who decides to seek a divorce and informs the other of their intent. Often denial is the first, instinctive response to this announcement. Even when there have been years of unhappiness and conflict, the partner who did not make the initial decision is overwhelmed by the request. Their immediate response will likely be disbelief. In many cases, the spouse will acknowledge problems in the marriage, but they did not believe the problems would result in divorce. There is also a certain amount of denial on the part of the initiator because they have yet to fully accept the decision they have made. Often, one partner is struggling to accept the decision and all that it means while the other partner is feeling a tremendous amount of guilt at having initiated the breakup of the family. During this initial phase conversations may take place over several weeks as the concept of divorce becomes a reality.

Dale and Martha were married 17 years with two adolescent girls, both adopted at birth. Martha, a stay-at-home mom, had devoted her life to their girls and spent little time or attention on her husband. Over the years she had gained a considerable amount of weight and quit having sex with her husband. Dale had made numerous attempts to discuss his concerns but Martha refused to acknowledge or address his unhappiness. Frustrated with his wife's spending on the girls and her lack of attention to his physical and emotional needs, Dale finally asked for a divorce. Martha responded with complete denial of any issues and refused to accept his decision. Further, she encouraged the girls to beg their dad not to leave. Martha would not contact an attorney and ignored Dale's efforts to discuss financial arrangements. She would walk away or cry hysterically whenever Dale tried to talk about moving out. His guilt kept him from making any decisive actions for several months. Eventually, he had his attorney serve her with divorce papers. Two weeks later, he moved out. Martha continued to insist that he was coming back. The girls were sad and confused by the events unfolding in their family.

In a sense, this denial softens the blow. For some, the denial is a form of disbelief in which they simply cannot accept that the other person is requesting a divorce. For others, this response is a protective mechanism that allows them to absorb the information without feeling overwhelmed. Denial creates a cushion between the announcement and the acceptance so that the initial response is usually not one of anger. Nonacceptance slowly gives way to acknowledgment that the upcoming events are actually going to take place. For many, the initial denial is followed by shock and an intense fear of the unknown

When the couple appeared to be happy, or at least content with the relationship, the request for divorce seemingly comes out of the blue. Couples in contentious relationships often throw the threat of divorce about as a weapon during an argument. These threats to "get a divorce" or "leave" have been levied so many times that when the actual decision is made and stated, denial is the first response. In some situations, one partner may request a divorce and then pull back from discussing the separation, allowing time for both to process the information. In most cases, divorce is initiated by one partner in the difficult position of having to inform the other of their choice to end the relationship.

While discontent can develop in either spouse, women are more likely to initiate the divorce. In a report presented at the 2015 American Sociological Association meeting it was reported that women initiated 69% of all divorces.[4]

Despite careful consideration over a substantial period of time, those leaving feel guilty. Guilt is a common response to feeling that your actions or emotions will cause another distress. These feelings can be debilitating and can delay the implementation of the decision, which is why the one being left will initially fight back by attempting to evoke shame in the spouse that wants out. Divorce rarely proceeds without one or both partners feeling that they have played some part in the failure of the relationship. Guilt may motivate one's actions. Some leave the marriage in an attempt to alleviate this uncomfortable feeling, such as in the case of infidelity or when a spouse feels responsible for their partner's unhappiness. Guilt is a difficult emotion to deal with and often leads to remorse over the breakup of the family. Hardening of feelings toward a spouse may alleviate remorse or shame for wanting out.

Guilt or denial motivate several types of actions. Those in denial or shock may attempt to reconcile with their partner, often begging for another chance or trying to convince the partner that their decision is faulty or harmful to the children. Feelings of guilt may result in a willingness to back down from the decision and to consider reconciliation. Some will agree to attend couples counseling.

Denial usually abates once the actual physical activities start taking place, such as contacting attorneys, requesting that somebody leave the family home or, in extreme cases, when bags are packed and put out on the front porch. The steps after the announcement and acceptance of the upcoming changes are very important in setting the stage for how family members handle the divorce. Care should be taken to proceed with realistic expectations and goals.

Anger

Anger is a multifaceted, powerful emotion. Even in the most amiable divorces, anger always plays a role. Anger can be the expression of intense rage, a form of disengagement, or a means of empowerment. It can be sarcastic, passive aggressive, or even violent. Sometimes, a sense of healthy anger can help an adult stand up for themselves to ask for what is fair and reasonable. Most adults have difficulty controlling or hiding their anger. Therefore, it is the parental behavior that adolescents must often witness. It can be the most frightening emotion for all family members. Movies such as *Dirty John: Betty (the Betty Broderick Story), Marriage Story,* and the classic *War of the Roses* are testaments to the extent anger can become a part of the divorce process.

> *Susan, married 17 years with four children between the ages of 9 and 16, recently discovered that her husband had been having an affair with someone at his office. Furious and reacting out of pain, she demanded that her husband move out immediately. He left that night and stayed at a hotel. A week later, he found an apartment. Susan packed up his clothes, golf clubs, and several plates and plastic cups and put them on the front lawn. She told the kids he was a cheater and was not coming back. Susan was too angry to consider the impact her actions had on her children. When confronted about this, she insisted that her kids had the right to know what "kind of man their father was." Susan continued to disparage him throughout the divorce and for years after.*

Anger almost always surfaces during the implementation stage, when the activities related to the divorce start to take place. Being served with divorce papers is often when many of those being left begin to feel and express their anger, which is often a result of feeling betrayed, rejected, or abandoned. In an attempt to hold on to what they believe is theirs, partners use anger to change the decision or to punish the spouse who wants out.

During the struggle and transition phase, primitive rage may surface and is borne out of tremendous hurt and fear. Rejection, fear of abandonment, loss of identity, and financial insecurity evoke differing levels of anger. Emotional expressions may include overt hostility, anger, verbal raging, impatience, sarcasm, and general irritability. Feelings of anxiety and episodes of uncontrolled crying can also result from anger. These complicated emotions show themselves in a variety of ways, such as disrespect, criticism, insults, disregard, and discounting. Ignoring phone calls, emails, and legal requests are indirect ways of expressing disdain. At its most primitive level, anger can result in screaming tirades, verbal abuse, physical threats, and even violence. While it is more common for men to be more physical with their anger, women have been known to be very destructive. One client threw her husband's beloved golf clubs in the neighborhood lake. Another soon to be ex-husband punctured his wife's tires when she was at her attorney's office. Episodes of destroying personal property are not unheard of as belongings are divided. Anger can result in increased criticism of the spouse, far too often in front of the children.

Controlling individuals often react by becoming more controlling by whatever means available. The need to reestablish some sense of power is the impetus behind refusal to allow visitation, refusal to pay child support or alimony, or excessive litigation. Closing bank accounts or canceling credit cards is common. Some spouses exact revenge by maximizing credit cards or allowing credit ratings to be damaged. One client reported that his soon-to-be ex-spouse took their two kids on a pricey vacation and bought them expensive electronics after he informed her he was thinking about leaving. Spending the money on the kids made it harder for him to complain or retaliate.

Passive-aggressive techniques are a way of expressing anger without necessarily having to take full responsibility for one's actions. For example, with the client previously mentioned, the wife stated she took the kids on vacation and bought them gifts so they would have happy memories during this difficult time in their lives. Many use the legal system as a way of expressing anger by creating roadblocks, seeking custody, and demanding an uneven distribution of assets. The old "I'll take you to the cleaners" is a well-known threat. In some cases, the couples turn to the legal system to battle it out in the courts, believing that this will legitimize their anger at each other. This very situation prompts many states and courts to insist upon several attempts at mediation prior to hearing a divorce case.

In some cases, a couple or individual is unable to let go of the anger. Hostilities can continue for years. Adolescents and young adults are often negatively impacted when parents argue during periods of teen transitions between homes, act openly hostile during teen activities, or even refuse to participate in or even attend an important function if the other parent is present. According to Dr. Ahrons (1994), "Continued, unrelenting hostility and anger are a clear indication that the losses that are an inevitable part of any divorce haven't been mourned" (p.81).[5] Anger becomes harmful when it feels like the only means to hold on to feelings that are no longer reciprocated. Relationships that were previously very combative may continue to connect through anger. These relationships are not psychologically stable, nor do they promote healthy adjustment for anyone involved. Everyone is aware of divorced couples that continue to be openly hostile to each other years after the divorce, even after both have remarried. Anger may dissipate over time only to resurface over minor disagreements or in the case of life changes.

Adults who have been controlled or dominated in the course of a relationship may find their anger empowering. They have felt intimidated for most of their married life and deciding to leave builds confidence and a sense of control over their own life. For Gail, mentioned previously, wanting to leave her controlling husband encouraged her to come in for therapy, helped her develop self-confidence, and empowered her to stand up to her husband. For others, anger can be a means of letting go. Justifiable anger over hurtful behavior during the course of a marriage can drive the decision to divorce and get out of an unhappy situation. It can also bolster the strength to fight if the other partner is being unreasonable during the divorce settlement. Anger can serve a functional role in divorce when it supports empowering actions. Unfortunately, it is often destructive, prolonging an already-difficult process.

Grief and Depression

Divorce is about loss: loss of love, companionship, identity, financial security, and dreams. Some find opportunities and freedom from unhappiness in divorce, but loss is always present. During the divorce journey, most experience some degree of grief. Grief is the process that we go through in order to accept the loss or the end of something significant to us. The stages of grief are denial, sadness, anger, bargaining, and acceptance. Many go through the stages and accept the ending of their marriage. Others get mired in the grief.

One overwhelming feeling associated with grief is sadness. Feelings of sadness vary in degree. Some experience occasional bouts of tearfulness while others can't seem to stop crying. Irritability, anxiety, or fatigue may be signs of sadness that is not acknowledged. Even those who feel ambivalent or relieved about ending the marriage find issues that elicit sadness. Some grieve the loss of the hopes and dreams of a happily-ever-after life together. Others feel sad for the impact divorce has on their children. Some may even feel pain over the experience that the partner is going through. Sadness and grief are usually experienced in the months following the announcement and dissipates as the process evolves.

Grief during a divorce is similar to grief over the death of a loved one. Denial is soon followed by a period of focus on the necessary details, such as planning the funeral, or, in the case of divorce, on the legal activities. When the initial changes subside, a sense of emptiness and insecurity may set in. Without focus or direction, one can become overwhelmed by this pain and loss. Being unable to see far enough ahead to know if life will turn out okay can bring up strong feelings of distress. While many will tell you that they are comfortable living alone, everyone is susceptible to feeling lonely. When you have shared your bed and home with someone for a number of years, their absence cannot help but create a kind of vague restlessness and sense of emptiness.

Prolonged grief can be debilitating and interfere with everyday functioning. When the sadness becomes intense, stretching over a number of weeks, it can result in symptoms of depression. Depression is a psychological condition in which the individual experiences unrelenting sadness, difficulty in everyday functioning, fatigue, problems with concentration, and a sense of hopelessness about their situation.

For those whose lives have been tied up in their family and marriage, the loss is traumatic. They may feel worthless, insecure, and pessimistic about the future. Suicidal thinking and even suicide attempts are possible during this time. The loss and stress of divorce can result in a depressive episode, but studies have found this is more likely to occur in adults who have previously suffered from depression.[6] Depression in a parent can be frightening for the adolescents in the home. Parents dealing with depression may have a hard time being available but should try to be cognizant of their teen's needs during this time. Many adults struggle with the losses and changes inherent in divorce, but most weather the changes over time.

Women initiate divorce most often and men are more likely to move out of the family home. Therefore, it seems likely that men will have to deal with more life changes and losses. Coming home to a small apartment with nothing on the walls can be disconcerting. Women often experience a greater change in socioeconomic lifestyle, especially if they were stay-at-home mothers. In a 2018 study by T. Leopold, he reported:

> Where gender differences emerged, they were mostly short-lived. Men experienced larger drops in satisfaction with life and particularly in satisfaction with family life observed in the year of divorce, but over the next years, the gender gap in these outcomes vanished. The same pattern was observed for women's larger declines in satisfaction with household income, suggesting that gender differences in the consequences of divorce are

> generally larger in the short term than in the medium term. (p. 791)[7]

As in any situation, individual and family differences override any gender issues.

Adults engage in a number of behaviors to deal with the grief and insecurity that divorce brings. Many will cry themselves to sleep, while others find their nights are filled with tossing and turning and obsessive thoughts of their ex-spouse. Some turn to alcohol and prescription drugs as a way of numbing their feelings. Others return to the wildness of their youth, trying to deal with their loss by socializing, partying, and spending a lot of time away from home. Others may throw themselves into their work, spending long hours at the office because coming home to an empty apartment is too difficult to face. Some immediately run into rebound relationships, trying to fill the love void. These excessive actions rarely work in the long run. Divorce and the accompanying grief are a process that is best dealt with slowly, with faith and hope in the future.

Physical Responses

The feelings divorce evokes are usually quite powerful and can affect the body. Additionally, people going through divorce often do not take good care of themselves. They may sleep poorly, eat inconsistently, and fail to get adequate exercise. Physical manifestations of divorce can include headaches, stomach distress, backaches, and any other kind of ache that the body can create to express emotional turmoil. Stress can result in a lowered immune system, leading to increased chance for illness.

There may be changes in physical appearance including weight loss or gain, new clothes, and hair styles. Some changes are due to neglect of self-care due to prolonged grief or depression. Others make a point of changing their look to reflect their new personal and social life. Some changes may be an effort to attract attention of a possible new partner, such as more revealing and sexual clothing, having breast implants, new hairstyles, or teeth whitening. Taking care of one's body during divorce is an important part of getting through this difficult period of time.

Relief

The last areas to consider in terms of emotional response are those adults who feel relief at the prospect of getting out of an unhealthy, unfulfilling marriage. This freedom may be tempered with concerns for their children and the future. Marriages that were dysfunctional with issues from outright abuse to emotional disconnection will find separation liberating. Many marriages have struggled with inequality in the relationship—perhaps one partner was controlling or excessively demanding and needy. Some families battled alcohol or drug abuse. Others have struggled with mental illness.

Getting the courage to leave brings relief and a stronger sense of self-worth. Some experience relief when the initial separation takes place; others find that time away from the relationship results in increased feelings of joy and peace. Being able to leave a marriage that has been unsatisfying can be empowering. This new-found strength helps to build a better life. Some celebrate the divorce as the beginning of an exciting new life. Families with teenagers may be relieved to be free from the parent-teen conflicts that have become a regular occurrence in the home. Not all divorces are journeys of pain; some are paths to self-worth and new beginnings.

Jane was married for five years. It was her second marriage and his third. She acknowledged that she had married primarily for financial security after a short courtship. Early on there were struggles due to her husband's drinking, anger, and controlling nature. Conflicts between her husband and her two teenage sons were common. When Jane tried to intervene, her husband would become angry with her for not supporting his authority, insisting she did not know how to handle boys. When her oldest moved out at 18, she moved into a two-bedroom apartment with her 14-year-old son. She finally found some peace for herself and her sons.

Types of Divorcing Couples

Several experts on divorce have created categories of divorcing couples for the purpose of illuminating the patterns of reaction and adjustment of these couples. While reactions vary, most couples fall into patterns of emotional responses and behaviors. Behavioral styles reflect the personality of the individuals, the reasons for the divorce, and the previously-established interactional patterns of the couple. The power of the negative reaction usually overrides the more positive and healthy responses. Therefore, in specifying the divorce type, the stronger personality and most intense reactions often defines the couples' divorce patterns.

In years of experience with divorcing couples, I have observed and conceptualized the following behavioral and response patterns: Outwardly Amiable, Business Partners, Angry Responders, and Vengeful. These are based on the couple's issues, motivations, emotional responses, and behaviors. Most consider the needs of the children in their responses. Some do not.

Outwardly Amiable

Frank and Joyce married after six months of dating. This was the second marriage for Joyce and Frank's first. Joyce had one daughter, Heather, age 15. Heather had continued to see her biological father for regular visitation. Frank was friendly and supportive of Heather and enjoyed his role as her stepfather. The couple had been married five years when they decided to divorce. Frank's job as a longshoreman kept him away from home for several months at a time and Joyce complained that she had not gotten married to be alone. The couple began to argue more frequently, primarily over finances and social activities. For example, Joyce wanted to go out dancing and Frank wanted to stay home and watch sports. Both agreed the marriage was not working.

The divorce was finalized in nine months with very few issues. Surprisingly the biggest conflict was over the living room furniture they had recently purchased. Minor conflicts were handled through e-mails and attorney negotiations. Frank requested to continue a friendly relationship with Heather. Both Heather and her biological father were agreeable to the continued relationship as Frank had been a kind and supportive stepfather. Joyce and Frank realized they had gotten married too quickly and had been looking for someone to take away the loneliness that each had felt.

Outwardly Amiable couples are probably the healthiest and strive to make the divorce proceed without too much controversy or anger. They are concerned with the well-being of their children, so these parents work to find a balance in their needs and wishes. This couple may utilize the same attorney or encourage both attorneys to present settlement offers that are equitable. Joint custody is the norm, and visitation is generous and flexible. There is an acceptance that the marriage is no longer working. At times, they may feel angry or scared, but they try and keep the expression of these emotions in check in order to minimize the impact on the family. When negative reactions arise, they find appropriate coping methods or seek out supportive friends to confide in. They do not use their teens as a sounding board. Some couples find a sense of relief when they realize they have been trying to keep a marriage going at the expense of their individual needs. These couples often become friends in a sense, allowing each other to move on to better relationships.

In these families, custody is usually shared and teens have open access to both parents. Family events involving the teen may be attended jointly, even if the couple does not sit together. These parents consult with each other when issues arise concerning their children. Holidays are evenly divided and some occasions may be shared. One family I worked with took several family vacations together. This category represents the minority of cases but should be a goal for families with children.

Business Partners

Bill and Sara were married for 20 years when they decided to divorce. They had one child, a 14-year-old son. Both had high-level positions in their respective fields. Bill was an oil company executive and Sara worked in Human Resources for a manufacturing company. Both were work-oriented and their work schedules often precluded much time together. Over the years, the couple had started arguing more frequently and found they had very little in common. About the only issue that they usually agreed upon was their son, who both adored. However, at times the son's extracurricular activities caused conflict as to who would be available to drive or attend the event. When asked, their son stated that he could rarely remember his parents being affectionate toward each other.

The couple agreed to use one attorney, kept their own 401k accounts, and worked out a joint custody arrangement. The primary conflict was over ownership of the house which they finally decided to sell and split the profits. Both spouses purchased smaller homes in the same school district, so their son could continue to attend his current middle school. In their efforts to protect their son and to be fair with each other, the couple never fully dealt with their emotional responses to the divorce and future interactions were cool and civil.

This category represents those couples who focus on the functional issues and hide behind the legalities. Difficult feelings are handled through emails, during brief squabbles, or angrily expressed to others. Denial and avoidance of conflict are the primary motivations behind this style of coping. Often this group accepts the marriage's end and neither have a strong need to fight for the relationship. These couples may seem to get through the separation in a low-conflict manner, but the emotions may surface later, such as when one partner decides to remarry.

Some issues or feelings may be handled in a passive-aggressive way. Both spouses seem intent on not sharing their level of pain with the other. Like business partners dividing the company they built together, they use the legal system to deal with their issues and disagreements. Mediations may result in brief clashes, occasional disparaging comments, and isolated tense interactions. However, most negotiations remain unemotional, respectful, and detached.

For these couples, the children are the shareholders and there is a need to present a facade of cooperation. These adults work hard to avoid bad-mouthing the other parent and encourage ongoing relationships with both parents. These couples want an easy transition for their teen. Teens may sense underlying tension between their outwardly-friendly parents; behavior which may seem confusing. Custody is usually arranged based on the state standard and both parents follow the guidelines consistently. Minor disagreements may arise, often concerning time or money, but are resolved within a reasonable period. Many of these parents invest their time and emotions on their relationship with their teens. They accept that the marriage may be over but the parenting relationship continues.

Angry Responders

Jerome and Lydia were married with four children between the ages of 10 and 16. The couple had been high school sweethearts and married one year after graduation when Lydia became pregnant with their first child. Over the years, the relationship between the couple had become more contentious with periods of cold silence permeating the home. Two years ago, Jerome had moved into the guest room. Shortly thereafter, Lydia became involved with someone at her office. Lydia, feeling guilty, informed Jerome of her relationship. The couple argued heatedly for months, eventually coming into therapy to see if they could save their fractured relationship. The couple stopped coming after only three sessions and opted to divorce.

The separation was dramatic with Jerome taking his half of all the furniture except what was in the kid's rooms. He moved into a small two-bedroom apartment, insisting that the kids stay with him during his visitation periods. He would become sarcastic or pout if the kids wanted to call their mother or their friends. The couple fought intensely and loudly, even in the presence of the children. The legal divorce took over six months, with numerous failed mediations. Finally, they reluctantly agreed on the usual state standards for custody, child support, and visitation. Finances were split, with Lydia getting the house and Jerome his retirement account. Neither were happy, but over time, they let go of old grievances. At their oldest child's high school graduation, they were able to sit together as a family.

The Angry Responders category is probably the most prevalent. These couples struggle with the process, experiencing a roller-coaster of emotions as the divorce unfolds. Anger is a normal part of interactions. Some of these couples may have had a low-conflict relationship, but when they begin dividing up their belongings and dealing with the sharing of their children, anger surfaces. Other couples have a history of irresolvable conflicts that escalate during the period of struggle and transition.

Many couples in this category feel misunderstood and unheard, with a strong need to be right. They need to win the battle even if they lose the war. These couples commonly have angry exchanges in the presence of the adolescent, thus the teen may be drawn into the conflict. Much of the anger expressed by this couple comes from a sense of abandonment, fear of the unknown, or betrayal.

Custody and financial support are key conflicts, which teens are often aware of. Litigation is often threatened or employed as a power play. Some of these cases are prolonged over inconsequential details. Once custody or support is established, minor changes become difficult negotiations. Requests may be denied if only as a means of retaliation. As teenagers are old enough to deal directly with parents, a lot of the changes in plans or requests for money are filtered through the teen. This may reduce the conflicts if teens are able to make decisions directly with a parent, avoiding the other parent's interaction. However, this may add stress for the teen. I worked with an older teen whose parents had each remarried. The two families did not speak and all negotiations went through the teens in the family. When I was finally able to get all the family together, they spoke with each for the first time in over three years and the teen was finally able to get out of the middle. Parents in this category may directly or unconsciously share information with the adolescent in a way that is disparaging of the other parent. Often teens in these families feel pressured into taking a side. This style of angry responders takes a toll on all family members.

Over time a lot of the anger in this couple subsides, especially after the divorce is finalized. The majority of couples in this group eventually work through their issues and find a way to adjust. Equitable and satisfying relationships with their teenage children take precedent over the parent's past issues. Some of these ex-spouses, however, have a hard time letting go of the anger. The anger may stay under the surface or at a low level for many years only to resurface at times of stressful interaction. A problem involving the teen may bring the animosity to the surface. A family event in which roles are unclear, and where a parent feels discounted or disrespected, can evoke anger. These families need to be aware of the minefields down the road that can cause anger or problems to resurface.

Vengeful

Steve and Diana had a particularly contentious divorce. The couple had been married for 21 years with three children, ages 12, 14, and 19. The oldest son was a college freshman. The couple and their children were referred to therapy by the ad-litem attorney, as the divorce process was exceedingly acrimonious and the children were expressing a lot of stress over the parent's conflict. Diana was closest to her younger children and openly encouraged them to refuse visitation with their father.

When the oldest son testified in court that his mother had been attempting to alienate his younger sisters from their father, Diana became enraged and accused her oldest of betraying her. Diana tried continuously to interfere with Steve's visitation with his daughters, including refusing to open the door, making last minute changes to the visitation schedule, and taking them out of town on his weekends. The girls expressed contempt for their father, claiming that he had abandoned the family and their mother. Any encounter between spouses resulted in loud and verbally abusive arguments.

The divorce took over two years and countless legal battles to finalize. The oldest son limits his visits with both parents to a few days during the holidays. Two years later, the couple is still unable to be civil to each other. Dad's visitation with his daughters is infrequent, erratic, and strained.

This category is the most destructive for everyone involved. In general, these couples were contentious prior to separation and the conflict escalates considerably during the divorce process. Many of these spouses cannot bear being left and anger serves as a way of holding on. Controlling spouses may seek to continue the relationship with threats and intimidation. The discovery of an infidelity may evoke intense feelings of abandonment and rejection; some of these issues may have their origin in one's childhood. Individuals in this category often use any means at their disposal to retaliate for perceived injustices or abandonment. These couples hide assets, destroy property, and denigrate the other partner to anybody who will listen, including the children. This kind of anger lasts for years and, even though there are times when it goes underground, easily resurfaces.

This category is particularly stressful for teens. Custody is usually carefully divided but often used as a means of retaliation against the other parent. These ex-spouses can't be in the same room together, even for five minutes, without causing tremendous stress for their teens and young adults. Birthdays, holidays, graduation, and even wedding planning, become a nightmare. Parents in this category are capable of alienation tactics and will use their adolescents as a weapon against the other parent. This category is the most damaging to a teen's development. Even when confronted with the possible harm their behavior may have on their children's well-being, these ex-spouses continue to act with disdain and anger toward each other.

Summary

Divorce is a journey of emotions punctuated by decisive, life-changing actions impacting all family members. The phases inherent in this process are Unhappiness, Decision, Implementation, Struggle and Transition, and Adjustment. These stages follow the path from the point of marital disruption to a new beginning. Many of the feelings are painful but necessary to the transition. As Wallerstein and Blakeslee, in *What About the Kids*

(2003), points out, "divorce is the end of love and the persistence of attachment. This enduring tie can be based on anger, tenderness, friendship, or any combination of powerful emotions" (p.9).[8]

Divorcing couples can fall into one of four pattern types four pattern types: Outwardly Amiable, Business Partners, Angry Responders, and Vengeful. At the end of the journey, a restructured family is established with various levels of connection. Divorce is a force of change, but the outcome is dependent upon the input of those involved. In families with adolescents, the parents' emotions and actions set the stage for the teen's response, but the teen's characteristics and strengths will also impact their adjustment.

2.

I Just Want to Stay with My Friends!

Custody and Parenting Style Changes in Divorced Families

I can rise to the challenge of being a divorced parent.
I did not divorce my children.
—Sefra Kobrin Pitzel, *Surviving Divorce*[1]

Beginning with the initial separation, shifts occur in the family structure. Some form of custodial arrangement must be made to clarify where and with whom the teen will live and to establish the specifics of visitation with the other parent. Custody may be a joint residential arrangement or one designating the mother or father as primary custodian.

Even early on, the adolescents will have opinions as to where and with whom they wish to live. Where is an easy choice; the with whom is much more complicated. Teens usually prefer to stay in their family home and remain in their current school. "I just want to stay with my friends" is a phrase often heard as teens cope with divorce. Statistically, most teenagers continue to reside in the family home with their mother. This is not to say that there are not situations in which the father becomes the primary custodian.

Parental separation results in each household becoming a single-parent home, though some parents opt to cohabitate with another person immediately. Divorce and the transitions that follow often result in restructured family roles, changed parenting styles, and disrupted parent-teen interactions. Single-mother households face issues including financial difficulties and parenting stress. Many of the same struggles are applicable to single-father-households. This chapter explores various custodial situations along with the particular challenges each one presents. Additionally, the impacts divorce has on parent-teen interactions and parenting style are addressed.

Custody

Custody, whether by temporary or final orders, is a legal ruling that specifies where the children will live, which parent has primary custody, and how often the other parent will have visitation. Custodial agreements also specify financial support and who has the right to make major decisions, such as medical or educational. Visitation is not the best term to describe the amount of in-person time the non-residential parent will have with their children, however it is the legal terminology. Both parents should spend quality connection time with their teens and maintain a parental role.

There are two basic types of custodial arrangements: primary (or sole custody) and joint custody. These terms and their meaning vary by state. Primary custody is usually the legal standard and implies that one parent has primary and physical responsibility for the teen and the other parent has varying degrees of time and rights allotted. In some cases, one parent has sole custody and the other parent has quite limited access to their teen. Custody agreements are usually achieved by legal mediation between the couple. When couples are not able to come to an agreement, an order by a judge will specify the custodial arrangement.

Joint custody is often the term used when the children live with one parent while the other parent has access to at least 35% of the time. Both parents maintain the right to make parental decisions, receive information about their teen (such as school records or medical), and share an ongoing connection (regular phone or text contact, attendance at the teen's activities, and ongoing supervision). Joint custody may also refer to families in which time and responsibilities are shared equally.

Shared custody, sometimes called dual residence, can be achieved in a number of ways. Teens may live with one parent for a specified period of time, such as a week, followed by an equal period of time with their other parent. In some families, one or more of the children live with one parent while another sibling lives with the other parent. Other teens move freely between the two homes. In a relatively new form of custody called nesting (or bird nesting), teens remain in the family home and the parents move in and out. A small apartment or house is obtained for the parent not in residence. There are pros and cons to each type of custody. Families should strive to find the arrangement that works best for them. Changes in custody and visitation may occur as situations change or as the teen ages.

Joint Custody

Joint custody is the most common and encourages the participation of both parents in the lives of the adolescents. The social standard is that the children live primarily with their mother and spend every other weekend, one or more evenings a week, and various holidays and vacations with their father. In joint custody, the emotional and physical needs of the teens are of primary importance. Teens need a relationship with both parents and joint custody acknowledges this. Shared custody often allows the teen a relationship with the non-residential parent that goes beyond the legally-specified time frames. Parents will often encourage the teen to call or see either parent as needed. Shared custody provides for open communication, maintains close parent-teen bonds, and affords adolescents a sense of family belonging. The shared responsibility in joint custody gives each parent a break, allows both parents to supervise teen activities, and fosters the belief that their ex-spouse will back them up on issues with the teen. In a 2014 article by Nielsen, she reported:

> Overall, the children in shared parenting families had better outcomes on measures of emotional, behavioral, and psychological well-being, as well as better physical health and better relationships with their fathers and their mothers, benefits that remained even when there were high levels of conflict between their parents. (p. 613)[2]

This form of custody, when handled responsibly and maturely, benefits both parents and teens.

Joint custody can create some challenges for the teen. In *Between Two Worlds* (2005), Marquardt expresses her concerns with joint custody:

> Divorce requires children to travel between their two parent's worlds. Joint physical custody, in particular, forces them to be almost constantly on the move between these worlds ... Joint physical custody also demands a great deal of cooperation between parents (p. 186).[3]

Teens may dislike having to pack and unpack between homes, especially if there is a significant distance between them. Teens can be frustrated when a needed or preferred item is at the other home. Adolescents are not happy when social activities are missed due to visitation. Joint custody works better when the parental residences allow the teen to be close to their school and friends. Being able to drive and having a car may ease the transitions.

One teenage client divided her time between both parents, who lived close, and was allowed to stay at either home at her discretion. My client appreciated her parents' effort to accommodate her need to have access to both parents but shared that having to continually choose between her parents was stressful.

Teens may also use the change in residence as an opportunity to manipulate or go around the rules. Problems arise when parental conflict interferes with each parent's access to their child. Arguments that take place during the periods of transition can keep the teen caught in the middle of the conflict. Parental interference with visitation or negative comments about the other parent are possible with joint custody. For joint custody to succeed, parents need to respect each other's role and involvement with their children.

Sole Custody

Custodial arrangements and terminology may vary by state. In sole custody, also referred to as sole physical custody, one parent has full responsibility for their teenage children. The residential parent is legally awarded all rights and decision-making responsibilities. The other parent may have limited or only supervised visitation. Sole custody does not preclude a parent from paying child support. This form of custody is decreasing in most states.

Sole custody is usually awarded when the other parent has been deemed unfit. This could be due to physical or sexual abuse, child abandonment, parental instability, incarceration, or extreme alienation. Sole custody may be awarded when the other parent is out of the country or incarcerated and not easily contacted when decisions need to be made. In the cases of physical or sexual abuse, the offending parent is deemed unsafe and supervised visitation may be granted as appropriate.

Unfortunately, some parents abandon their adolescents following divorce and sole custody allows the custodial parent to make all relevant decisions. In cases of severe parent/teen alienation, courts may temporarily award sole custody to the alienated parent in hopes that the teen will develop a healthy relationship with the alienated parent. Nielsen (2018) reports that sole custody may be beneficial for some teens from high-conflict families when the parent-teen relationship is unhealthy.[4] There may be limited visitation schedules that allow for a continued connection while avoiding some of the ongoing conflict patterns.

Sole custody may be temporary. As situations improve, a change in custody may occur. Joint custody is the norm, as society now encourages the ongoing relationship between teens and both parents.

Nesting

Nesting is a new form of custody that allows the adolescent to remain in one home while the parents move in and out and share parental responsibilities. Staying in the family home provides adolescents with stability and security. It also allows teens to avoid some of the social discomfort of having to explain the changes in their lives to peers and teachers.

Nesting may be beneficial for older teens who will be moving out on their own in a few years. This form of custody requires parents to work together to maintain the family home, keep similar rules, and share necessary information. Negative aspects include the possibility of parental disagreements over everyday issues, such as who should clean, grocery shop, or pay for broken appliances. Additionally, teens end up watching a replay of one parent moving out on a regular basis. This type of arrangement may fall apart when a parent begins a new relationship. Nesting aims to put the needs of the adolescent first but may not work long-term with couples who continue to be in conflict.

Single Parents

Separation of households is one of the first steps a couple takes during a divorce. This may be decided by the couple or the legal system. Temporary court orders usually specify where the children will live, who remains in the family home, how visitation is handled, and how finances are allocated. The final divorce decree may take years, so the temporary orders are critical to the initial family changes.

Usually, mothers receive primary custody, especially early on. In certain situations, the father will have primary custody. In a report citing the 2017 U.S. census data, Pearce et al (2018) highlight that while father-only families have increased in number, mother-only families are still nearly six times more common than father-led families.[5] This section will address the issues faced by single parent families, with primary focus on mothers. Many studies have addressed the problems these mothers face. Areas of impact include economic disadvantages, increased parental responsibilities, emotional and behavioral reactions to the divorce, and changes in the parent-teen relationship.

Financial Concerns

Divorce frequently puts women at an economic disadvantage. In a 2018 report from the Pew Research Center, it was noted that 27% of single parents are living below the poverty line, with single mothers twice as likely to struggle financially as single fathers.[6]

A number of stay-at-home mothers seek employment in order to support their families after the divorce. Some were absent from the workforce long enough to make going back to work difficult. They often start at lower-level positions than their ex-spouses, who have been gainfully and securely employed for many years.

Single mothers may end up moving if they cannot afford to stay in the family home. The neighborhood they move into may not be as educationally or socially advantageous or as safe as the one they lived in previously. Some parents end up with two jobs to cover expenses. Socioeconomic concerns impact parental well-being, teen supervision, and family lifestyle.

When a divorced parent is financially required to go back to work, they are likely to be more concerned about work hours and location than pay scale. Mothers who were already in the workforce often find that more of their income goes toward household bills. Child support does not always cover the family expenses. Adolescents are expensive; food, clothes, school activities and entertainment are all costly. Car insurance and gas are often an additional expense for older adolescents. Even if they are aware of financial constraints, teens want and push for those items their peer group deems essential. Some mothers work two jobs just to afford cell phones, computers, and satellite TV for their teens.

Economic issues can further strain a stressful home environment. Aside from getting all the bills paid, single parents feel pressure to provide their adolescents with electronics and an adequate entertainment allowance. Single moms and non-custodial dads often struggle over who pays for what. The parent who initiated the divorce may feel responsible for their teens' financial needs and may be hesitant to enlist financial help from their ex-spouse or other family members. Requests for additional funds can become a point of contention between the ex-spouses. Parents who are still bitter may use the requests to disparage the other's lack of ability to take care of their responsibilities. Many single moms have a need to be able to make it on their own. Asking the biological father or grandparents to pay for extras such as a car, homecoming dance, or cell phone plan may be difficult.

When a parent divorces during their children's adolescent years, child support is limited. Financial support is usually only awarded through their teen's 18th birthday or the end of high school and often does not include continued education. While couples may have established college accounts, the divorce may consume these funds. In too many cases, the college fund becomes the attorney's fees.

On the other side of the picture are those single mothers who have sufficient financial resources to take care of their teens. Many of these mothers were already in the work force making decent salaries with good health and leave benefits. In some states, women are required to pay alimony if they were the primary family breadwinners. These mothers find divorce easier financially, but the emotional and logistical issues may still produce distress. Money does not ease the emotional pain of divorce. Divorce divides family assets. It always creates financial strain and requires adjustment.

Parent's Emotional Health

Another challenge of divorce adjustment is the emotional well-being of the parent. Mothers, in particular, often feel betrayed, rejected, and abandoned. Even when the mother initiated the divorce, the emotions are ever-changing and surprisingly intense.

Parenting alone is an overwhelming task. Adolescence brings heightened awareness of the impact of emotions. Thus, adolescents will be cognizant of their parent's emotional well-being and level of functioning. Teens who perceive a parent as distraught may feel responsible for taking care of that parent. Mothers are often viewed as fragile by teens. In some cases, this protection is expressed through anger toward the other parent. I have known many adolescents to send angry texts to their father demanding to know why he is treating their mother so badly or why he is not providing enough support money.

Single mothers may depend too heavily on their children to meet their social and emotional needs. After years of being married, divorced mothers might have few friends or outside interests. Single mothers are unlikely to go to singles events alone. Church social groups tend to be primarily older women and may not be appealing or appropriate for everyone. Dating is often not a focus for mothers who recently separated. Single moms, with the task of childrearing yet to be finished, hesitate to start dating or seek outside activities when they feel it conflicts with time at home.

I have worked with mothers who felt guilty about attending a divorce recovery group in the evening. Social engagements may conflict with their teen's scheduled activities. Some single moms focus on and even indulge their teens in order to make up for the divorce. Lonely and unable to make friends due to parental and household responsibilities, these parents become focused on their teen's friends and activities. Some even encourage teen gatherings at their house in order to have noise and company.

Another struggle parents with adolescents may face is extended periods of time alone. Teenagers are notorious for preferring to be either in their rooms or out with friends, especially on weekends. Every other weekend is often a period of visitation with their father, leaving mothers home alone. While younger children are willing playmates for mom or dad, teenagers prefer their peers. When a single mother lets her unhappiness and loneliness become obvious to her teen, the teen could feel the need to be mom's confidant. These adolescents may sacrifice some of their own needs for their parents' needs.

Divorce may precipitate depression and anxiety. Even parents who do not meet the clinical definition of major depression experience grief and sadness over the loss of the marriage. This loss may relate to missing their spouse, the end of their marital identity, or the loss of their dreams. Depressive symptoms and grief can last for weeks or months, with intermittent periods of relief. Feelings of despair are strongest in the initial period of separation and may resurface when the actual divorce is finalized. Teenagers will be dealing with their own grief reactions and working on their necessary developmental tasks while living with parental grief and depression.

A glass of wine or three can make a lonely evening seem less lonely, at least initially. Alcohol and prescription medications have long been a means of coping for adults dealing with the upheaval of divorce. Adolescents watching parents deal with difficult emotions by drinking or using pills are learning unhealthy coping methods. A 2018 report by McCutcheon at al. found that parental alcohol use disorders in association with parental separation was a predictor of early substance use (alcohol and cannabis) by adolescents.[7] Teens in these households must deal with parental substance abuse on top of their own issues during the family transition and adjustment period. Alcohol and substance use diminishes parental affection, attention, and supervision.

Bitsy had been a stay-at-mom for over twenty years. She had married her high school sweetheart at age 19 and had three children within six years. She had attended college briefly but dropped out after getting pregnant. Her husband had received a degree in accounting (with Bitsy working to support the family) and worked long hours climbing the corporate ladder. After twenty years, he requested a divorce, claiming they had outgrown each other.

Bitsy was ill-prepared for being on her own. She went to work as a receptionist at a car dealership and soon started drinking after work with co-workers. Within a year, Bitsy was spending a lot of her evenings at the local bar laughing and drinking with those younger than herself. She claimed that she was making up for the years that she had missed by becoming a mother and wife so young. Her teenage children soon learned how to fend for themselves. Bitsy was not able to deal with her husband's rejection and turned to alcohol and younger friends to cope.

Alcohol or drug use in response to a divorce sets a poor example of coping. In worst case scenarios, the teens become children of divorce and adult children of alcoholics.

Parental Supervision

One of the most notable concerns in single-parent homes is parental supervision. Research has shown that parental supervision deteriorates in single-parent homes under the stress of divorce.[8] Monitoring adolescents' activities is not an easy task. Older teenagers are not simply in the next room watching TV or playing with their toys; they are out driving around with friends, attending parties, or on the Internet. Teens may say they're going to be at the high school football game, but they can easily end up at a party.

Keeping tabs on a teen, even with phone GPS apps, and being familiar with their friends requires a vigilance which can overwhelm a single parent. Custodial parents may lack the energy to follow up on the specifics of their teen's plans; many feel inadequate in supervising their teens. Mothers, especially those new to the workforce, may find that they are physically exhausted at the end of the day when they are needed for homework and extracurricular activities.

Some working parents struggle with balancing work and family when there is not another parent available to help with scheduling matters. Additionally, younger adolescents are often home alone after school. Summer is another extended period of time when parental work hours make it almost impossible to monitor a teen's activities. While older adolescents may be responsible with their free time or may even have part-time jobs, younger teens are more at risk when left alone.

Mothers are traditionally considered more of a pushover. Single mothers often have difficulty exercising their authority over teens. When they do assert their authority, single moms often have a hard time with follow-through with no male figure in the home to back them up. This reluctance concerning discipline may stem from prioritizing the adolescents' happiness and emotional well-being rather than structure. Often these mothers struggle with guilt over the impact that coming from a broken home may create for teens. It has been noted that single fathers may have difficulty supervising their teenage children. According to a 2009 article by Breviak et al.:

> Single fathers are assumed to be especially prone to having problems with the monitoring of their offspring, both because they seem to have less knowledge about their children's friends and activities throughout their development and because they might have a less intimate and open relationship with them. (p. 418)[9]

Inadequate supervision can result in teens, especially younger teens, becoming involved in questionable, unsafe activities.

Some single-parent homes do very well and the environment is relaxed. Rather than focusing strictly on the rules, these parents emphasize the smooth functioning of the household. Single parents may provide a more democratic atmosphere, focusing on the important issues while letting the little stuff slide.

Effective parenting is easier when ex-spouses are no longer fighting over decisions. Teens typically cooperate under authoritative parenting which is responsive, fair, and consistent. In single-parent homes, arguments should be minimized and efforts focused on getting along rather than on power struggles. Adolescents function best in homes where rules are based on safety and healthy development. Consequences should be age-appropriate and fair.

Custodial and Non-residential Fathers

In some families, fathers assume the responsibility of primary custodian. While not the norm, this is more likely to occur during a child's adolescent years. Adolescents may request to live with dad, especially if he remains in the family home or can provide more financial support. Some fathers are ingrained as the primary parent and fight to retain that role.

When fathers seek custody, it may be that the mother has significant challenges, such as psychiatric problems, substance abuse, or financial instability, which may interfere with her parenting ability. In other situations, the mother may request that the father assume custody of the children—perhaps in the case of teenage boys who are difficult to control. Some families split custody, with fathers retaining custody of the sons and mothers taking care of daughters.

Non-residential fathers have some form of visitation and various legal rights. Some agreements are the mutual decision of the divorcing couple while others are court ordered. Not all non-custodial parents are happy about the final agreement as pertains to their access to their children. Many fathers remain actively involved in their teenagers' lives. Some distance themselves over time. A close relationship with both parents is important to an adolescent's healthy development.

Custodial Fathers

Fathers assuming primary custody for their children has become more commonplace. In some families, while active in a parenting role, fathers may not have been the primary parent prior to divorce. Traditionally, fathers are viewed as providers and disciplinarians while mothers are considered more nurturing (although many family roles are now more equally divided). Primary custody requires fathers to assume multiple roles juggling work, household care, and parental responsibility.

Sam and Diane had been married for 19 years, with two daughters, aged 13 and 17. The relationship had been strained for many years, primarily due to the wife's emotional struggles. Sam initiated the divorce after discovering that his wife had been involved in relationships with men that she met online. Her sexual addition resulted in frequent unexplained absences from the home. Concerned with his wife's emotional stability, he sought and received primary custody of his daughters. The adjustment has been difficult for everyone. Sam decided against sharing any of his wife's difficulties with his girls, who are confused by the family changes. Diane has accepted the custody arrangement but remains bitter. She pressures the girls to request a change of custody yet visits inconsistently. Over time, the daughters have been able to figure out that their mom has emotional problems and living with their dad provides them with more stability.

There is conflicting information on how adolescents fare when the primary custodian is the father. Monitoring teen's social activities and dealing with teen mood swings may be areas where fathers fall short. Studies have indicated that single fathers are not as emotionally close to their children, communicate less, and are less likely to know their teen's friends.[10] Additionally, studies show that adolescents in single-father homes are at higher risk for substance abuse and antisocial behavior.[11]

Lack of supervision over peer connections and social activities can leave teens, especially those adjusting to parental divorce, vulnerable to peer pressure. Another research finding is that fathers are more likely to be granted custody when the teens are already exhibiting behavioral problems or when the mother has been deemed legally unfit. Teens that are hard to handle may be sent to live with the father after problems arose in the mother's home. Teens may request and be allowed to live with their father, sometimes because Dad is more permissive or his home is in a coveted location.

Adolescents involved in unsafe activities need and may even want a parent to intervene and provide external controls. Nielsen (2011) reports that fathers provide more discipline and routine and are better at handling difficult teens.[12] Peer pressure may be hard to resist and a strong parental figure can be a safe out. I have often encouraged teens to use the "my dad will freak out if I..." as a reason to say no to peer pressure. Teens may find living with Dad less stressful and more conducive to their individuation. Many dads function well as primary parent and establish a healthy home environment for their children. They provide emotional connection, financial support, and adequate supervision for their teens' activities. Father-based homes are also likely to encourage an ongoing relationship with their non-residential mother.

Non-Residential Parents

Custodial agreements vary from state to state, with mothers being more likely to get primary physical custody and fathers receiving varying degrees of visitation. Some specify joint custody with flexible visitation. The majority of fathers live separately from their teenage children and the quality and quantity of time spent together is dependent upon a number of factors: legally regulated visitation schedules, father's efforts toward keeping the connectivity, living within easy driving distance, the mother's opinion of the father, and the level of father-teen conflict. Money can also be an issue which affects the father-teen connection.

Some fathers, especially workaholics, focus on their careers. They have seen their provider role as the expression of their love and have difficulty shifting from this focus. Fathers may mistakenly believe that providing child support and having their teens visit every other weekend is enough of a relationship. Some parents move for work or to be closer to their family of origin, believing that long summer visits or Christmas holidays are sufficient to maintain their relationship with their adolescents. Relationships take work, especially when you are not together daily. Regular contact indicates a level of care and concern on the part of the father that is advantageous for teen development. In discussing divorced parenting Nielsen (2011) writes:

> Children of divorce benefit most when their father is actively engaged in their lives across a wide range of daily activities ... These ordinary routines and rituals including cooking together, running errands, getting ready for school, working together on homework, shopping, doing chores, and being together in spontaneous, unstructured ways. (p. 590)[13]

Quality of interaction can make up for a lack of quantity, especially when teens perceive an honest effort at maintaining a relationship. Even when regular and consistent visits are not possible, perhaps due to work schedules or travel distance, the father can find ways to be involved and show his love. Regular phone calls, texts, attendance at activities, and interest in a teen's life all indicate love and commitment.

The father sometimes chooses to distance himself from the family after divorce. Perhaps he feels overwhelmed by the loss and being around his teenagers only exacerbates his pain. These fathers fall away as a way of protecting themselves. Other fathers mistakenly believe they are not needed in the adolescent's life, especially with older, independent adolescents who spend a lot of time focused on friends and their own activities. Unfortunately, some fathers simply decide that they no longer wish to participate in the family. Instead, they focus on creating a new family for themselves.

Brian started divorce proceedings after 17 years of marriage, leaving his ex-wife and two teenage children in the family home. He claimed that he was no longer in love with his wife and wanted to be free to pursue new interests. Six months after separating, Brian began dating a younger woman from his office. The conflicts between the ex-spouses intensified as the final divorce was negotiated. Within two months, he had moved in with his new girlfriend and her 7-year-old son. Brian stated that his new family needed him more and that as long as he paid child support and saw his kids periodically, he was meeting his obligations. Brian's girlfriend did not get along with his teenage children. His time with his children began to taper off. The kids, hurt by his actions, reacted by refusing to have any contact with their dad as long as his girlfriend was living with him. Brian chose his new life, claiming that it was not his decision but his children's.

Non-custodial fathers who are well connected with their adolescent children usually share several characteristics. They make a point of being available and involved, which is shown by attending their teens' activities, calling or texting on a regular basis, asking about and keeping informed on the teen's activities, and keeping a consistent and routine visitation schedule. Visitation times need to be seen as a priority in the parent's life: no last-minute cancellations. Caring fathers monitor and maintain discipline when the teens are in their custody, allowing for age-appropriate freedom and activities. In effective co-parenting relationships, fathers work with their ex-spouse to handle significant events or behavioral problems should they arise.

Lastly, money plays a significant role in the relationship between fathers and children, specifically non-custodial fathers. Despite the widespread, societal belief that deadbeat dads abound, the overwhelming majority of fathers pay reasonable child support on a regular basis. Most have no issue with doing so. Many fathers pay above and beyond the required child support. Unfortunately, some mothers talk to their teens about financial concerns as a way of passive-aggressively attacking the father. As a rule, teens should not be given full information as to the financial arrangement between the parents as these negotiations are often complex and involve a number of factors which are not necessarily pertinent to the adolescent-parent relationship.

Parent-Teen Relationships

All families, whether married or divorced, experience a shift in the relationship between parent and child during the teenage years. The developmental stage of adolescence modifies the child's perception of the parents' infallibility, making teens more critical of parental behavior. During this time there is a pulling away from parents. Most teens are less than forthcoming about their feelings, thoughts, and activities. A comfortable parent-teen relationship will have a positive impact on the teen's psychological development while negative or distant interactions may be detrimental. Close relationships are characterized by warmth, open communication, sincere interest, encouragement, and mutual respect. Negative relationships are critical, dismissive, and disrespectful. In spite of their appearance of independence, teens need support, affection, and supervision to function well in the adolescent years.

Custodial arrangements impact parent-teen relationships. The character of the everyday interactions with primary custodial parents can set the stage for teens' adjustment. Parents who are concerned, involved, and nurturing will have an easier time parenting their teens. Adolescents respond better and share more in the context of a respectful, fair environment. They also are more amenable to supervision and likely to cooperate with parental rules. Single mothers cannot depend on strong-arm tactics to elicit compliance with family rules; they need to have an emotional connection and mutual respect. Custodial fathers need to provide structure and a nurturing environment in order to assure a stable home environment.

Father-teen Relationships

Divorce often takes a father away from the daily lives of his children. Most researchers agree that it is the father-adolescent relationship that suffers the most in divorce.[14] In more recent years, it appears that fathers are more likely to put in the effort to maintain relationships with their children after divorce. Some of this is due in part to society's belief that both parents are equally important in the child's development. Adolescents, in particular, benefit from having their fathers in their lives; sons need an ongoing and appropriate male role model and daughters benefit from a healthy model for their own male-female relationships.

A primary ingredient in the father-adolescent relationship is that of the mother's opinion of him. Mom's opinion of Dad impacts the mother's interactions with her ex-spouse, the teens' connection with their father, and the relationship she has with her children. Mothers help teens adjust when they support teen engagement with the non-custodial parent. Mothers, even without intending to do harm, may fail to facilitate teen closeness with their non-custodial parent.

Some of the struggles between fathers and their children can be directly attributed to the mother's intrusion and negative comments. Adolescents, especially daughters, tend to be protective of their mother's feelings and may take on the burden of feeling angry and distant from their fathers. On the other hand, mothers who are encouraging of the relationship and try to separate their own emotional feelings about their ex-husband from their teens' opinion of their father set the stage for healthy relationships. Likewise, the father's opinion of the mother can interfere with the parent-teen relationship. A father who disparages the mother may create distance between himself and his teens. Adolescents are generally very protective of their mothers. Acceptance and respect between all family members can benefit family adjustment in the short and long term.

Another important issue impacting the father-adolescent bond is the amount of conflict between them. Arguments with daughters are somewhat less volatile and are often focused on the daughter's activities and choices of friends, while conflicts with sons were generally about their level of respect and responsiveness to parental authority. Usually father-son clashes become more heated and can result in physical exchanges. For some highly contentious relationships, divorce provides a way to escape some of the ongoing conflict between father and teen. In some cases, parental separation takes some of the issues out of play and may even provide for a better relationship. When the disagreements between the non-residential parent and teen continue after the divorce, adolescents often resort to withdrawing contact rather than remaining engaged in the struggle.

Bodie and his father had a history of negative interactions. Jerry (dad) had been raised by a controlling father and as a parent he adopted a lot of his father's parenting techniques. During Bodie's childhood, Jerry had a quick temper and punishment was often in the form of a spanking or screaming lectures. Bodie's mom tried to intervene but this resulted in conflict between the couple. When Bodie turned 14, he started pushing back at his dad's control. The home became more contentious and Bodie and his mother moved out when Bodie was 16.

Initially Jerry tried to maintain control which was met with anger and withdrawal by Bodie. After a year of strained and limited interactions, Jerry decided to enter therapy and try an establish a better relationship with his son. Jerry came to realize how angry he was at his own father and that he did not want to alienate his own son. It took a while but Bodie and his father slowly connected. Dad was seating in the front row as his son graduated high school.

Conflict between parent and teen has a detrimental effect on teen emotional well-being. Adolescents in continual disagreement with custodial parents have poorer outcomes, as the other parent is no longer available as a buffer for the tension. For some families, the stress in the home is decreased by divorce, particularly when the emotions the parent was directing at the teen were a diversion for the frustration they felt in their unhappy marriage. Parental separation allows some of this atmosphere of tension to diminish.

Struggles with non-residential parents may lessen after separation. Research has found that adolescents in conflict with the same-sex parent benefit by a degree of separation from that parent.[15] Mothers are likely to allow teens to distance themselves from the father when the conflict is ongoing and the teen is complaining about their unhappiness. While adolescents need ongoing contact with both parents for optimal development, forced visitation when parent and teen have a history of volatile interactions can result in more problems for the teen. Decisions concerning custody and visitation benefit from an awareness of the relationship that each parent has with their teen.

Divorce Disclosures

When a parent is adjusting to a divorce, their teen may become an available confidant for parental emotions. These disclosures have a fine line dividing appropriate and detrimental information sharing. Afifi et al. (2007) report that:

> Inappropriate divorce disclosures typically constitute private information that a parent reveals to a child about the divorce that is negatively valenced, hurtful toward the other parent, too sensitive for the child's age, or that places the child in an uncomfortable position as a mediator, counselor or friend. (p. 80)[16]

Negative disclosures are more likely when parents feel a lack of control over the stresses of the divorce.[17] Parents may share information as an outlet for their pain, as a way of explaining the divorce, or to help shape a teen's perceptions about relationships.

Alienating parents share information that is intended to interfere with their teen's connection with their other parent.

Blaming the non-residential parent for financial woes creates anxiety for the teen. While adolescents are often aware that money is tight, believing that they caused the financial problems or that they are seen as only worth so much by their father is highly stressful. "Your dad isn't paying his child support on time. I don't know how we will pay the rent this month."

Many parents make comments in the midst of painful reactions which they regret when they realize the information could harm their teen's emotional well-being. Inappropriate information may diminish the trust and respect that the teen has for the parent that is sharing too freely.

Allowing conversations about the divorce that help a teen cope is conducive to their adjustment. Parents who answer questions about the divorce or their emotions honestly but without unnecessary negativity, blame, or details can be helpful in the teen's adjustment. Teens benefit from a parent's acknowledgement of their struggles with the changes in their life, making the teen's own feelings more acceptable. Pretending that everything is okay or that feelings cannot be spoken is not helpful to anyone.

Despite the verbal and intellectual abilities of adolescents, they are not adults and conversations should be age-appropriate. Older adolescents may handle more detailed information than younger teens. It is also helpful if the information provided concerning the divorce is consistent between the parents. Parents rarely have the same version of the marital problems.

Healthy Interactions

A healthy relationship between both parents and their adolescents results in better self-esteem, less depression, and less delinquent behavior. Continued contact with both parents is needed, as long as the interactions are positive.[18] Divorce diminishes a parent's emotional and physical energy, making it hard for overwhelmed parents to listen to and monitor the drama that is a teen's world. However, listening to a teen's daily chatter can go a long way to making the home life easier. Parents who put in the effort tend to have cooperative teens. Ideally, each parent will make an important imprint on the teen's psychological development through supervision, care, and encouragement.

Parenting Styles

Parenting style is the fundamental interaction between parent and teen. It includes the patterns, actions, personal motivations, and emotional reactions that guide a parent's choice of rules, expectations, and consequences. For a minority of parents, the patterns of parenting they exhibited prior to divorce continue with only a few changes. For most, the impact is greater.

The concept of parenting style was initially identified in 1971 by Diana Baumrind. The three main types were designated as authoritarian, authoritative, and permissive.[19] These conceptualizations have been the basis for social research on parenting behavior. In 1983, Maccoby and Martin expanded the permissive category into indulgent and neglectful.[20]

In my book, *The Parent Effect: How Parenting Style Affects Adolescent Behavior and Personality Development,* (2011), I identified five categories of parenting styles: controlling, permissive, disengaged, enmeshed, and healthy.[21] Parents who focus primarily on adherence to a specific and often inflexible set of rules and consequences are considered authoritarian. They are usually controlling and have a strong need to be respected. Parents who are lax in supervising their teen due to their own issues, a need for teen acceptance, or a busy life are exhibiting a permissive style of parenting. Disengaged parents pay too-little attention to their adolescents, usually due to their own busy life or emotional issues. Enmeshed parents live their lives through the accomplishments of their teens, over-identify with them, or feel the need to indulge them. Healthy parents provide a good balance of warmth, attention, and structure. These categories provide a blueprint for exploring the changes that occur during the course of separation and divorce.

Disengaged Parents

During a divorce, parents may become disengaged from their teen and many of their parental responsibilities. Some withdraw to the point of neglectfulness. I refer to these parents as "not now, I'm busy" parents. During divorce this takes on a whole new level—these are the "not now, I am going through a major life change" parents. In *For Better or For Worse,* Hetherington (2002) stresses, "Disengaged parenting is a form of emotional, psychological, and sometimes physical desertion. Essentially, the parent abandons children to cope with stresses of divorce on their own. Disengaged parents are focused on their own needs or survival" (p.133).[22] Parents can easily find themselves overwhelmed by the demands of coping with divorce and have little emotional strength left to deal with the difficult period of adolescence.

The disengaged style of parenting occurs more frequently with adolescents than with younger children. The pain of divorce, demands of work, or the efforts that go into establishing a new life drains parents of the energy to give their teens the needed attention or supervision. These parents focus on their own drama and often do not want to hear about the teen's stress. Single parents have limited time or ability to monitor teen activities. Ongoing conflict between the divorcing parents (referred to as interparental conflict) can cause a parent to disengage from their teen. Inadequate parental attention or supervision may be borne out of mistaken beliefs concerning the maturity and needs of adolescents. Older adolescents may appear ready to take on the majority of their own care. They may present themselves as functioning well even when they are not. Depressed parents have a need to trust that the teen is functioning well without a lot of parental intervention.

Changes in the lives of divorced adults impact parenting ability. Some stay-at-home mothers find themselves required to work in order to support their families. Non-custodial parents may move too far away from the family to participate in day-to-day parenting. Some parents become workaholics to deal with the grief of divorce. Yet others avoid parental responsibilities as a way of getting revenge on the ex-spouse. "You wanted the divorce, so you deal with it" is a means of retaliation. Non-residential parents all too often become disengaged from the everyday lives of their teens either by choice or by circumstances. Avoidance of the emotions associated with leaving the family home can lead to disengagement. Some parents are unwilling to put in the effort staying involved requires. Disengaged parenting can result from work schedules, job relocation, or economic constraints.

Non-custodial parents often slip into a neglectful parenting style when they focus on establishing a new life. This can include new social activities or dating. Disengaged parents may make plans with their teen but then cancel at the last minute. Some cannot keep visitation schedules consistent due to work obligations, while others simply find other activities more appealing. Non-custodial parents who move away require more dedication to maintain contact. Generally, any parent who lives more than three hours away tend to visit less frequently.

Christopher and Laine had been in a pattern of disintegration for years. Chris had been laid off from work twice and each time he took over a year to find another job. Laine, a nurse, had been the primary breadwinner for years. Often Chris spent his free time drinking with friends. His relationship with his two teenage kids was distant. Laine finally demanded a divorce with the support of her two kids and family. Chris opted to move out of town to live with an old friend who promised him a job. His visits with his teens were erratic and he often cancelled at the last minute. He continued to be under-employed and his child support was inconsistent. Neither partner had money for a divorce, so the marriage remained in limbo for years.

Finding activities to do with a teenager is not always easy. This can become a non-residential parent's excuse to disengage from their teen. Adolescents have little interest in spending the weekend at their father's place watching TV. Dinners out can become expensive or too routine. Teens prefer to be out with their friends and may push back against plans with the non-custodial parent. These parents can become little more than a chauffeur for their teen's activities. Without warmth and attention from their teens, these parents may withdraw from regular visitation.

Many adolescents find ways around parental rules or may seek permission for activities that initially appear acceptable to busy parents. Teenagers argue, manipulate, and cajole, making it difficult for parents to maintain a strong position on issues. Many stressed-out parents simply give in to demands in order to focus on other problems in their lives. "Do whatever you want" is a common response in these homes.

Families where neglect becomes the norm face the danger of adolescents becoming parentified. Parentification occurs when the teenager assumes the role of primary caretaker in the family as a result of parental expectations or neglect. These teens take on the responsibility for younger siblings, household chores, and even their parent's emotional well-being. Teens adopt a pseudo-maturity role which interferes with the developmental tasks they need to undertake.

Permissive Parents

In divorce, some parents become more permissive. These parents get more lax, inconsistent, or indulgent due to the emotional demands of dealing with divorce. They often try to remain engaged, but circumstances and emotional stress make it difficult. Hetherington (2002) writes, "Mostly, our permissive parents were recent converts to the style, and their conversion was prompted by physical and emotional exhaustion, or by guilt" (p. 130).[23]

Parents who were previously involved in their teenager's life or who maintained healthy boundaries for their teen often have little emotional strength to deal with the teenager's push for independence after divorce. This permissiveness often means giving in or not being strong enough to say no. Teen demands that escalate to arguments require too much of the parent's energy, so the parent acquiesces. This parenting style can lead to teen manipulation. The stress of living with divorcing parents may create increased rebellion and demands from the adolescent.

Some adults may have previously been strict parents in response to the expectations of the ex-spouse. The more intimidating, authoritarian parent set the tone for the family. This difference in parenting style may have been a major source of contention. Once the controlling parent is out of the home, the other parent may become more relaxed and even overly permissive, if only for a short period of time. Parents who feel guilty about the controlling parent's years of reign will overcompensate by becoming more permissive. Permissive within reasonable boundaries can make the transition to a single parent household less stressful.

Parents become more permissive in order to decrease the stress in the family. Some parents want a peaceful environment after years of struggle. It becomes easier for the parent to acquiesce to the adolescents' demands or let more issues slide. These parents are trying to get away from a home fraught with strife. They don't want power struggles with their teen. Teens may take advantage of this situation. Parents need to assess their laissez-faire approach and provide sufficient supervision to keep their teen safe

Other parents are permissive in order to have a friend and ally during this difficult time. Parents may cross the boundary between friendship and parenting when they start relying on their teenagers for companionship and comfort. Some adults regress to a pseudo-adolescence and start partying to avoid the loneliness that separation can bring. These parents may start allowing and even participating in teenage parties, complete with alcohol and drugs.

One of my teenage clients, Jill age 17, shared that her girlfriend's father often allowed parties and underage drinking. She stated that the dad was divorced and traveled frequently and his parties were his way of spending "quality" time with his teenager. Even my teenage client realized that this was distorted thinking on the dad's part, but reported that lots of kids ended up at his house when he was home. It was unclear as to whether the girl's mother was aware of the parties at her ex-husband's house. During one of these parties, Jill ended up drunk, throwing up in the front yard of his house. Another concerned teen called her parents. My client's parents were furious when they found out and wondered if they could report him for serving alcohol to minors.

In some cases, the more permissive parent wants to be considered cool by the teen and the teen's friends. As the non-custodial parent has less daily contact, they tend to be the more permissive parent. These parents make the life of the custodial parent harder. The teen goes home to the uncool parent, who deals with the day-to-day activities and provides the bulk of the supervision.

If both parents are too permissive the teen may feel abandoned. They can become involved in unhealthy activities and act out as a way of forcing their parents to pay attention. Teens usually know what a parent deems important and may act up in that arena. Parents who stress academics may end up with teens who are failing. Parents who push athletics will have a teen who refuses to continue participation in these activities. A teen's acting out may confuse those parents who see themselves as good parents and their teen's friend. Teens need a caring parent, not a friend.

Enmeshed Parents

There are those who are enmeshed with their children either by being over-involved or over-identifying with them. Parents with high expectations can devote too much attention to what the teen is doing or accomplishing, not to who the teen is. These parents need their adolescents to be the primary focus of their lives. This devotion may have played a role in the divorce. Typically, enmeshed parents continue to be so throughout the divorce, some becoming even more obsessed. Boundaries may get lifted when divorce takes the other parent out of the daily interactions.

Divorce and its emotional repercussions may intensify a parent's need to live their own life through their teen's accomplishments and activities. Some parents turn to their children for companionship, developing a bond that is not always healthy, as it is developed out of the parent's needs and is not in the best interest of the adolescent. When this type of unhealthy relationship develops between the parent and a teen of the opposite sex, the teenager essentially becomes a substitute spouse for the parent. This relationship is extremely unhealthy for the adolescent. Parent-teen closeness that crosses a healthy family boundary can seriously interfere with the development of the teen's own interpersonal relationships.

Controlling Parents

Authoritarian parents have a controlling parenting style. In *The Parent Effect, (2011)* I refer to these parents as the *my house, my rules parents.*[24] During a stressful divorce, authoritarian parents may find it very difficult to maintain the same rules and expectations they had previously held. Mothers, in particular, have been shown to have more difficulty controlling their teenagers once the father is out of the home. Fathers may have been the enforcer of discipline or the mere presence of both parents may have induced teens to accept previous parental limits. Teens struggling with divorce may be harder to control or more disdainful of a parent's authority. Control of an adolescent assumes a level of routine and consistency in the home which is hard to achieve during the transitions that parental separation and divorce brings.

Previously easy-going parents may become stricter. They need to feel some control over their life and may mistakenly believe what they can control is their teenager. Others need a way of proving to themselves that they are being responsible parents even if their marriage is falling apart. Divorce leaves some parents with very little emotional connection to offer their teens and they may compensate by being more involved and rigid because it is the one thing that they feel they can do for their children. For these parents, control becomes synonymous with caring. Control works for the parent but not necessarily the teen.

Non-residential parents, often the father, may attempt to maintain their position with their children by holding a tight rein. However, their irregular contact makes this is a difficult position to maintain, especially with adolescents who quickly realize that their fathers have very little power over their day-to-day lives. In other situations, non-custodial parents may interpose themselves in the custodial parent's interactions with the teen as a way of fighting with their ex-spouse.

Jason, divorced less than one year, has two teenage children who live with their mother. He has liberal visitation, but the couple often disagree over his time with his teens. Jason believes his ex-wife is too lenient and that the kids don't want to visit him because their mother's house has few rules. Jason frequently argues with both of his kids, his son in particular, over issues which he feels are important to their supervision. His response is often punitive and his actions include refusing to pay for his son's gas or turning off his cell phone. Jason came into therapy expressing anger at his ex-wife, concern for his children, and frustration with his lack of closeness with his teens. Jason believed that his children needed him to be the disciplinarian, as his ex-wife was lax in monitoring their behavior. He failed to understand that he was allowing his relationship with his kids to suffer because of his anger with his ex-wife.

The personal upheaval that divorce brings makes it difficult for parents to maintain control consistently. Out-of-control spouses can become controlling parents. Typically, established rules and consequences become inconsistent, rigid, and even irrational. What is disallowed one day may be completely acceptable the next. Consistent expectations and appropriate consequences for behavior often shift to strict demands for behavioral compliance for the sake of control. These shifts become confusing for the teen. Over time, after many unsatisfying conflicts, these authoritarian parents may discover that respect and cooperation are more realistic goals for their relationship with their teenagers. With adolescents, being in control is not the same as controlling. Supervision and realistic expectations are an important form of parental care.

Authoritative Parents

Authoritative parents most likely were parenting in this style prior to the divorce. These parents find ways to supervise teen activities, give nurturing attention, and provide positive encouragement. These parents have the best relationship with their teens. According to Parra et al. (2019):

> The children of authoritative parents have higher levels of self-esteem, moral development, interest, motivation and academic performance: they also have an internal attributional style, consume alcohol and other drugs less frequently, and are less likely to succumb to negative peer group pressure and have fewer behavioral problems. (p. 2)[25]

Healthy parent-teen interactions that include both parents are the most beneficial for teen development. These parents usually share custody and co-parent well. Even when disagreements occur, the parents focus on the needs of the teen.

Excessive marital conflict and divorce can drain a parent's emotional resources and limit their parenting abilities, but many parents find ways to cope without involving the teens. Some are better parents once freed from an unhappy marriage. Some, when no longer compelled to support a spouse's strictures, are now able to parent in a way they consider healthiest for their adolescents. The changes of divorce allow some parents to refocus on their teenagers. Many of these parents enjoy the teenage years and do not stress over the small stuff.

Healthy parents maintain family routines and provide structure within the home. Rules are established, behavior is monitored, and appropriate consequences are given for infractions. Most importantly, attention and affection are available and unconditional. Parent-teen skirmishes are kept in perspective. When an issue arises, the non-residential parent is informed and involved. Both homes agree to follow a similar set of expectations and consequences. For instance, if a teen is grounded from the phone at moms, dad will enforce this at his house. This may be difficult for divorced parents, but the effort is made to do what is best for the teen. If the couple cannot co-parent well, they may opt to parallel parent, which is a style of divorced parenting that stresses respect for the other parent's decisions and a curtailing of conflict for the sake of the children. In these families, parental interactions are kept to a minimum and an agreement is made to share important information with each other.

Divorce does not necessarily impact all families in the same way. For some families, it becomes the opportunity to restructure their parenting style into one that is psychologically healthier and beneficial for both parents and teens. There have been situations in which controlling, permissive, and even neglectful parents have adjusted their parenting styles to a more balanced method of raising their teenage children. Parenting does not always suffer with divorce, nor are all children damaged by the experience; some are better off when the parental conflict stops. Healthy parents may still struggle with the feelings created in a divorce, but they do not sacrifice their teens to deal with it.

Summary

Separation and divorce results in numerous changes in the dynamics of a family. The majority of divorced families are mother-custody households with the father having various amounts of visitation. Non-residential parents may remain actively involved or drift away from their teenage children. Notwithstanding custodial arrangements, parents and teens are family and regular interaction is key to adolescent well-being. Parent-teen relationships are crucial to the adjustment of families during and after divorce. Adolescents should have access to and closeness with both parents for optimal development.

Additionally, divorce often creates changes in parenting styles and abilities. Some parents become focused on their own issues and become disengaged or permissive. Other parents are able to focus on their teens, providing stability and warmth. Some spend too much time on rules and forget to provide support and nurturing. Authoritative parenting style creates the best home atmosphere and outcome. Most parents want to be good parents, but divorce is an emotionally powerful life force.

3.

I Said I'm Fine—Now Leave Me Alone!

Teen Responses to Parental Divorce

Just as there is no one common adult experience of divorce, there is also no universal adolescent experience of divorce.

—Michael Riera, Ph.D.

Uncommon Sense for Parents with Teenagers[1]

Adolescence is a time of significant physical, cognitive, emotional, and social change. The developmental tasks of adolescence (individuation, autonomy, separation, and achievement) are accomplished through a progression of changes over the teenage years. Most teens successfully progress to adulthood. Some get stuck during certain developmental stages, while others make only superficial changes and appear pseudo-mature. Rushing through these steps can affect healthy development and create problems with functional maturity later in life. Maturity is best accomplished slowly and carefully, not a common style of teenagers.

Parental conflict, separation, and divorce during the adolescent years will inevitably create special challenges for teenagers and their family. For the purpose of this work, younger adolescents are those ages 12 through 15 and older adolescents are those ages 16 through 21. The impact depends upon factors including the teens' individual personality, their developmental stage, and their parents' handling of the divorce process. The level, nature, and continuation of parental conflict are particularly salient to an adolescent's responses. Before we delve into teenagers' reactions to divorce, it is helpful to briefly familiarize ourselves with the universal changes that occur during the developmental period of adolescence.

Adolescent Changes

Cognitive and Emotional Changes

Cognitive changes during adolescence are significant. Recent research has shown that there is ongoing brain development throughout the adolescent years; the most noteworthy is that the prefrontal cortex continues changing into the early twenties.[2] This area is responsible for problem solving, considering consequences, and most importantly, impulse control.

Teens tend to process information with the amygdala part of the brain, which functions through emotional responses. Adolescence brings a shift from concrete to abstract thinking. Jean Piaget's (1896-1980) theory of cognitive development refers to this as the formal operational stage, which involves the development of abstract, hypothetical thought and the ability to reason through situations in a more complex manner.

Teens become more thoughtful overall—often referred to as metacognition. They think more deeply and abstractly about themselves, others, and the world around them. They are likely to analyze situations and make judgements based on their perceptions and emotional reactions.

These cognitive changes often lead teenagers to feel that they are the only person who has ever experienced thoughts and feelings the way they do. This self-focused thinking partially accounts for the deeper significance teens place on their feelings. Also, adolescents are more likely to misunderstand social cues and overreact to stressful, unfamiliar, or uncertain situations. Teenagers have a heightened emotional response due to the cognitive and hormonal changes taking place.

Personal Changes

Adolescence is a period of social and personal growth. Teens develop their own identities, become increasingly independent, and engage in more intense social and intimate relationships. They identify more with peer groups and less with family. This transition is often filled with emotional turmoil for the teen and for their family.

Some of the necessary social changes occur within the context of the family. Parental reactions to teen changes contribute to the success that adolescents experience in their developmental endeavors. Teens need to try out new styles, interests, and personal opinions. Parental support of healthy choices goes a long way. Too much control or indifference from parents can result in rebellion and a distorted sense of self. In families where change is discouraged, teens may become secretive and withdraw emotionally. Appropriate responses to adolescent actions are difficult in well-functioning families—in divorcing families they are even more complicated but also more crucial.

Adolescents naturally strive to become emotionally, cognitively, and socially independent from parents. They need to identify with peers while learning to think independently. Autonomy and individuation are terms often used interchangeably, but actually they refer to separate but interconnected aspects of the transition from child to adult. Autonomy means being able to make one's own choices, to plan and to follow through on decisions, and to develop a personal value system. Individuation is developing an identity separate from parents and peers, attaining a clear sense of self, and becoming personally and socially capable. Teens want and need to make their own decisions concerning friendships, activities, clothing, hairstyles, and music. During this time, teenagers spend more time alone in their room, on schoolwork or hobbies, on the Internet, or out with friends. Accomplishing these developmental tasks allows individuals to become independent, self-sufficient, and emotionally healthy.

Sexual and Social Roles

Adolescence is a time for developing and clarifying one's masculine or feminine social role, becoming comfortable with one's sexuality, and developing and maintaining interpersonal relationships. These tasks correspond to Erik Erikson's (1902-1994) young adulthood developmental stage of *intimacy versus isolation*. Practice relationships, which lead to long-term adult intimate relationships, take place throughout the teen years.

Also, romantic interests are established, social skills are practiced, and sexual confidence is established. Clothing, hairstyles, activities, and music choices become important, as these define teens as part of a particular social and sexual group. Peer interactions prepare teens for adult social interactions and obligations. During this time, one's sexuality is developed through various sexual activities designed to test these sexual feelings. This aspect of development can be frightening and stressful. Parents, as role models of successful interpersonal relationships, are an important resource in these developmental tasks.

Achievement

Achievement is an important developmental task that gives rise to a teen's sense of purpose and accomplishment. Teens find themselves drawn to certain activities or interests. They align their identity and social group with these pursuits. Examples of these are high school athletes, art students, band members, or the school gamers. Aspects of these activities often merge into their adult career choices. Schoolwork and extracurricular activities provide adolescents with a sense of achievement.

Ownership of one's grades and personal accomplishments are extremely important during this time. Part-time jobs and extracurricular activities encourage adolescents to organize their time, manage money, and develop negotiation skills. However, teens may end up overscheduled and exhausted when they find themselves juggling school, work, and activities. Parental intervention is often needed to help teens realistically balance their busy lives. This task of developing a sense of achievement and accomplishment is important to becoming a productive, responsible, and self-sufficient adult.

A Day in the Life

Another important component to consider in looking at teen reactions to parental strife is what a teen's daily life is like. Most teens begin their day very early. Even though we know teens need a good night's sleep, school usually starts at 7:30 a.m. or 8:00 a.m., necessitating a wake-up of around 6:00 a.m. to get ready and catch the bus or drive. Some teens even have practice or tutoring before school.

At school, they are expected to follow a restrictive set of rules aimed at maintaining a controlled, safe learning environment, not at individuality. Teens have six or seven teachers (think bosses), each with their own set of rules and academic expectations. Adolescents have less than ten minutes between classes to get through the social maze of the hallways. Never mind if you need to go to the bathroom or are having a fight with your boyfriend. They sit in uncomfortable chairs for approximately one hour and quietly pay attention to all the information presented. After all, they will be tested on this knowledge. Tests, papers, and projects are continually assigned. Due dates are not negotiable. Teens also are required to be creative, analyze literature, learn a new language, and understand algebra. At the same time, they are not to disagree with any of the adults or policies that define their day.

Then, there is lunch. For many this is a time of uncertainty, loneliness, or superficial bravado. Social interactions are guided by a predetermined set of norms that can make or break an individual's sense of self. After school, many teens have practice or a part-time job. Some go home to an empty house and may have household chores to manage. Some care for younger siblings. Evenings are filled with homework, household chores, and social media. Many teens have two to four hours of homework. Evenings are also time for social contacts, which is often an emotional minefield. Way too often teens do not go to bed until 11:00 p.m. or later. This daily schedule is all taking place while a teen is undergoing the important tasks of adolescence.

Add to this the upheaval of their family environment, as the home they once felt safe in is in a state of conflict and transition.

Kristi is a 16-year-old in high school. Her parents are currently separated and have started the process of legal divorce. Kristi and her sister, Amy, who is 12, spend every other weekend with their father, who lives in a two-bedroom apartment 30 minutes from their family home. Her parents are working hard to make the transition easy for their daughters.

Kristi starts her day at 6:00 a.m. so that she can shower, put on her make-up, and pick out the right outfit. Her mom is now working as a nurses' aide at a local nursing care facility and starts work at 6:30 a.m. Kristi is responsible for making sure her sister is up and has breakfast before she catches the bus at 7:00 a.m. A quiet girl, Kristi has only a few close friends and struggles socially. She has not revealed her parents' divorce to her peers. Kristi's first class is algebra, her worst subject. Her father used to help her with her homework but since he moved out has not been available. Her second class is social studies. Her friend is in that class, so Kristi begins to be a little more comfortable with her day. Her third class is biology, followed by lunch. There is one friend she feels comfortable with and the two girls sit on the edge of one of the lunch tables. They rarely socialize with the other kids at the table and feel like outsiders during lunch.

Due to her parents' separation, Kristi has to bring her lunch, as her mom can no longer afford for her to buy lunch, like the other kids. Next is physical education, where Kristi often feels awkward and clumsy. Her last period is English. She secretly likes a boy in this class but knows he will never notice her. After school, Kristi goes home, where she is responsible for cleaning the dishes and starting dinner. Homework often takes three to four hours, especially without her dad to help her. Kristi is sad and lonely but does not want to burden her mom, who seems stressed out by the separation. Nights find Kristi struggling to sleep as she worries about her school life and her family. Her next day begins at 6:00 a.m.

Adolescent Reactions

The accepted myth is that adolescents are overly emotional, impulsive, and often act irrationally with little provocation. Even though teens may have an elevated emotional response to situations, the reality is that most teenagers are responding to specific events in their environment. That stimulus may be an upcoming exam, a slight by a friend, a rejection by the opposite sex, an unacceptable parental decision, or the awareness of marital problems.

Clearly, some perceptions impact responses, however most reactions are directly connected to what is going on around them or with the people they care about. Teenagers may be able to understand the issues, emotional struggles, and other nuances of their parents' divorce, but this awareness does not protect them from the emotional repercussions. When a teen is trying to understand the changes happening in their family, they may exhibit their emotions in a straightforward manner, in a passive-aggressive way, or hidden within other actions. Especially during divorce, it is important for parents to listen, look behind the obvious, and help their teenager deal effectively with their emotions and reactions.

Parents who separate during their children's adolescent years may mistakenly believe their teens will be able to understand and adjust well to the changes occurring in the family. Teens often request and may be given detailed information about the parents' marital problems. When they do not receive sufficient information from parents, teens will create explanations from their observations and analyses of the situation.

When knowledge is lacking, people tend to imagine worst-case scenarios. Fears about the future may interfere with the teen's development of autonomy and individuation. When parents have worked hard to keep disagreements behind closed doors, teens may be unaware of the problems in the marriage. However, adolescents will often notice when their parents are emotionally distanced from each other. Other teenagers end up with a front row seat to the drama unfolding as their parents separate and dismantle the life they built together. For many teens, the parental conflict may look more like an encounter between Godzilla and Mothra than a resolvable disagreement. All of these situations result in a myriad of emotional and behavioral reactions.

Most studies on parental divorce have shown that teenagers ultimately adjust to the changes in the family, but none are unaffected.[3,4] As previously noted, responses are dependent upon the individual teen's issues, temperament, strengths, and the manner in which their parents handle their divorce. Interparental conflict and the parent's emotional health will be key factors in a teen's choice of responses.[5] Outside resources, including extended family, friends, and professionals can also influence the teens' adjustment. Let's explore the possible emotional and behavioral reactions of teenagers dealing with parental separation and divorce. Even when a teen exhibits a particular emotion or behavior, they may be unaware of the connection between their response and its antecedent.

Denial

Most teens take their parents' relationship for granted; to the teen the parents' marital issues are secondary to the parent–child relationship. In situations with ongoing and overt conflict, the teens are not only aware but may even be drawn into the marital problems. Other teens are blissfully naïve concerning problems in their parents' relationship. No matter what level of awareness the teen has, the first reaction to the announcement is denial.

Denial is the inability to acknowledge the parents' problems or the upcoming separation as a reality in their life. Surprise and shock often accompany this response. Teens will often feel confused or ambivalent about the news. Some may listen quietly and then withdraw to their room. Other teens cry openly. Many adolescents insist that this is not happening. Teens may express anger that their parents are not trying hard enough to stay together.

Whatever the initial response, the teen is reeling from the news, often hoping that it is not true. As Wallerstein and Blakeslee in *What About the Kids (2003)* states, "While you should be prepared for an initial cool, almost detached response to your announcement about the divorce, be aware that still waters run very deep ... Your announcement evokes powerful fears and passions that lie very close to the surface" (p. 100).[6]

It is not unusual for teens to remain in denial even as the changes start to happen around them. Many, especially younger teens, maintain the fantasy that their parents will stay together. Older teens may accept the information but continue to hope for reconciliation. Even teens who have witnessed their parents fighting hold out some hope for a resolution to the discord. A few are relieved and have actually hoped for an end to the conflict that permeates their home. Even when teens deny that they have any questions or concerns, they need time to adjust and an opportunity to talk more in-depth about what is happening. When a teenager says they are FINE, be sure they are not.

Sadness and Grief

Parental separation brings about a tremendous sense of loss for all family members. This family upheaval and the subsequent changes that occur will result in grief and sadness for the adolescents. Even when separation brings some relief from the conflict at home, there is loss: loss of family identity, loss of daily interaction with both parents, loss of financial stability, and even loss of the family home. Adolescents feel heartache when they see their mothers cry. They are sad that their dad is alone in an apartment with nothing on the walls, sad that summer vacation is ruined and heartbroken that they may have to move out of the family home. Teenagers are let down when a parent does not show up for their visit or to their game, as promised. Teens may hide behind "It doesn't matter, I am sure he was busy," but the absence is felt.

Grief, of which sadness is a common characteristic, is the process of acknowledging and coming to terms with a loss one often did not expect or want. All family members grieve the loss of the family they were accustom to, even if that family was one of high conflict. Teens mourn the loss of childhood memories and future possibilities. This process of grief brings up many emotions and can take years to work through.

Sadness is a natural response to a loss or change in one's life. Sad feelings will ebb and flow as the divorce proceeds. The degree of sadness and its expression depends on the dynamics of the divorce and the teens' age and temperament. Studies have shown that when parental conflict was low and the teen is surprised by the separation, sadness is more pronounced.[7]

Youth from high-conflict homes may find the news less of a shock but still feel the loss. When one parent become less accessible following the separation, many teens feel anguish at the absence of regular contact. As divorce is a great stressor, the primary custodial parent may also be less available. Parental divorce inevitably alters the amount of attention a teen receives from their parent. There is also a special kind of sadness connected to the teens' awareness that their parents no longer love each other and that love does not last.

Younger teens may be more likely to feel the loss, as they are still dependent on the family for their social activities and interactions. Older teens struggle with the disruption of their family identity and the lack of security that comes from knowing that their childhood home is there for them as they venture into the world. College-age teens have the difficult choice of which home to go to during summers and holidays. Older teens are more likely to have established interests and peer associations which help them deal with the family changes.

Teens handle their loss in a number of ways depending on their personality and emotional style. The family's norms about expression of emotion come into play as the teen attempts to find an outlet for their reactions. Many adolescents will not openly acknowledge their pain and will need encouragement to talk about their feelings of loss. Teens may seek to protect their parents by hiding their feelings and putting on a good face. "I am fine!" is the common response to questions about how they are handling the parental separation.

Often the sadness is expressed alone in their room. Some cry openly but refuse to talk. Teens might suppress these feelings by becoming angry or withdrawing from family. Others push themselves into schoolwork or other endeavors as activity can quiet the thoughts and the emotions associated with grief. These outlets may be a healthy way of coping for some, while others are running away from their feelings. Irritability or acting-out behavior are less obvious expressions of sadness. Empathy for parents' pain will result in similar emotions from the teen, even if they are not able to fully appreciate what they are experiencing. Some talk with parents, peers, or school counselors about the family disruption; others struggle alone.

Depressive Symptoms

When a teen is unable to work through their sadness and grief over the losses created by the divorce, they can experience depressive symptoms. Divorce, in and of itself, does not cause depression but is a significant life change that may precipitate depression in teens predisposed to depression. Individual temperament, the degree of parental conflict, parent-teen relationship problems, and the number and severity of transitions experienced all interact in the development of clinical depressive disorders. Those teens who contend with significant changes, such as a move away from friends or estrangement from the non-residential parent, have more difficulty managing the sadness and grief. Depression should be considered when a teenager has become withdrawn, believes they have no one to turn to for help, or does not have activities that provide an outlet for them.

Anger

Anger, a complex emotion, is a normal part of adolescent emotional development. Becoming more aware of the world around them and developing their own perceptions and opinions, may trigger teens to experience various types of anger-based emotions. Anger has an extensive range. It can be expressed as irritation, annoyance, impatience, displeasure, contempt, frustration, and rage. Life's injustices and perceived hurtful and inappropriate behaviors (especially bullying) may create a healthy sense of anger. How anger is acknowledged and dealt with is critical to its healthy development. How to handle anger is often learned from parent modeling and peer behaviors.

Parental conflict and separation will always invoke a degree of anger. Anger at parents for splitting up their family. Anger that their parents can't get along better. Irritated that parents are fighting over stupid things. Bitterness at having to visit their other parent on a scheduled day. Frustration at not having enough money for extra things. Pissed off at having to miss a party due to visitation schedules. It just isn't fair! Realistically, there isn't anything that is fair or easy about trying to figure out who you are while your parents are yelling at each other and dismantling the family home.

Anger that surfaces during a teen's parents' divorce will be expressed in a variety of ways. Some teens are verbal and direct. Others will hide behind doors or a fake smile. When anger feels unacceptable, some may pull away from family, react passive-aggressively, or become depressed. Teens may strike out at others to hide their real feelings from themselves. Increased irritability, frustration, and disrespect are signs of anger not directly acknowledged or expressed. Anger can be a helpful feeling giving teens permission to dislike the changes, empowering them to speak up, and ultimately helping them to make a healthy adjustment.

Younger adolescents may have more difficulty accepting their angry feelings and struggle with appropriate expression of these feelings. These teens may look to parents for guidance in handling their anger. Older teens may be able to intellectually work through their anger and find acceptable ways to share these feelings with parents and friends. However, older teens may also express their unacknowledged anger in passive-aggressive or immature ways. Sharing their angry feelings with peers, parents, or counselors may help teens deal with anger's intense and sometimes scary feelings. It is important to be aware that anger is always a possibility during the many transitions that will take place during a divorce. Parents have a responsibility to recognize the signs of anger and to support their teens as they deal with their natural feelings of anger.

Seth was a quiet 16-year-old who enjoyed video games and had a few close friends that he had known since childhood. He had an older sister, who was in her second year at college. His parents had recently decided to separate after 20 years of marriage. The couple had no overt conflicts but simply felt that they were no longer in love. His father worked long hours and was a bit of a loner. His mother, 12 years younger than his father, had decided that she wanted more from her life than her marriage could provide her. The couple told Seth together and insisted that the divorce would not impact his relationship with either parent. Seth listened quietly to the news and, after asking a few questions, stated he was okay. Both parents were relieved that he had taken the news so well. They checked in with him several times over the next few weeks, but he continued to insist that he was okay. Seth's father moved into an apartment 15 minutes away. Both parents made themselves as available as possible, even getting Seth a car so he could travel between homes. Two weeks after his dad moved out, Seth was suspended for fighting at school, which was out of character. Over the next year, he became increasingly irritable and disrespectful with his mother, often spending a lot of time in his room or with friends. After a year, the couple requested counseling for their son, who was obviously struggling with his parents' divorce.

Anxiety

Parental divorce is the source of many interconnected concerns and fears. Changes in the family situation creates stress and anxiety. This feeling is experienced by many teens as excessive worry, nervousness, restlessness, or fear. "Research has shown that stressful life events—for example ... having parents who are separated or divorced—can raise the risk of social anxiety disorder. The more such factors teens have in their lives, the greater the risk seems to be" (p. 51).[8] Anxiety is often confusing for teens. They often don't have an accurate assessment of what they are feeling.

Adolescents may have trouble concentrating and become easily frustrated. They may be irritable or restless. They may have trouble sleeping or experience nightmares. Teens worry that the physical manifestations of anxiety indicate something is medically wrong with them, adding to their stress.

What teens do not realize is that anxiety is often a way for the body to tell you that something is frightening or confusing. Many are apprehensive about what will happen in the future, as their family has been their primary security base. Teens who already feel anxious in social settings may become more distressed. Many do not share with family or friends what they are feeling because they do not want to be seen as weird or crazy. Younger adolescents may find the changes in the family more stressful than older teens, who are more differentiated from family.

Anxious teens may have difficulty expressing themselves. As anxiety can intensify fears and increase negativistic thoughts, teens may hide what they are going through. Anxious teens will withdraw and spend more time alone in their room. They may avoid social activities and even miss school due to physical complaints. These teens may develop headaches and stomach distress. Parental conflict adds to the stress the teen is dealing with and makes the home no longer a safe place. Seeking out other connections may be helpful or backfire. Girls may become involved with an older male for security. Alcohol and drugs may be used to calm anxious feelings and worrisome thoughts.

Guilt and Blame

Complicated feelings, such as guilt and blame, can occur during the upheaval of a family. There is natural tendency to find someone to blame in a painful situation. Teens are often in denial during the early stage of parental separation and want to find a reason to explain or to alter the home situation. When the parents had fought openly over parenting issues, teens may develop a sense of guilt or self-blame. Even when the conflict or stated reason for the separation is not related to the teen's behavior, they may feel responsible. Children and adolescents may believe that they can encourage parental reconciliation by behaving differently. Some act out as a way of diverting attention from parental conflict, others try to become the perfect kid.

Another reaction common in divorcing families is to allocate more culpability for the marital problems to one parent. Siblings, especially those who are the source of parental concern or conflict, may be seen as responsible for the separation. Often teens are swayed by the emotions and statements of their parents and end up taking sides. A parent's anger at their ex-spouse can influence a teen's perception of that parent.

Other teens make their own assessment and blame one parent more than the other for the issues in the marriage. A discovered infidelity can provide a villain easily blamed for the break-up. Assigning blame may help teens to mistakenly believe that reconciliation is possible if only the guilty parent would change. When a teen is protective of a parent, they will hold the other parent responsible for the favored parent's pain. In this situation, teens may be outright rude and dismissive with the rejected parent. Disrespect and withdrawal of affection can indicate that the teen is blaming a particular parent.

Teens may be vocal about holding one parent responsible, especially if it aligns with their preferred parent. Other times, teens will tell their perceptions to friends but not say anything to parents. "I think my mom's drinking is why my dad is leaving." "Dad is always working and doesn't have time for us." "That stupid blonde woman destroyed our family!" Finding someone to hold responsible may help a teen feel more in control of a distressing situation. However, anger at a previously-loved parent or feeling responsible for the divorce can be difficult for a teen to manage and may lead to additional emotional problems.

Finding Another Home

Home is usually a place of love and security. Adolescents want and need a home base where they can feel cared for, relaxed, and protected. When this home is being upended by conflict and divorce, they will often seek an alternative home base or, at the very least, other adults to connect with.

Some teens may feel like an outsider in their non-residential parent's home, especially if that parent is now living with someone else. Teens may spend more time with extended family, as they are familiar and comfortable. Often a friends' family will fill the need for a home base and teens will gravitate to these houses during times of stress. A friend's mother or father may be a supportive resource during family instability.

In selecting an alternative family, the teen can easily perceive the other family in ways that meet the teen's needs, rather that realistically. There may be anger at parents for not being like the Joneses, whose family seems happier. Often extended family or close family friends are available to help the teenager deal with the emotional fallout of the parents' divorce. Professionals, perhaps a therapist or youth minister, may also provide temporary security or support while the family is being restructured.

There is the possibility that teens will look to peer relationships that are not necessarily healthy alternatives. Teenage girls may become sexually active and even have a child in hopes of creating their own family. Other teens may become involved in gang activity, as gangs stress the family component of its members and may be very appealing to adolescents who feel disengaged from parents. Parents need to be aware of the friends their teen is associating with. Teens will be secretive and defensive of peers they think parents will not approve of. They will find ways to spend time with these peers without parental knowledge or approval. Parental disapproval may lead to intense conflict between parent and teen. The "they are there for me" is often decried. Healthy relationships outside of the family during a parent's divorce can be a way for teens to cope, while negative associations can be harmful.

Acting Out

It is not uncommon for teens to react to their emotions in a behavioral format. A certain amount of rebellion and pushback is normal and conducive to the tasks of adolescence. Teens undergoing the stress of the parental divorce will normally feel a variety of uncomfortable, intense emotions.

When teens do not feel they have options or outlets to address these emotions, they will end up acting out in a variety of ways. Teens act out by becoming more oppositional at home, being disrespectful, being sullen, or isolating. More intense ways of acting out include skipping school, hanging out with unacceptable peers, becoming involved with alcohol and drug use, engaging in minor and even major types of criminal mischief, and becoming sexually active.

Angry teens will argue, insult, slam doors, and hit walls. Some teens may even resort to running away or other methods of escaping the home. In an often-cited study by Wallerstein, Lewis, and Blakeslee (*2000, The Unexpected Legacy of Divorce),* it was reported that:

> One in four of the children in this study started using drugs and alcohol before their fourteenth birthdays. By the time they were seventeen-year-olds, over half of the

> teenagers were drinking or taking drugs. . . . Of those who used drugs, four in five admitted that their schoolwork suffered badly as a result. ... Early sex was very common among girls in the divorced families. . . In our study, one in five had her first sexual experience before the age of fourteen. Over half were sexually active with multiple partners during their high school years. (p. 188)[9]

While these statistics seem frightening, it is important to remember that acting out and alcohol use during the teenage years occurs in all family situations. Some acting-out behaviors may be short-term reactions to family upheaval.

Other types of acting-out behaviors include minor acts of mischief, skipping school, or self-harming. Self-harm, such as cutting, may be an expression of the pain one is experiencing. Eating disorders are another way of trying to be in control of something at a time when one's world feels out of control. Research has found an increase in compulsive spending by teens dealing with divorce.[10] Other teens may become obsessively involved in an activity, such as chronically exercising or playing video games all night.

Often negative behaviors are eventually noticed by parents, school personal, or even the police. Teens who act out need attention, supervision, and an opportunity to work through their emotional issues. Parental intervention is important at this junction in a teen's adjustment to divorce. Acting out during adolescence can become a path to difficulties in adulthood.

Manipulation

Manipulation is a means of obtaining a desired outcome from another by influencing or coercing their response. For teens, manipulation is usually aimed at parents and focused on getting something desired or an affirmative response to a request. There are positive forms of manipulation, such as cleaning one's room before asking to go out. However, in most cases manipulation is considered a negative or underhanded method of getting one's way. Early in life, children learn effective ways of getting what they want—a tantrum that gets a cookie is a quickly-learned lesson. Parental divorce or separation can result in increased use of manipulation by teenagers. An article titled *I've Kept It That Way on Purpose (2008)* states:

> Adolescents after divorce or separation do not simply absorb parental resources as sponges absorb water; rather, they gather and interpret information about their parents, dodge questions, engineer images of themselves, parry parents' probes, maneuver between households, and cut ties with parents in efforts to exert their own authority and to secure their individual identities. (p. 615)[11]

Adolescents manipulate in several ways. The most common way is to simply ask one parent or the other for preferred activities. Teens usually know which parent is more lenient. At times, teens will move from one home to the other to keep parents unclear about their activities. Another form of manipulation is to withhold information from one parent in order to receive a favorable response or to avoid a negative reaction. Having a project that is due on Monday or failing a class may be kept from the parent while visiting for the weekend. Another typical form of manipulation is to threaten to move out of the parent's home if desired activities are not allowed. "I will just go live with my dad. He will let me go to the concert!"

In many families, divorce means less-direct communication between parents, as information is often passed through the teenagers. While this may seem like an easy alternative for conflicted couples, using teens as messengers is risky and a bit of a setup for the teen. This allows adolescents to manipulate the information to receive a preferred response.

Divorce, and the lack of communication between the parents, is a breeding ground for learning how to manipulate a situation. It is understandable that adolescents will figure out how to best work within the structure of the family. However, the potential for misuse of this ability is increased in the context of parental division. Parents need to co-parent effectively to avoid being manipulated by their teens.

Responsibility and Maturity

Divorce and the establishment of two separate households will usually result in changes in responsibilities at home. Working parents necessitate care for younger siblings and the house. Household responsibilities may include cooking, laundry, housecleaning, and even grocery shopping. Adolescents may be left to care for themselves, including getting ready for school and managing their own schoolwork. Some may take a job for extra household money.

This increased responsibility and maturity allows some teens, especially older teens, to feel control over the changes going on in their family. Teens function better when the added responsibilities are age-appropriate, acquired over time, and support family functioning. Difficulties arise when the teenager becomes too bossy with younger siblings or disrespects parental authority. Teens may also become caught up in feeling that they need to care for their distressed parents. Assuming too much responsibility (parentification) is detrimental to the healthy development of the adolescent.

Maturity is developed through series of experiences and accomplishments. As parents focus on the complexities of their own lives, teens may feel the need to become more independent. Dr. Pickhardt in *The Everything Parents Guide to Children and Divorce* (2006) emphasizes:

> The teenager may accelerate her separation from family in response to the parent separating the marriage ... some teenagers may feel driven to act more grown-up because, deserted by the unified family they could once count on, they now feel more impelled to grow up quickly and operate on their own. (p. 115)

Important steps in the developmental process may be skipped when teens push themselves to assume age-inappropriate responsibilities, resulting in a superficial identity that lacks important core characteristics. Younger teens taking on the tasks of older teens and adults may feel overwhelmed and insecure. Adolescents who grow up too fast may miss some of the nuances in the development of their adult self, and this will show up later in life.

In general, older teens are better equipped cognitively, socially, and emotionally to become more self-sufficient. Handling life's tasks without appearing, feeling, or reporting being overwhelmed may indicate that the teen is maturing in a healthy manner. Pseudo-maturity and rushed independence will be noticeable, as these teens will begin struggling in many of their areas of functioning. Parental responsibilities include encouraging their children to take their time growing up.

Negative Perceptions

Adolescence is a time of changes in thinking, the development of personal perceptions and opinions, and moral judgements of others. Adolescents become aware of their parents' imperfections and are quite critical of the mistakes that they see their parents making. This perception of the fallibility of authority extends to teachers and other adults.

How adults handle the divorce process provides teens with many opportunities to critique their parents' behavior. Divorcing parents may disparage the other parent, hide assets, lie, or engage in other unscrupulous behaviors. Too often, teens are given or overhear details about the legal process of divorce, including emotional conversations with lawyers and others. Teens may be reluctantly drawn into the custody issues. This enables the teen to form impressions about how the legal system works—often unfavorable perceptions. Noticing how parents and other adults behave during this stressful period can create a level of cynicism in the adolescent.

Somewhere around ages 12 through 14 there is a slow shift from concrete thinking to abstract thinking. Younger teens engage in more black-and-white thinking, which often translates into more negative beliefs about their family situation. Their reactions to the divorce may be confusing and unsettling for them. Having a parent move out may feel like complete abandonment. "My dad is gone." "What did I do wrong?" "We are not going to have enough money." Younger adolescents are more likely to form opinions based on their parents' reactions and responses.

Teens aged 15 and over are likely to develop their own perceptions of the family's issues. Older teens are able to abstractly consider such issues as love, trust, fidelity, security, and other factors that they once considered a given in their family.

Sometimes, in an effort to form their own opinions, teenagers will lean toward the opposite or more negative aspects of an issue. Hurt, angry teens are likely to develop a viewpoint or value that is in direct opposition to what their parents espouse. Therefore, it's understandable how upsetting it can be for a teen to witness their parents argue and to watch the divorce unfold.

Particularly contentious divorces create intense negativistic perceptions. Negative thoughts developed during this time period may include love isn't real, people don't stay around, my parents can't be trusted, problems can't be solved, love brings pain, adults cheat, and women are too demanding. Teens may question the meaning and importance of commitment to love and to family. For many teens, these negative perceptions are altered as they go through some of their own positive life experiences. Other adolescents may develop ingrained, unhealthy perceptions and end up with lifelong difficulties.

Negative observations of their parents can harden a teen's feelings, making them more cynical about the world. Teens may express these emotions through rude, dismissive, and argumentative treatment of others. They will disregard authority figures and question rules. Some teens may even become involved in anti-establishment causes, even if only superficially. Worst-case scenarios are when teens become involved in gangs and/or engage in delinquent behavior. Fortunately, most teens of divorce adjust relatively well after the family settles into their new normal. The development of beliefs and values is an important aspect of adolescent development with long-term implications.

Interactions with Parents

Adolescence is a period of increased parent–teen conflicts as the teen struggles to individuate. Disagreements over activities, curfews, clothes, school, and computer use are normal. However, divorce can exacerbate normal conflicts into unhealthy battles. Teens may become disillusioned with parental authority. Refusing to follow rules, not seeking parental approval for activities, being outright rude, and refusing to attend family events are all possible teen reactions.

In some families, the conflicts may escalate into volatile arguments that may become physical. When parents fight with each other, they are modeling how to handle conflict, and teens may treat a parent with the same disregard or disdain. "You talk to mom that way, why shouldn't I?" "I don't care what you think!" Another reaction is to sabotage or refuse visitation with a parent. Elements of parental alienation can seep into the parent-teen interactions when interparental conflict is center stage in the family dynamics.

Healthy Coping Skills

Numerous studies have found that most teens ultimately adjust well to parental divorce and the restructuring of the family.[12] While divorce is difficult in the best of situations, many teens are able to work through the challenges in a way that develops their strengths and positive attributes. Healthy adjustment includes acknowledging and working through difficult feelings. In handling the changes inherent in divorce, many adolescents develop resilience and the realization that they can handle life's changes. Teens who are socially confident and connected to peers may handle the changes better. High-functioning teens are also able to handle school work, have friends, be involved in extracurricular activities, and get along with parents and siblings.

In a 2015 research review that examines coping styles that result in positive outcomes, Mohi found that:

> Of the coping styles ... reciprocal support, or the act of establishing a two-way support system between offspring and parents, yielded the best results in terms of positive long-term outcomes ... Participants who reported primarily using the support coping style experienced a greater sense of responsibility, maturity, self-confidence, and inner strength, as well as a higher acceptance of their parents' choices, weaknesses, and strengths. (p.51)[13]

Teens with parental support have a good chance of developing healthy ways of coping. Well-adjusted youth adapt to the altered family structure while maintaining a close relationship with their parents. Adolescents can be realistic about the family situation and understand that relationships don't always work out. These teens continue to have a belief in love and commitment. Healthy adolescents may accept more responsibility for their own self-care, decisions, and activities. They usually feel more in control, even with the changes going on in their family.

How the adults in the family manage their sadness and anger can set an example for the teen. Healthy teens are capable of communicating what they are feeling and make reasonable requests of their parents. They are able to articulate that they do not wish to be brought into the middle of the parental conflict and will not take sides. Home life and interactions with parents often stabilize after the conflicts have subsided, allowing teens to become more relaxed and comfortable in their homes. Understanding and feeling compassion for a parent's distress without getting too caught up in the drama is important for adolescent adjustment. When they feel overwhelmed, teens will talk to parents, peers, or request professional help. Psychotherapy and support groups can help teens deal with their emotions and develop their inner strengths.

Academic Impact

Adolescents spend more than half of most weekdays in school which, as described earlier, carries a lot of expectations, social stress, and academic challenges. When a teen's home life is characterized by parental conflict, uncertainty, and packing and unpacking between residences, schoolwork may not be a priority. A shift in academic performance—with lower grades, missed homework, excessive absences, and early drop-out rates—is a known effect of family restructuring.[14]

Parental monitoring and support for schoolwork is hard to maintain during stressful times. Distracted teens may delay preparing for college by not studying for the SAT or not filling out college entrance forms in a timely manner. Alternatively, there are teens who respond to family upheaval by becoming hyper-focused on school, especially if they feel successful or safe in that environment. Some of these teens may obsess over doing well in school. Scholastic success can be a diversion, a chance to get something right, or a way out of the family. Disruption in educational functioning can have long-term implications. Teachers, coaches, and school counselors may identify and intervene with teens who are struggling and alert parents of the changes in academic functioning.

Impact on Developmental Stages

The developmental tasks of adolescence may be impacted by parental divorce. According to Lansford (2009):

> It may be that divorce has effects on particular outcomes that are salient during the developmental period during which the divorce occurs. For example, academic achievement, identity development, emerging romantic relationships may be affected by divorce that occurs during adolescence because these domains of functioning are developmentally salient then. (p. 143)[15]

Divorce during the early adolescent period (ages 12 to 13), usually jump-starts some of the dramatic emotions and behaviors associated with this developmental stage. The negative attitude typical of early adolescence is intensified and directed at the parents, who teens believe are taking away the security of their home. Teens may also be angry at one parent for making the other parent leave. There is also a strong hope for reconciliation. These age-related responses correlate with the younger adolescent's more concrete than abstract thinking process. These teens struggle with their emotional responses without the cognitive ability to fully understand their reactions.

Young teens may feel pressure to grow up before they have the time and prerequisite activities to easily make the transition. Some adolescents may regress to an earlier emotional age as they become frightened of venturing out into the adolescent world.

Regressive behaviors include becoming clingy and emotional with their parents and playing with childhood toys. Teens may unconsciously believe that if they remain children, their family will continue as it was when they were younger. When there has been significant parental conflict there is a natural sense of relief when the divorce process is started. However, young teens may feel guilty or responsible for the conflict. Relief gained by parental separation may carry its own struggles.

The middle adolescent age group (ages 14 to 16) responds with action. Normal developmental activities during this time involve experimentation with style and interests. There is a move toward identification with peers and a moving away from parent-centered activities. Angry and confused about the change going on at home, this group may turn to their peers for emotional support, thus becoming vulnerable to peer pressure. This may lead to early experimentation with alcohol, drugs, and sex. Teens may also disengage prematurely and develop a pseudo-maturity. This identity will be lacking some important characteristics, as it is developed out of anger and fear rather than growth and life experiences. Still needing the security of home, mid-range teens will often escape to friends' houses, allowing these families to provide them with a stable family model.

Teens in the mid-adolescent period often react to parental separation with anger and engage in more conflict with parents. Disillusioned with their parents' actions, these teens may balk at accepting parental authority. Some behaviors may be aimed at making their parents pay more attention to what the teen is going through. As adolescents are developing their sense of right and wrong, they may find themselves morally outraged at the parent they deem responsible for the divorce. Awareness of a parental infidelity may create intense feelings of anger toward a parent and shame about the parent's actions. These teens may not share their parents' divorce with friends due to fear of being judged. Shame about a parent's actions, especially if an affair is uncovered, may keep teens from spending time with friends or having friends over to their home. Acting out can reach the extreme level at this developmental stage and teens will often feel out of control.

The following case example is a composite of three families. All of the families had three daughters between the ages of 12 and 17. The families were in various stages of divorce and were involved in family therapy. Two mothers and one father were the primary custodial parent. The similarities of the age specific reactions were remarkable.

Byron and Judy had been married 20 years with three daughters. Prior to separating, the couple had tried marital therapy in hopes of making their relationship work but eventually decided to separate. Conflicts were kept private but they reported that the girls were aware that the couple had been arguing recently. The couple decided to tell their daughters together. The parents stressed that the problems were between them and that both of them would be there for the girls. The youngest daughter, Cindy, age 12, initially cried and begged her parents not to get a divorce. The middle child, Penny, age 15, listened quietly, stated "whatever," and went to her room. The oldest daughter, Kristen, age 17, asked questions about the upcoming changes, stressing that she did not want to have to make any changes in her busy schedule. Prior to talking to the girls, the father had arranged to get a short-term lease at a nearby apartment. He moved out one week later. Visitation was the state standard.

Shortly after dad moved out, the youngest daughter began to push for reconciliation. Cindy became clingy and tearful, having difficulty with transitioning between homes. She would cry frequently, claiming to miss whichever parent was not with her. Penny continued to insist that she was okay and that the changes were not a big deal. However, within several weeks, she started fighting more with both parents. She also blamed her father for the breakup and openly accused him of not trying hard enough to come back home. No matter what activity he planned, she was bored and disrespectful of him. The oldest daughter, Kristen, was unwilling to spend nights at dad's apartment, instead arranging to sleep overnight at friends on his weekends. After several months, she did agree to spend some time at dads but stayed fairly aloof. Shortly after the separation, Kristen started dating a guy who was two years older. Unbeknownst to her parents, she started having sex with her new boyfriend and talked about moving out after graduation.

During the early months of transition, both parents spoke regularly and worked together to help their girls deal with the family changes. The couple continued in therapy and encouraged all three girls to have individual sessions. In therapy, Cindy was tearful but struggled with understanding her reactions. She held on to the hope for reconciliation. Penny was reluctant to talk and even denied being bothered much by the divorce. When she did talk, there was a lot of anger about the changes in her life. Kristen was the most articulate but dealt with the divorce by moving her loyalties to her peers, especially her new boyfriend. In time, the family settled down and all three girls established a connection with their dad and he, in turn, worked with their busy adolescent schedules.

Late adolescence is the period of time from 17 through 21 years of age. Many parents mistakenly believe that older adolescents have the cognitive and emotional ability to weather the storm of divorce. This may be true if the teen has sufficiently individuated and is not heavily dependent upon the family to meet their physical and emotional needs. However, all ages struggle with the family restructuring.

Parental divorce may interfere with the healthy development of peer and intimate relationships. Teens in late adolescence are primarily focused on developing interests, making life choices, and building their own relationships. Teens may react by creating their own "families" as they feel betrayed by their families of origin. Romantic relationships during this time may end up being patterned after their parent's problematic relationship; teens may become involved in highly conflicted interactions. Teens may become more cynical and mistrustful of relationships and fear their own relationships failing.

The emotional upheaval of the family may impact the teen's ability to make decisions that take them away from the family, such as attending college or joining the military. Older teens may also experience strong emotional reactions, such as depression and anxiety. These feelings may forestall the development of autonomy and impede their move into adulthood.

Gender and Race

Recent findings have been mixed and there is no consistent pattern regarding the effect of divorce on girls or boys. General studies have indicated that girls tend to internalize their reactions while boys are more likely to externalize.[16] Typically, females express a wider range of emotion while males respond with action. This indicates that girls will be more likely to be sad, depressed, confused, and anxious. Girls may act out their emotions by becoming sexually active and seeking a male security relationship. Boys act on their feelings and are more prone to anger and aggression. Boys will also lean more toward peer interactions and may engage in minor acts of criminal mischief. Emotionally, males may be less forthcoming with their feelings. In terms of coping, it has been reported that "females seek more social support, whereas males use more physical-recreation strategies and relaxation" (p. 98).[17]

Very little research has addressed the issue of race in regard to parental divorce and adolescent adjustment. Studies have indicated that African American children may fair slightly better than others during their parental divorce.[18] Reasons for this include that African American culture is more likely to accept and support single-mother households. There may also be less of a change in socioeconomic resources. Additionally, American teens fair better than European or Middle Eastern teens, as divorce is not seen as a stigma in American while other cultures may be more likely to discourage divorce. Hispanic families also receive more extended family support and therefore may experience fewer negative effects.[19] Overall, the impact of divorce is more related to conditions within families and the amount of resources available to the teens than to ethnic or race considerations.

Summary

Adolescents are emotional and reactive by nature and divorce during this period in their lives is complicated. Even if adolescents appear to be handling the divorce well, they need an opportunity to talk about and express their feelings concerning the changes in their lives. Responses to parental conflict and divorce can include denial, sadness, anger, and guilt. Acting out occurs in a variety of ways including drinking, minor mischief, and conflicts with authority figures. Academic impact is seen in the majority of teens. Positive, growth-promoting responses are seen in many adolescents.

In general, most teenagers adjust well, with the primary impact occurring during the early stages of separation and divorce. The more changes that the teen endures, the more struggles are experienced. As one teen in *Surviving Divorce* states: "Divorce itself is a terrible thing, but when you go through it and come out the other side, you realize that the peace you've found is worth all the sorrow" (p.100).[20]

4.

Why Can't You Just Get Along?

Special Situations in Divorcing Families

The message that our spouse is to blame for the divorce, therefore carries three hidden requests: Don't be mad at me. Pity me. Join me in being angry at your other parent. None of these serves our children.

—Richard A. Warshak, *Divorce Poison*[1]

Parental divorce can create significant changes in a household. Parents may be overwhelmed with managing home and family on their own. Adolescents may step in to help with the care of siblings and household chores. When these newly-acquired responsibilities unbalance the parent–child roles, it is referred to as parentification. Teens who assume the emotional care of a distressed parent can experience difficulties in their own development.

Adolescent development and adjustment can be severely impacted by ongoing, intense conflict between parents. Fighting that occurs before, during, and after divorce is called interparental conflict. Anger can lead a parent to actively encourage their children to disrespect and reject the other parent. Parental alienation is an emotionally damaging experience for any adolescent. These situations can develop during divorce and have long-term implications for teenagers.

Parentification

Separation and divorce often diminish a parent's ability to fulfill their parental role. Parents may become so overwhelmed by the loss of their marital relationship that they are unable to manage household responsibilities. Other parents lose interest in maintaining the home that is now causing them so much stress. Some parents handle their unhappiness by turning to their teen for comfort and companionship. These changes may result in a role reversal in which the teenager takes over many of the parenting responsibilities—referred to as parentification.

There are two basic forms of parentification: instrumental and emotional. Instrumental involves taking over the household tasks, while the emotional type refers to assuming care of the parent's emotional well-being. The level of parentification varies in families, with the more developmentally damaging forms occurring when teenagers become a substitute spouse or companion.

Divorce is not the sole cause of parentification in a family. Physical issues, financial problems, mental health challenges, or alcohol and drug abuse can result in a teen assuming more of the household responsibilities. Emotional parentification is more likely when a parent is particularly devastated by a separation. Additionally, some cultures are more likely to encourage adolescents to take on responsibility for the family and care of siblings. Parentification is more than just about teens taking on household responsibilities, it is a distortion of roles that can interfere with a teen's emotional development.

Instrumental Parentification

Separation results in two households. Parents may ask teens to help care for younger siblings and to assume more of the household chores. Prior to the divorce, most teens could barely manage to keep their rooms clean. Dirty dishes, piles of laundry, and uncooked meals require attention, and the teen may step in to help. Care for younger siblings is often taken on by older teens. Parentification occurs when the teen assumes these chores as their primary responsibility. Even as the family stabilizes, the parent fails to reassume the parental role. These changes can become ingrained in the new household's identity.

Often in parentification, the teen begins to view these tasks as their domain and the parent as the one requiring care. Parentified teens struggle with balancing home, school, and social activities. For many, the expectations of the home override school and friendships, and their development in these areas suffer. Younger teens, in particular, will have more difficulty handling all of the responsibilities. Younger children, also upset by the divorce, may cling to their sibling or resent their authority. Adolescents should not be expected to run a household and will struggle to manage these responsibilities. Torn by the various expectations, these teenagers are frequently unable to find a sense of accomplishment in any arena. Teens may end up feeling that they are not doing a good job running the household or caring for siblings. As Dr. Emery (2016) in *Two Homes, One Childhood* states:

> Caretaker kids suffer from the weight of developmentally inappropriate responsibility. Under a surface of competence, hyper-responsible kids often are anxious about making everything better—or depressed about

their failure to do so. Even when they "succeed," parentified teenagers still lose. (p. 259)[2]

Parentification involves a role reversal. Teenagers often strive to meet the expectations of parents and other adults. Parents may work and then expect to come home to a clean house and a cooked meal. In many cases, parentified teens are not provided with acknowledgment or praise for their actions. Teens may even experience criticism and anger from a parent for not handling the tasks well. "I work all day and all I ask of you is to start dinner!" "Your grandmother is coming over and I don't want her to see the house a mess!" Outside sources may praise the teen for assuming more responsibility. "Aren't you wonderful for helping out your mom!" Additionally, overwhelmed parents may withdraw from providing guidance and supervision for the teen. Growing up too quickly without validation and parental support has long-term implications.

Positive outcomes can be seen in some parentified teens when the added responsibilities are age specific, valued, and supported. In these situations, the expectations of household help are short-term and the parent maintains a level of authority and caretaking. Some studies have indicated that parentified teens may develop resilience from having coped well with the divorce and successfully handled the additional responsibilities.[3] These teens may develop their caregiving skills and a sense of purpose. Closer connections to their younger siblings are possible. Some parentified teens feel more in control of a chaotic home and come to value their own strength and independence. While some adolescents develop positive characteristics in stressful family situations, it is preferable that teens develop their strengths without having to sacrifice some of their childhood.

Emotional Parentification

While instrumental parentification can create problems for the teen's development, emotional parentification is more complex and damaging. Emotional parentification involves crossing important parent–child boundaries and inducing the teen to assume responsibility for the parent's well-being. As stated in *The Unexpected Legacy of Divorce (2000):*

> It is an overburdening that seriously inhibits the child's freedom to separate normally and to lead a healthy adolescence. Bound to the troubled parent by unbreakable strands of love, compassion, guilt, and self-sacrifice, the child is not free to leave home emotionally or follow her heart in love or marriage. (p.9)[4]

In some situations, the adolescent assumes the role of caretaker for a lonely, emotionally fragile parent. A parent may initially request that the teen keep her company due to her loneliness but then she begins to treat the teen as a friend or confidant. In other situations, the teen witnesses the parent's pain and feels the need to provide compassion and companionship. In more intense cases, the expectations from the parent that the teen fill the void left by their ex-spouse is explicit and nonnegotiable. Parentified adolescents become caregivers and companions. They function as friend, confidant, and therapist. Often these teens act as envoy for the conflicted couple, purveyor of negative messages, or peacekeeper. When the bond between parent and teen is based on the emotional needs of a distressed adult, the teen becomes a substitute spouse. In some cases, an element of sexual behavior develops that is extremely unhealthy and inappropriate.

The parentification role becomes entrenched and is difficult to back away from. For some adolescents, the power of the role fuels their need to be important and loved by the parent. Rarely can this relationship be sustained and satisfying for the teen or the parent. As a parent begins to seek out other companions or the teen attempts to differentiate, these roles shift and become emotionally complicated. These changes will often occur at different times and create conflict. In some ways, the divorce trauma is repeated in the parent–child relationship.

Lucy was 14 when her parents Roger (48) and Linda (39) separated. Mom moved to an apartment closer to her work. The parents decided to keep Lucy at her current school and in her home. Early on, mom's visitation was erratic and the conflicts between the couple were volatile. Roger had married later in life and was particularly confused and distressed by the separation.

Alone and floundering, he turned to Lucy for support and companionship. Friday nights became their special night. Lucy, hurt and confused by her mother's lack of involvement, clung to her father's special attention. Roger became increasingly dependent on Lucy and would share his feelings of hurt and rejection by Linda. He also allowed Lucy to handle many of the household chores and even helped her get her driver's license early. Lucy soon began defending her dad and blaming her mother for the break-up. After a year, the mother moved out of town and gave primary custody to Roger. Relationships between all three were strained.

Two years after Linda moved out, Roger decided to start dating and signed up for a dating app. Lucy found the app on his phone and became hysterical. Any attempts by dad to date were met with anger and acting-out behaviors. Lucy stated that "this was her house and no other women was coming in to take over." Roger started dating a woman from his office, but Lucy refused to interact civilly with her. At 17, Roger moved Lucy into her own apartment, but she continued to frequent her dad's house, demanding attention and arguing with Roger's live-in girlfriend. By the time the family came into therapy, the emotional issues were extensive.

Studies indicate that mothers are more likely to parentify their daughters, either as support for household tasks or as a friend and confidant, while fathers may turn to their daughters as substitute housekeepers or companions.[5] Boys are susceptible to "becoming the man of the house" and feel the need to protect or comfort their distressed mother. One mother (with 5 children) I worked with was emotionally unable to deal with her husband's leaving. She would sit in her room crying hysterically that she could not handle all the kids alone. Her oldest child, a son, soon took on the responsibility of his siblings at the expense of his own schoolwork and social relationships. Parentification is more likely with older teens, who appear capable of assuming the adult tasks. All parentified teens struggle under the weight of adult responsibilities and the long-term effects are seen in many areas of their adult lives.

Interparental Conflict

Conflict is a complicated, multi-faceted issue. In all families, a degree of normal conflict allows for individuality and expression of differences. Disagreements may occur between any family members. Adults may argue about money, household responsibilities, or parenting decisions. Conflicts over video games or time in the bathroom may arise between siblings. Parents and teens may differ over curfews, homework, household chores, or computer time. These ordinary conflicts are easily resolved and family equilibrium is quickly restored. When families manage these minor disagreements well, the children learn to resolve conflict in a reasonable manner. Conflict resolution skills help adolescents accept and manage their emotions. In some families, the level of discord intensifies as the unhappiness with the marital relationship increases. In some marriages, the conflict has been at a high level for many years prior to the couple considering divorce. When conflict involves high-intensity emotions and behaviors, the well-being of all family members is affected.

Conflict Styles

There are two basic types of conflict: overt and covert. Overt conflict indicates an exchange that can be heard and observed. Mild overt disagreements are usually resolved by agreement or mutual withdrawal. Moderate conflict includes arguments that are verbal with passion for one's position. More high-intensity conflicts turn into battles with shouting, interruptions, and a more adamant position on the issues. These intense discussions often evolve into personal attacks with a concerted effort to dismiss or denigrate the other's opinion. Overt arguments may include screaming, cursing, name calling, and even physical aggression. Adolescents living with ongoing overt conflict will either be drawn into the issues or find ways to escape.

Covert anger includes periods of silence, passive-aggressive actions, and withdrawal of affection or attention. There is often an attempt to manipulate, control, or hurt the other partner through indirect, subtle methods. In mild conflict, a parent may withdraw affection but deny the behavior. "I'm not mad, I'm just tired." "I don't know what you are talking about." Negative comments to the children or other family members may encourage disrespect of the other parent. Sarcastic or cutting remarks are brushed off as "just kidding." Mild covert styles may include indirect actions, such as excessive spending or neglecting household responsibilities. In moderate conflict, the covert actions may be more noticeable, such as moving out of the bedroom or damaging a spouse's beloved item.

When marital conflict becomes chronic, spouses have difficulty masking their anger. The methods, while still primarily indirect, become more blatant and hurtful. Examples of this type of covert conflict is allowing the spouse to be served divorce papers at work without advance warning or removing all their personal items from the home while they are at work. Covert conflict styles may be less upfront but still noticeable to teens living with their parents' problematic interactions.

When a marriage is not functioning well, arguments may occur on a more frequent basis. When these disagreements take on a personal, emotional component, the marriage's stability is affected. Struggles between couples with children are referred to as interparental conflict. These conflicts rarely go unnoticed by adolescents. A 2016 study noted that "increased sensitivity to interparental conflict, along with the stage-salient developmental tasks and changes ... may increase adolescents' vulnerability to interparental conflict." (p. 77).[6] It is well documented in social research that interparental conflict before, during, and after divorce is the most detrimental factor in an adolescent's emotional development and well-being.[7, 8]

A range of issues can cause conflict in a troubled marriage. Couples can disagree over finances, sex, drinking, household tasks, time together, parenting decisions, extended family, and leisure activities. When the topics become more personal—such as perceptions of the other spouse, lack of intimacy, or parenting styles—conflict increases. Often the possibility of divorce is thrown out as a hurtful tactic. In the case of infidelity, reactions can be volatile. These discussions may take place in the living room, behind bedroom doors, or on the phone. Even if parents attempt to hide these arguments, teenagers can sense problems in the marriage.

Disagreements can range from mild to extreme. Mild conflict may include verbal disagreements, periods of silence, sarcasm, and a general sense of tension. Minor disagreements are usually resolved and the couple resumes comfortable interactions. As couples become increasingly dissatisfied with their relationship, arguments may intensify. There becomes a point when the issues become secondary to the anger and dissatisfaction between the couple. Moderate disagreements may slowly evolve into heated conflicts. Differing opinions, personal accusations, verbal assaults, cursing, and even door slamming become common. Unresolved conflicts may subside only to surface again later.

In some marriages the fights become exceedingly volatile. These are referred to as high-conflict relationships. The disagreements quickly spiral out of control, and the intent is to hurt their partner rather than resolve differences. Loud, hateful, and even physical altercations occur without regard for who is listening or observing. Even a closed door or headphones cannot protect the teen from noticing the fighting between their parents.

High-conflict battles may escalate into physical altercations. Spouses may throw objects, threaten harm, or damage walls. One or both may physically assault, including pushing, slapping, or punching. For some, the suggestion of divorce creates a heightened degree of danger. Abusive spouses are triggered to become desperate and violent by the possibility of separation. These couples are in the minority. However, adolescents who witness these altercations will undoubtedly struggle emotionally and may fear for their own safety.

Spousal disagreements may become a competition. Some partners need to be right and will continue the conflict until they feel they have won. Winning the fight is more important than any issue. Some refuse to acknowledge the other's opinion or emotional pain. One spouse may try to withdraw from the argument but is pursued by the more dominant partner. Giving in is seen as weak or subservient. Conflicts may become entrenched in the interactional style of the couple. Parents are role models and teens learn from observation. Additionally, the possibility of increased discord between parents and teens exists in high-conflict homes.

As the divorce unfolds, the levels of conflict fluctuate depending on the couples' ability to negotiate differences. There are often variations in the couples' conflict styles. Couples may be screamers, avoiders, or criers. One spouse might be a pursuer who is relentless and confrontational. Another may be passive and prefer to avoid, hide their feelings, or withdraw from the conflict. A parent attempting to compromise or decrease the conflict level may find themselves up against the more dominant partner. When both are avoiders, the tensions are palatable.

Certain personality-based characteristics are connected to a parent's tendency to escalate during disagreements. Alcoholism or substance abuse in a partner can create more irrational behavior. Partners who struggle with mental health issues, including narcissistic, borderline, or paranoid personality disorders can be particularly destabilizing.[9] These individuals are more focused on the conflict than the impact that it may have on their teens. Parents with psychological disorders have a difficult time shielding their teens from their marital and personal issues.

Research indicates that "what matters is not simply that an argument occurred, but how it is *handled* by the parents" (p.444).[10] Parents who disagree respectfully and find a way to resolve their differences teach their children an important life skill. Low-conflict families often find ways to mediate their differences. However, during a divorce, parents rarely fight fairly and conflict resolution is inconsistent at best. Teens may observe parents agree to a compromise but not follow through. Bitter spouses may refuse to resolve a conflict out of spite. In high-conflict families, conflict "resolution" is usually achieved by intimidation, deceit, or icy silence. Rarely is compromise actually achieved.

Many parents turn to the legal system to resolve disputes. Failed mediations and custody battles can result when parents become entrenched in their respective positions. Teens do not attend lawyer appointments or court hearings, thus they are limited to the parent's perception of the process or overheard bits of conversation. These observations are instructive. Few parents think to directly teach their teens conflict resolution skills in the midst of divorce.

Changes in conflict usually precede a couple's decision to separate. In low-conflict families, teen may be unaware of the problems, with no warning about the upcoming changes. When conflict levels change, teens may begin to feel concerned but will rarely ask questions. High-conflict marriages elicit the most response from teens, as it is nearly impossible to deny the dysfunction in these homes. High-conflict divorces take the greatest toll on adolescents.

Interparental Conflict and Divorce Phases

The phases of divorce are unhappiness, decision, struggle and transition, and adjustment. During these stages, the level of conflict can shift considerably. Divorce may diminish the conflict or open the floodgates of anger and resentment. During the initial stage of unhappiness, couples become more aware of their differences. Disagreements can grow more personal and emotional. In some marriages, the relationship is unsatisfying and the couple start to pull away from each other. Initial actions, such as a parent moving into the guest bedroom, may signal the declining relationship.

When conflict patterns change, teens may notice that their parent's marriage is struggling. Lessening of conflict may be mistakenly viewed as a sign of improvement in the relationship. Increased conflict can lead to teenagers asking questions; though they may not be emotionally prepared for the information. As the unhappiness becomes more obvious, parents may begin to share some of their issues with their teens. This gives the parent a sense of the teen's response to separation. Parents often hope their adolescents will accept the separation, thus assuaging their own guilt over breaking up the family. Other parents provide personal information to manipulate the teen into taking their side in the split.

The decision and implementation phases bring the reality into the family. Decisions will include where each parent will live, temporary custody, visitation, and child support. Many parents begin legal proceedings, adding a whole new level of stress. The level of marital conflict dictates how well this stage is handled by the parents and the family. If decisions are made with anger and custodial conflicts begin early, the separation can be traumatic. According to Felder and Victor (2011) in *The Good Divorce:* "the demise of a marriage begins with the breakdown of all rational communication, leading to arguments, recriminations, sometimes even violence, until the final death blow when one or the other parent walks into a lawyer's office to begin divorce proceedings" (p.12).[11] Teens may be drawn or insert themselves into the drama.

Family conflict also plays a role in the manner of separation. Low-conflict couples will allow a reasonable, fair transition of belongings and arrange for visitation aimed at joint access. Mid-range conflict couples may struggle with some aspects of dividing assets and belongings. High-conflict couples need to separate with a degree of anger and do not always consider the damage to the other family members. The manner of departure of one parent from the home will always be memorable for the teen.

Struggle and transition is the phase in which parental conflict will either intensify or calm down as new households are established. Transitions are easier with low-conflict marriages—arguments may soften, becoming more respectful with periods of calm. If the couple can work toward more cooperative parenting, their teens will have an easier time adjusting. During this time, the family stabilizes and ex-spouses come to respect each other's role in the lives of their children.

In high-conflict families, the fighting may continue and even worsen. Some couples battle throughout the process. Discord can become centered on the children, pushing the teens to take an active role in the conflicts. Visitation schedules, school activities, finances, and holidays can become a competition, if not an outright battle. Teens may be given too many personal details, asked to carry messages, pushed to take sides, and turned into spies.

Even after the final divorce papers are signed, high-conflict couples continue to rage at each other. The anger between the couple often shifts to arguments over the kids. These loud, disrespectful battles occur over the phone, in person, or are sent through the teen. Often conflict occurs when the teen (and even their friends) is present. Continual legal filings extend the battle and are often portrayed as fighting for the teen's best interest. Most teens quickly realize that they are not being fought for but are a means of victory for the parent. For high-conflict families, the issues never fully get resolved and the teen's life remains stressful.

The adjustment phase may take years for some families. Interparental conflict is particularly important during this time. For many couples, disagreements surrounding the divorce have settled down and they have worked out a consistent, if not ideal, schedule for custody and visitation. There is often less need for ongoing communication between the parents and the reasons for conflict have subsided. However, some couples continue to find issues to fight about, often centered on the teens and financial arrangements.

Carol and Brad had been married for 18 years and had two sons, Jake age 12 and Mike, 16. For the majority of their marriage, Carol, an oil company engineer, was the primary earner. Brad worked erratically and made a couple of attempts at starting his own business, none of which succeeded. Carol was working overseas and the couple initially agreed that the children would stay with their father in the family home.

While overseas, Carol had started dating a co-worker after she and Brad had separated. Brad was enraged when informed of the relationship and started complaining bitterly to his sons that Carol had abandoned her kids and that she had been having an affair. In anger, Brad petitioned the court for full custody claiming that Carol had abandoned her sons. The younger son, Jake, was particularly susceptible to Dad's manipulation. Phone calls with his mother were strained and Jake often spoke disrespectfully to her. Brad could be heard in the background encouraging Jake's negative remarks. During Mom's absence, Jake's schoolwork declined and his behavior problems escalated.

Carol immediately returned to the states and petitioned the court for shared custody. Brad said he would agree to shared custody if Carol continued to pay full child support to him. She declined and the couple ended up in a protracted court battle. The court appointed ad-litem attorney requested therapy for both boys. Carol eventually received custody, but Brad continued his relentless attack on her. Financial issues remained a major point of contention. Over the years Jake and Mike transitioned between homes, struggling to handle the parental arguments. The older son left for college and came home as little as possible. Jake continued to have emotional and behavioral difficulties throughout high school.

Parental alienation is a distinct possibility in these families. Teens whose parents cannot let go of the animosity between them will continue to find reasons to argue for years to come. Adolescents in these families struggle with adjustment as the parental discord precludes their home life from stabilizing.

Impact on Parenting

Interparental conflict can impact one's style of parenting. The stress of divorce and ongoing disagreements can affect a parent's ability to supervise teen activities, to provide consistent and loving attention, and to offer reasonable consequences for inappropriate behaviors. As reported by Michael, Torres, and Seemann (2007):

> Parents in conflict tend to show their children less affection … communicate less with their children … and become more irritable and emotionally unavailable. … They also engage in less monitoring of their children's activities … and methods of discipline may change, becoming harsher, ineffective or inconsistent. (p. 158)[12]

Distressed parents may find monitoring a teen's whereabouts or activities too emotionally taxing and time consuming. Unresolved anger may overflow and end up directed at their teens. Animosity between ex-spouses interferes with a parent's level of connection and emotional availability.

Interparental conflict can ripple into the interactions between parents and their adolescents. Teens, in particular those whose responses to the divorce are anger and withdrawal, may not comply with parental requests. Increased arguments often occur as teens react to separate households with differing rules. When a parent, especially the non-custodial parent, feels less involved or even rejected by the teen, their level of affection and supervision will decline. Teens who witness the conflict style of their parents will learn to handle their differences in a similar style. Physical altercations between teen and parent are more likely in families where parents have had volatile interactions. This role-modeling will have implications for the teen's future relationships.

Adolescent Reactions

According to a 2018 research review, "new evidence highlights that children's emotional, behavioral, social, academic outcomes and future interpersonal relationships are adversely affected by conflict between parents/careers whether adults are living together or not (i.e., married or separated)" (p. 374).[13] Teenagers are often cognizant (degree and acceptance may vary) of interparental conflict and this awareness intermingles with the developmental tasks of adolescence.

In some families, conflicts are out in the open with screaming, arguing, and disrespect between parents. Teens may experience one parent being intimidating and controlling. Some adolescents may also witness physical altercations. They may hear their mother cry behind closed doors or watch their dad move out. Teens may overhear threats of divorce or accusations of infidelity with little opportunity to ask for clarification. There are families who argue behind closed doors in the mistaken belief that their adolescents will not be aware of the conflicts. Moreover, teens are naturally curious and not above listening through doors or from their room. Periods of cold silence, moving out of the master bedroom, or snide and disrespectful comments are passive-aggressive techniques of conflict that can pervade the home. For teens, silence and tension only create an opportunity for them to develop their own perception as to what is happening. Lack of information likely results in worst-case scenarios in the teen's imagination.

The teens' adjustment to the divorce is largely contingent upon their perceptions of and response to the interparental conflict. Adolescents will assess the validity of the issues, the person they deem most responsible for the argument, and the possible outcome. In high-conflict situations, they also gage the degree of danger to themselves, to a parent, or to siblings.

Teens may ask what is happening and if divorce is a possibility. Parents often want to protect their teens and, in doing so, respond with "It is nothing for you to worry about." Teens do worry and they need information to help them understand the issues. Frustration with parental fighting is possible. Teens often ask "why can't you just get along?" Even when teens are trying to deny the problems evident in their parents' arguments, awareness is inevitable.

Some teens may attribute the disagreements to outside sources, such as a bad day at work or a parent's drinking. Doing so may allow the teen to minimize the conflict and to believe that their family is stable. Other teens may withdraw to their room or go out with friends to avoid acknowledging conflict. Once the decision to divorce is made and shared with the teens in the family, their awareness creates more intense emotional and behavioral responses. The conflict now directly impacts the teen's family life. Sadness and a sense of loss about the family unit develops. Anger or grief often replaces denial or indifference.

Some adolescents become overly focused on their parents' conflicts. They may attempt to referee the arguments or beg their parents to stop fighting. Acting out behaviors may be an effort to provide an alternative problem for the parents to focus on. Often parental conflict, especially after separation, will focus on parenting differences. Teens may feel responsible for the conflict when the fight relates to them. Even when teens understand that the problems are within the marital relationship, a degree of self-blame may develop. Feeling responsible allows an adolescent to believe they can exert some control over the chaotic parental relationship. Tired of the conflict, some adolescents may encourage the separation. For many families, the divorce can decrease the level of conflict, at least in their everyday lives. For other teens, it can be extremely frustrating when the divorce does not provide a reprieve from the interparental conflict.

Some of the primary emotions experienced by teenagers witnessing parental conflict are fear and insecurity about the outcome. Home is no longer a safe place in which to try out their individuality. Teens will also experience a sense of hopelessness and frustration when they are unable to manage the conflict. In a 2003 study by Afifi and Schrodt, the authors state:

> Adolescents may not have developed the skills necessary to persuade their parents to comply with their request to modify their conflict styles. Thus, they may engage in avoidance because it is the only available response, or the one that produces the least anxiety (p.147).[14]

Teens who live in the midst of ongoing parental conflict develop a heightened sense of danger and may come to expect conflict and tension in their own interactions. This heightened sensitivity adds stress and anxiety. Some teens need to escape the conflict at home. They stay behind closed doors or withdraw into video games or other activities. Avoidance is also accomplished by spending more time with friends or at friend's homes.

There are a number of reactions exhibited by adolescents dealing with interparental conflict. Some act out as a way of deflecting the conflict in their home. Others become angry and engage in more intense conflicts with one or both parents. Conflict at home can result in aggression and bullying aimed at peers. In a sense, these teens are replaying the situation at home. Disrespect for parental authority may lead to teens being rude, dismissive, or flippant with teachers or other authority figures.

Teens dealing with parental conflict are more susceptible to alcohol and drug abuse and delinquent behavior.[15] Academic decline is also seen in these adolescents. It is really difficult to get homework completed when a battle is going on between your parents or when you left your laptop at your father's house. Stressful home environments have a physical impact on teens, such as disrupted sleep patterns and physical complaints.

There is evidence that teens who experienced parental conflict are more likely to become involved in contentious relationships. The conflict styles observed at home become a model for the interactional and conflict styles of the teens in their peer relationships. According to a 2010 study by Simon and Furman:

> Adolescents exposed to marital violence have more conflictual romantic relationships, more often use aggressive conflict styles, and more often view dating aggression as justifiable. . .. interparental conflict could

> predispose adolescents to non-aggressive, destructive conflict tactics. For instance, adolescents exposed to interparental conflict may seek to minimize conflict altogether by avoiding negative expressions, yielding to partner's preferences, or expressing positive affect when conflict clues are perceived. (p. 189)[16]

Typically, males tend to respond with more aggression in relationship conflicts while females withdraw or try to appease. Learned conflict styles may be revised as adolescents interact and gain perspective from peers.

Some teens try to manage the discord in their homes. Some become caretakers, trying to comfort and provide companionship to the parent they perceive to be most hurt by the conflict. Teens may side with one parent against the other. Some teens will instigate or foster the conflict in hopes that the end result will be to their advantage. Manipulation of parental conflict can be a way to secure favors from a parent. Some teens, weary of the continual conflict, may push for separation or refuse to visit the non-custodial parent. Parents need to take notice of their teens' reactions and take measures to help them understand and cope.

When teens are able to understand and avoid feeling the need to intervene in interparental conflict, their responses may have a positive impact on their emotional well-being. "The problems are in my parents' relationship and not my responsibility" Parental fighting that settles down after separation allows teens to feel that it acceptable to step away from unhappy relationships or situations. Success in other areas of their lives can allow teens to develop confidence and self-esteem. Developing peer relationships—both social and intimate—can reinforce a belief in love and commitment. Parent–teen closeness can help teens feel safe and supported. This relationship allows individuation to continue successfully.

Long-term Outcomes

Many long-term emotional repercussions result from being subjected to conflict between parents. Conflict beyond the divorce can be particularly harmful. It keeps homes from stabilizing and erodes a teen's belief in love and commitment. Some families struggle for years, even as these adolescents have families of their own. "Sorry, Grandpa won't come to your party because Grandma is coming." Areas of impact can include ongoing relationship with family, acquired conflict styles, attitudes toward romance and marriage, and self-perception.

Though teens may seem independent, family relationships are of great importance for their emotional development. Marital conflict can interfere with the bond between teens and their parents. Teens will often detach prematurely and seek security outside of the family. Some become estranged from one parent following divorce and continued interparental conflict. Choosing one parent and disengaging from the other is a means of simplifying and decreasing stress. The relationship with one or both parents can be strained for years, if not permanently.

Over-involvement with a parent, especially if that parent does not remarry, can interfere with peer attachment and disrupt future adult relationships. These teens sacrifice their own relationships to care for a distressed parent. In other situations, adolescents may feel overwhelmed and need to escape the parents' conflict. Romantic relationships can be a diversion from the parental conflict. Teens may form early romantic relationships and rush to establish their own family. These intimate connections can be a replacement for family affection or a reassurance that love is real and lasting. However, many of these teen connections end up being unsatisfactory and have similar problems with conflict management to those their parents had. These interactional styles can affect adults in their intimate relationships, at work, and with friends. Additionally, interparental conflict affects a teen's long-term perception of love, fidelity, and marriage.

Many adults have been able to work through and move beyond the conflict that pervaded their early lives. Most children of divorce acknowledge that they struggled with their parents' negative interactions. Many have memories of traumatic parental fights. Adolescents who adjust well and came to adulthood relatively unscathed often had good self-esteem, found alternative sources of support, and were able to understand that the conflict was not their responsibility. Positive experiences, such as extracurricular activities, social gatherings, and school achievements can offset some of the stress. Additionally, protective factors that act as a buffer to parental conflict include a close parent–teen relationship, peer and sibling support, and positive self-esteem. Support may also come from a trusted adult, a therapist, or support group.

Parental Alienation

One of the most damaging experiences for a teen is when a divorcing parent actively advocates for a teen to reject their other parent. Parental alienation is the term used when one of the parents has become disrespected, rejected, and even estranged from their child. In most cases, one parent actively works to discourage and even destroy the relationship between the other parent and their child. Alienators hope to create an alliance with the teen that has, at its core, an unwritten agreement to reject the other parent.

High-conflict divorces and custody battles are often a trigger for the alienation behaviors. Remarriage may also be a trigger for alienation, as the ex-spouse may feel replaced. Custodial parents are often the initiators of the parental rejection and will have more opportunities to brainwash the teen against their ex-spouse. The level of alienation is dependent on the degree of pathology and vehemence of the alienating parent, the reaction of the rejected parent, and the teen's level of cooperation. In a 2012 study by Godbout and Parent they report:

> A child's rejection of one parent and close association with the other has many determinants, which include both (the rejected and the alienating) parents' behaviors, the child's level of vulnerability (separation anxiety, lack of social skills, behavior problems), and parent-child role-reversal. (p. 36)[17]

While there are situations in which the alienation is initiated by the adolescent, it is the adults' responsibility to encourage a healthy relationship with both parents. Teens may be reacting to an ongoing negative relationship with a parent or as a means of protecting a distressed parent.

Alienation usually develops over time. Behaviors will escalate as the instigating parent becomes increasingly obsessed with creating the dysfunctional relationship. Alienators utilize a number of attitudes and behaviors to seriously disrupt the bond between a parent and their teen. Actions may include negative comments and distorted accusations about the ex-spouse. They will share intimate and often inaccurate information about the other. Comments are made to undercut the parent and teen's relationship, such as "your mother was having an affair before we separated" or "we could get you a new phone if your father was paying his child support."

Other tactics include belittling, cursing at, or making fun of the other parent. Teens are encouraged to disrespect, ignore, or hang-up on the rejected parent. The alienating parents will ask the teen to keep secrets or to spy on the other parent. Spying can include reading parent's texts or emails, listening in on phone calls, searching rooms, and accessing private financial information.

Parents will encourage or even require the teen to take sides or blame the other parent for the family's dissolution. Claims of abuse or alcohol and drug use are made against the other parent. Alienating parents manipulate information to make the other parent appear neglectful or abusive. Parents will engage in heated arguments with their ex in front of their teens to highlight misconceptions. They make statements to the teen that claim that the other parent does not love them or will not keep them safe. "Your father is not there for you. He does not love you like I do."

Interference with visitation is common, with parents "forgetting" that the parent was coming, making last minute changes, or encouraging the teen to refuse to see their other parent. Often these tactics are then used to alter or remove parental visitation rights. Custody battles with ongoing contempt of court filings become a norm for the divorcing couple. There is some disagreement among the scientific and legal communities as to what defines parental alienation and its use in legal proceedings, specifically as it pertains to custody disputes.

Types of Alienators

Dr. Darnel (1998) in *Divorce Casualties* specifies three types of alienators: naïve, active, and obsessed.[18] Naïve alienators do not necessarily want or need the teen to totally reject the other parent. They will, however, create conflict for the teen's loyalty in a number of ways. They may make comments that indicate their disrespect or complain openly about their ex-spouse. The parent may inadvertently push an angry and confused teen to reject a parent. Rejecting a parent may be a way of coping with complicated feelings for the teen. These parents may create some loyalty issues for their teen but do not intend to prevent the parent and teen from having a relationship.

Active alienators have an emotional need for the teen to reject their other parent. With these parents, obvious, targeted statements and actions are intended to create a negative perception of the other parent. Alienating parents will share information that is personal and harmful to the other parent's character. Sometimes the parent may regret their comments, realizing that they came from a place of hurt and rejection. Even when these parents try to take back their comments, the teen has already heard them and made their judgement.

Parents may need to discourage a teen's relationship with their other parent in order to avoid being alone or abandoned by the teen. When their anger surfaces, comments and accusations are made that reflect disregard and disrespect for their ex-spouse. Active alienators have a need for the teen to take sides and be loyal to them. They may want the teen to empathize with the pain and anger that they feel. These parents encourage their adolescent to adopt many of their own feelings toward their ex-spouse.

Obsessed alienators are determined to destroy the parent–teen relationship. They will take every opportunity and use any tactic to ensure that the teen rejects their other parent. These parents are obsessed with the need to have their child align with their view and share their hatred for their ex-spouse. Motivated by their need for retaliation, these ex-spouses are focused on destroying the teen's connection with their other parent and the teen's emotional well-being is secondary. Even when confronted with their alienation behavior, they will cling to the belief that they are protecting the teen from a worthless and evil person.

Jessica and David married young and had two children, George, 19 and Jerilyn, 14. David was very successful engineer (working long hours) and Jessica was a homemaker. The couple had a fairly contentious relationship for a number of years, often arguing over money, David's work hours, and Jessica's need for attention. The separation was at the request of David, who offered generous monthly support for Jessica and the kids. Prior to the separation, David had enjoyed a close relationship with his children. Jessica responded with considerable anger and distress. Even prior to the separation, Jessica and Jerilyn's relationship was rather enmeshed.

Shortly after the separation, Jessica stared refusing to allow David to see his daughter. She blocked his calls and started badmouthing him to Jerilyn. Quickly the alienation escalated with Jerilyn beginning to make claims that her father was emotionally abusive, with mom backing up her claims. The court intervened and ordered visitation for the father and therapy for the family. During the custody hearing, the older brother (in college) testified on behalf of his father. After the hearing, the mother attacked him in the parking lot, screaming at him for being disloyal to her and Jerilyn and telling him he was never welcome back home.

During the Court-ordered therapy sessions, the mother raged about her ex-husband and demanded that he not be allowed access to her daughter. Even when the session was focused on her daughter's emotional well-being, the mother focused on her husband's abandonment of her. In an individual session, Jerilyn reported many of the same claims and insisted she didn't want anything to do with him. Mother continually blocked visitation by not being home, scheduling activities during his time, and literally standing at the front door screaming obscenities at him while his daughter refused to come out. When she did visit, Jerilyn often brought friends along, ignoring her dad, or spent time on the phone with her mother. Jerilyn would refuse to talk with him and made a point of making a mess at his house and refusing to clean up after herself. She also asked repeatedly for extra money, stating that she and her mother were financially strapped. The father paid all basic household expenses and the mother was receiving over $7,000 a month in support and drove a Lexus. Despite the ongoing efforts of the mother to keep David from his daughter, he continued to call, send notes, provide support, and to show up for every visitation and therapy session.

Alienated Adolescents

There is the question as to how adolescents become alienated when they have the cognitive ability to question messages from parents. Teens that are alienated are vulnerable to parental manipulation in part because of the developmental changes they are going through. They perceive their parents as fallible and are quick to judge behaviors. That plus the high emotions that are possible during a parental divorce create an atmosphere where the teen is open to becoming estranged from a parent.

When a teen has not been particularly close or often clashed with a parent, they are more susceptible to alienation. Alienating parents may need their teen to prove their loyalty by agreeing with their negative beliefs. When teens feel pressure to take sides, they may accept the alienating parent's claims as a means of alleviating the interparental conflict and bringing some peace to their own conflicted emotions. Once an adolescent begins to buy into the negative assessments of the other parent, the teen will assume these beliefs as their own.

Teens often claim that they are not being influenced by the alienating parent and that these thoughts and judgments are their own. Teens do not readily admit to being manipulated by a parent. When a teen is discussing their perceptions of the other parent, the stories or statements will often be very similar to the parent's report or even word for word in each retelling. Once a teen has accepted the negative assessment, there is a need for them to defend and ultimately believe what they are feeling.

Alienated teens will disrespect, argue with, ignore, and refuse to visit the rejected parent. It is more difficult to require a teen to spend time with a parent than it is with a younger child. One of my families had two teenage sons who would take off when their mother came to pick them up and refuse to return home until she left. Another client put liquor bottles in her father's trunk and claimed he was driving drunk even though he was an alcoholic who had been sober for years. Ongoing alienation makes it difficult for a teen to know what to believe or to be able to trust their own perceptions.

Teens who are subjected to alienation and lose their connection to a parent will struggle with a number of psychological effects. According to a 2011 study by Baker and Ben-Ami reported that alienation "strategies inevitably and directly result in children feeling worthless, flawed, unloved, unwanted, endangered, or only of value in meeting another's needs" (p.473).[19] Emotional repercussions include low self-esteem, incomplete identity development, and insecure attachments.

Alienated Parents

Alienated parents are often in a difficult situation. Depending on the level of rejection and disrespect, some parents try to remain connected to their teen while others back away. One client asked if it was okay to stop seeing his children because the conflict with his ex-wife was so stressful. Parents should make the effort to continue a relationship if at all possible. Staying connected without engaging in retaliation is difficult. Keeping a line of open communication is important. Parents should help the teen reconsider the information provided by the alienating parent in a way that allows the teen to feel comfortable and maintain loyalty to both parents. At times, pulling back may be necessary to protect the teen from the alienator's rage and pressure, especially with parents who are obsessed with driving a wedge. It is important to let the teen know of their regret at limited contact. Some adults become engaged in a contest of wills, both pulling on the emotional vulnerabilities of their teens. The actions of the alienated parent can help heal the parent–teen relationship or push the teen away.

Summary

Divorce can create unique and stress-inducing changes in a family's dynamics. When a teen assumes the household responsibilities of the parent, they may be experiencing instrumental parentification. Emotional parentification is a level of role reversal in which the teen becomes responsible for the care of a distressed or needy parent. Parentification interferes with the adolescent's developmental tasks and will result in the loss of some important educational and social experiences.

Conflict in families can be either overt or covert with most families exhibiting both types. Of particular concern for adolescents is the conflict between their parents known as interparental conflict. Parental conflict styles are often dependent on several factors: personality of the individual, conflict style of partner, topics of disagreement, and stage of divorce process. Interparental conflict can range from mild to intense. High-conflict couples argue emotionally, attack their spouse's identity and character, name call, curse, and even become physical. Overt styles may be quieter but can be just as damaging to the family functioning and stability.

Parental alienation is the effort of one parent to disrupt the teen's relationship with their other parent. Having the teen reject the other parent is the primary focus of the alienating parent. This behavior can reach extremes and result in significant emotional distress for the adolescent. Parentification, interparental conflict, and alienation usually have long-term emotional and personality consequences for adolescents

5.

I Don't Have to Listen to You!

Creating Stepfamilies

Becoming a stepfamily is a process, not an event, counted in years, not days or months.

—Patricia Papernow,
Surviving and Thriving in Stepfamily Relationships[1]

Parental divorce during the teenage years is stressful and the issues that develop when parents begin to date and remarry add even more layers of complexity. Teens rarely welcome new adults into their parent's lives and their reactions can range from indifference to open hostility. It is unrealistic to assume that a parent will forgo adult companionship until their children are settled into their own adult lives. Some divorced parents begin to date immediately, while others wait several years. Most parents eventually date and many remarry. Some prefer to cohabit, often expecting this arrangement to be less complicated, while others engage in long-term committed relationships while maintaining separate households. The creation of newly formed stepfamilies, through marriage or cohabitation, requires adjustments on everyone's part.

Stepfamilies may be considered simple or complex. Simple stepfamilies are when a biological parent with children marries and the new stepparent moves in. In simple stepfamilies, the non-biological adult may have children of their own but these children do not reside with the newly formed family. Complex stepfamilies involve the joining of two biological parents, each bringing children into the household. The term blended family is another term for stepfamily. The development of a new stepfamily takes time and the process is as complex, if not more so, than the divorce. Adolescents will always have an opinion and an emotional reaction to new family members. This reaction is dependent upon factors including their feelings about the new spouse, the stepparents interactional and parenting styles, the addition of stepsiblings, the reactions of their other parent, and their level of acceptance of their parent's divorce.

Parental Dating

At some point after the divorce, one or both parents will begin to date. Older teenagers may move out prior to their parent beginning to date. Younger teens are more likely to end up dealing with the entrance of a new adult into their lives. Parental dating, even if done discretely, will not go unnoticed by the teenagers in the family. To complicate matters, the adolescent will also be developing their own peer-based relationships. According to M. Gary Neuman (1998):

> Deep down, many teens believe there is something "weird" about parents' dating, and in a way, there is. It's unusual for a parent and child to be on the same footing,

> in the same phase, doing the same things for the same reasons. (p. 365)[2]

In continually married families, parental interactions (communication, affection, respect) are a model for a teen's romantic relationships and home is a safe base from which to begin dating. For most teens, a new person in their parent's life is met with apprehension and disdain. The parent may be ready to date, but the teen may not be ready to accept a new adult in their parent's life.

Dating after a divorce is complicated. Some parents avoid socialization for fear of becoming involved in another problematic relationship, while others seek companionship to help them deal with loneliness. Non-residential parents, usually the father, are more likely to begin dating after the divorce, while custodial mothers may avoid new relationships. Residential mothers' lives tend to be more centered on their children and jobs. They rarely have time or a need to date. Custodial parents may be more sensitive to the reality that a new adult in their teenager's life will be disruptive. Additionally, time for dating and access to other single adults may be limited.

Non-custodial parents (usually fathers) have more alone time and may seek out adult activities to keep from sitting in an empty apartment. In either situation, adults will, at some point, develop an interest in adult companionship. Sometimes new feelings develop with someone who previously was a friend, co-worker, or neighbor. Some adults end up reconnecting with a former romantic partner, such as their high school sweetheart. As dating becomes a possibility, the question arises as how to inform the adolescent about their decision to begin dating or that they have met someone.

Dating within the first year after the separation can create emotional confusion and distress in adolescents who have yet to come to terms with the family breakup. Even when teens were aware of the severity of the problems in the marriage, they often hope for reconciliation. When a parent begins dating shortly after the split, the teen's response is usually negative. This new person will be viewed as an interloper and as an interference to the possibility of reconciliation. Dating too soon may lead a teen to question if the current relationship was initiated prior to the separation, and therefore the cause of the marital discord. Dating becomes a threat to reconciliation and provides a scapegoat for the teen's anger and confusion.

Parents, who were in a relationship prior to the separation, may introduce this person to their teenage children way too quickly, hoping for acceptance. Adolescents in the process of establishing their own romantic relations can be very judgmental and critical of a parent's perceived marital infidelity. Teens want to believe in love and commitment. A known parental infidelity destroys this belief. Even if the marriage was highly conflicted, infidelity is seen as a betrayal of their other parent and not as an experience of love. Acceptance of a parent's new relationship is unlikely when the introduction comes before an adolescent has had time to come to terms with the end of their parent's marriage.

Divorced parents may seek out a new relationship to deal with the pain of a divorce, avoid feeling lonely, or to feel loved. Some look for relationships that help them financially or with the burden of single parenting. Unfortunately, some may ultimately end up in another unsatisfying relationship. Not all marriages or cohabitation are entered into solely for love. New relationships that are poorly thought out or hastily entered into can cause additional stress for the family's teenagers, especially when they unfold and then collapse in front of the teens. Recently divorced adults should proceed slowly for their sake and that of their teenagers.

Jeff and Barbara had recently decided to separate and came into therapy to help their two teenage daughters deal with the changes in the family. The separation was at the mother's request as she had been unhappy in the marriage for several years. The couple had worked hard to keep their conflicts private, although the girls were aware that there were issues in the marriage. The couple jointly told the girls they were temporarily separating, citing only "some issues we need to work through," even though both parents expected that they would ultimately divorce. The youngest daughter, Amy, 12, cried while Sara, 15, listened quietly, stated "whatever" and then went to her room. Shortly after telling the girls, the father moved to an apartment near his work, 30 minutes from the family home. Visitation was every other weekend and Wednesday nights.

After dad moved out, Amy immediately began to push for reconciliation. She even wrote "love notes" to each parent about how lonely the other parent was and pleading with them to work it out. Sara maintained that she was okay and that the changes were not a big deal. Two months after the separation, Sara looked at her dad's phone and found recent texts and a selfie of her father and a blonde woman. Dad explained that he had started dating a woman at his office and offered to have the girls meet her. Sara was angry and upset, refusing to even meet dad's new friend. Within several weeks, she started fighting more with her father and blamed him and the "stupid blonde in dad's life" for the family breakup. No matter what activity dad planned, Sara was critical of him and the activity. Amy expressed more interest in spending time with her father but usually looked to Sara for her response. On several occasions, dad brought Sara home early due to the conflicts between them. Mom tried to intervene on his behalf, expressing support for dad's decision to date.

Despite efforts by both parents to keep regular visitation, the girls ended up seeing their dad inconsistently on his weekends but continued with Wednesday night dinners. The "stupid blonde" was still not welcome even after the couple had been dating regularly for several months. The father struggled with balancing his new girlfriend and his relationship with his teenage daughters.

While some resources may recommend that the parent date discreetly and wait before introducing someone new to the family, this may not work well with adolescents. Teens are intuitive and often notice if a parent is talking on the phone to someone, going out frequently, or dressing up more for work or other activities. They will also see past your insistence that you are just friends. It is a good idea to approach the topic of dating with teenagers and allow them to ask questions and discuss their feelings. Be assured, teens may initially act as if this is not a big deal but, in reality, it is. Teens may understand the need for peer companionship but will still struggle with a parent's dating.

It is not necessary to introduce every person you go out with to your teenagers. Teens should be informed about any date you are seeing regularly and believe may become a long-term commitment for you. Provide basic information about the new person and allow the teen to ask questions. Introductions should be well thought out. Allow the teen to pull back as needed. Permitting the teen to develop a relationship with the parent's new adult friend at their own pace is easiest for all involved. Don't expect your teen to welcome your new friend readily. Most teens will be critical of the new adult and respond with aloofness, superficial politeness, or even outright hostility. Even if a teen is accepting of a parent's dating, they will not be interested in double dating or joining you and your new friend at the movies.

Depending on the teen's age or dating history, they may have a difficult time separating their own relationship experiences with those of a parent. A recent heartbreak in a teen's life will make accepting new love in a parent's life harder to handle. Even adults can be quite immature in newly formed relationships with all the intense emotions that love brings. Sharing your excitement about an upcoming date when a teen is crying over a recent breakup is inadvisable. Adolescents need a parent's support during their foray into young love. Do not compete with your teen over your dating experiences. Fathers should not brag to their sons about all the "hot chicks" they are dating. Letting your daughter help you get ready for your date is different than sharing the details of your recent romantic encounter. Being too demonstrative with your new love interest will make your teen uncomfortable. Handling the adult relationship maturely and honestly (but not with too much detail) can make acceptance easier for the teen.

Sexual Issues

Sex is a significant issue for developing adolescents. Parental dating may influence the adolescent's own sexual attitudes and behaviors. Teenagers are often uncomfortable confronting a parent's sexual activity. Even if they suspect that you are having sex, they don't need to have a visual of it. Allowing someone to sleep over creates an awkward situation, especially when the teen has only recently become aware of the new relationship.

Adolescents, with their own sense of budding sexuality, may find some of their interactions with a parent's date uncomfortable. Teenage girl's style of dress may create tension for the mother's new friend. Boys may be uncomfortable when dad's date is attractive to them. Awareness of their parent's intimate relationships and perceived parental permissive attitudes toward sex can influence a teen's sexual activities. Knowledge of a parent's sexual behavior can be seen as permission for their own sexual activities. When a divorced parent engages in sexual behavior as a response to the loss of their spouse, or an infidelity was the cause of the divorce, teens can view sex as a recreational outlet rather than a healthy part of love and commitment. Parent–teen communication concerning healthy sexual attitudes and activities plus appropriate monitoring can support a teen's sexual development. A parent's sexual relationship should be managed discretely, away from the teen's home.

However, another difficulty may surface when a parent shows no interest in interpersonal relationships and avoids all acknowledgement of one's natural sexuality. According to Nielsen (1999):

> Some mothers ... have problems in regard to sexuality and to emotional intimacy ... if their mother acts as if she has never had any sexual or romantic needs or if these aspects of life are unimportant, shameful, or

> embarrassing, then her children may eventually adopt these same feelings and attitudes. (p. 554)[3]

Divorce can result in teens losing their parents as role models for healthy, satisfying intimate relationships. Dating by a parent can reassure a teen that romance is possible. Keep public displays of affection to a minimum.

As an adult relationship develops the couple may spend more time together, which may decrease the time available for the teen. Adolescents need to feel that the new relationship is an addition to their lives, not a loss. Joint family activities are recommended and will help the teens get to know the new adult. Ask the teen for input on activities or ways for them to get more comfortable with the individual you are dating. Also, be careful not to ask your new significant other to assume parental responsibilities. Picking up a teenager from school or attending a teen's extracurricular activity may be acceptable if the teen is comfortable with it. Disciplining or making decisions about a teen's activities is never appropriate. Adolescents are quick to point out that "I don't have to listen to you, you are not my parent." Dating relationships may progress quickly, but making a connection with the family's teens should always be taken slowly.

Despite experiencing a divorce, many adults will take a chance on love again. Letting the children in the family know when a relationship is moving toward a commitment of some type is important. When the new relationship becomes serious, the teens should be encouraged to spend time with their parent's new significant other in order to develop a level of comfort with the new adult. When the boyfriend/girlfriend also have children, the two families need to be introduced. When a decision is made to marry or move in together, allow plenty of time for the teen to get used to the idea and to express their concerns and questions. Surprise weddings in Las Vegas are a terrible idea. Do not have the new partner move in while the teen is away for the weekend. Additionally, it is a good idea to let the teen know if the relationship is not working out and that a breakup is possible. Teens may be surprisingly upset if they have invested emotionally in the relationship working out.

It is advisable to introduce the new partner to the ex-spouse. Support from their other parent can aid teens in their acceptance of the relationship. In some families, a parent's new romantic relationship can stir up old issues between the ex-spouses. No matter how well the parents have adjusted to the divorce, seeing one's ex-spouse with another love interest is difficult. As a parent's relationship moves forward and a commitment is made to live together, all family members need to be involved in establishing a new family system.

The Wedding

There is the distinct possibility that one or both parents will remarry within several years of the divorce. A wedding ceremony, no matter what size or style, has meaning for extended family members, as this marks the joining of two families and the acceptance of a new family member. When divorced parents remarry, a wedding is a statement as to the beginning of a new family. Custodial parents are bringing a new adult and possibly new children into the teen's home. When a non-custodial parent marries, the changes may be less drastic.

The children in both families need to be involved with the ceremony in some way. Wedding plans should be shared with the teenagers. Asking for their involvement signifies their inclusion in the new family. The wedding ceremony may include the couple's children as bridesmaids, groomsmen, ushers, or ring bearers. Some families ask the oldest son to escort their mother down the aisle. If both adults have children, they should be included as equally as possible. When a non-residential parent marries, their biological children could feel as if their father is taking on a new family and leaving them behind. Inclusion in the wedding gives the message that the new family system will find a place for everyone.

Cohabitation has become more commonplace. Many second (or third) relationships begin with a couple moving in together. Residing together as a family needs to be marked by some form of statement and/or activity. A special dinner or small family gathering can act as a statement for the family changes. All too often, this change of living arrangements happens with little discussion and the new family roles and relationships are ambiguous. Cohabitation, when couples bring biological children into the household, is the beginning of a stepfamily.

Stepfamily Development

Following an adjustment period, divorced adults often take another chance on romance and commitment. Some adults are seeking companionship and financial or household stability. In a 2020 article, *Divorce, Repartnering, and Stepfamilies: A Decade in Review* by Raley and Sweeney it is reported that "In recent years, about 40% of all new marriages were remarriages for one or both spouses ... suggesting to some that Americans remain strongly attached to marriage even when their first (or second) marriage dissolves" (p. 85).[4]

Second marriages or cohabitation create a new family that brings together a variety of personalities with different expectations and needs. Stepfamily configurations may consist of any combination of parents and their residential or part-time children. Stepfamilies can also include children born of the new union, non-biological but legally adopted children, and same-sex couples with biological children and new partner. Shared residence and a desire to function as a family are the key components of a stepfamily.

Cohabitation

Cohabitation is two adults who decide to live together as a form of commitment and a statement to others that they are in a long-term relationship. Many cohabitating couples eventually decide to marry. For some same-sex relationships, marriage is not a legal option (although this is changing in many states) so cohabitation, often with the couple having a commitment ceremony, results in a stepfamily. Living together is increasingly common in our society and is sometimes seen as less complicated than marriage. It allows the couple to live together, share expenses, and divide household responsibilities. It is also a means of keeping finances separate, maintaining primary responsibility for any children, and avoiding another divorce should the relationship not work out.

Some custodial parents may be concerned that marriage will interfere with their receiving financial support from an ex-spouse. Often divorce decrees specify that alimony is terminated when a spouse remarries. Biological custodial parents (usually the mother) may desire an adult relationship without having to relinquish any of their parental rights or control. Live-in significant others have no legal rights or responsibilities for non-biological children. Adolescents may feel that cohabitating relationships are tenuous, as the couple are not legally wed. Teens are wary of making emotional connections to an adult who may leave at the first sign of problems. They will also be less respectful of an adult who is not technically their family. There is some evidence that adolescents in cohabitating versus married stepfamilies fare worse in terms of emotional well-being, school achievement, and antisocial behavior.[5]

There are also other studies that conclude that teens in cohabitating stepfamilies adjust as well as those in married stepfamilies.[6] As with any form of a stepfamily, the issues that are salient to the well-being of adolescents include closeness with custodial and non-residential parents, presence of and supervision by caring and authoritative adults, low levels of household conflict, and adolescent personal strengths. More about these factors in the upcoming sections on stepfamilies. Even without a formal title as stepparent, these cohabitation families often establish themselves as stepfamilies with strong and enduring emotional ties.

Brian, 14, and David, 16, lived primarily with their father and spent every other weekend with their mother, Betty. The parents had divorced three years prior due to numerous differences and Betty's drinking. Their mother claimed to be sober since the custody hearings. The father had remarried two years previously and the boys had a good relationship with their stepmother. Recently, mother's new boyfriend, Joe, had moved into her apartment. The couple had only been dating for three months and the boys were uncomfortable with the boyfriend's drinking and his controlling behavior. The boys told their dad that Joe often yelled at them, dominated the television, and even controlled the food they ate. Mom insisted that she needed Joe's support to handle the stress of dealing with two teenage boys. Brian and David stated that they resented Joe's bossiness, claiming, "he is not my father."

One weekend, Joe accosted the older brother over a minor issue. According to both boys, the mother had told her boyfriend to "beat his ass." David ran off and called his dad, who came to pick up the boys. Mom denied that her boyfriend had touched her son despite obvious bruises on David's arm. After that incident, the boys refused to go back to their mother's as long as the boyfriend was there. When the mother (with the boyfriend in the car) came to pick up the boys for her weekend, they ran away. The mother called the police, who located the boys but said they could not force the boys to go with her. The father eventually sought a court order for sole custody. David testified: "It is just easier not having to go stay with her, I am doing better, I am happier at my dad's." Mother was granted limited visitation. Additionally, the court ordered individual and family therapy for the boys. Despite the change in the custodial agreement, mom refused to stop living with her boyfriend.

Stepfamilies

Stepfamilies are created when a divorced parent with children marries or cohabitates with a new partner. According to Jenson (2017), "Before 18 years of age, an estimated one third of youth in the United States will reside in a stepfamily household. (Pew Research Center 2011) … Most stepfamilies—roughly 80%—are reared by a biological mother and stepfather" (p. 1051).[7]

Simple stepfamilies refer to a biological parent, their biological children, and a new partner. Fathers can also be custodial parents and their marriage to a new partner brings a new stepmother into the family. In some situations, the stepfather has biological children with visitation rights. Weekends in simple stepfamilies can bring the children of both families together or the mother's teens may go to their dad's house while the stepfather's kids move into the family home. Holidays and summers become complicated and the house can become congested when visitation brings both sets of children into the home. Visitation schedules can create issues over shared space, privacy, and use of belongings. New stepfamilies may opt to live in the mother's home, move into the stepfather's place, or acquire a new residence together. Increased challenges occur when the family relocation results in a change of school district.

New households that bring both spouses' children into the home are complex stepfamilies. These blended families bring about the most issues and complications. The couple may move into a new home or live in the previous residence of either partner. In complex stepfamilies, at least one set of children will be leaving their family home and possibly their school.

Moving into one parent's residence can create an immediate imbalance in the stepsibling dynamics; some teenagers remain in their home territory and the others become "the invaders." The children may end up sharing rooms and belongings, which may hinder harmonious interactions. One client with three teenagers married a father with three same-aged teens. The couple bought a home in the same school district and remodeled the upstairs into six bedrooms, allowing each teen to have their own space. They also bought a big van. In most situations, the couple has been dating for a while and the children in both families have had an opportunity to meet and interact prior to moving in together. Even when the various family members have developed a connection prior to the marriage, the challenges of being a stepfamily are present.

Stepfamily Challenges

In *Surviving and Thriving in Stepfamily Relationships: What Works and What Doesn't* (2013), Dr. Papernow identifies five major challenges that are salient to the healthy development of stepfamilies: family inclusion, the child's struggles with loss and change, parenting roles and styles, family culture, and involvement of ex-spouses.[8] These challenges vary in style and intensity, as each stepfamily is unique.

Belonging

Family inclusion centers on an individual's sense of belonging. In stepfamilies, the biological family members are insiders and the new partners are considered outsiders. Children of the stepparent are also outsiders. According to Papernow (2013), "The insider /outsider challenge emerges very early in the step-couple relationships and threads its way through all of the other challenges. It often remains present, though in somewhat softer form, even in mature well-established stepfamilies" (p. 28).[9]

Fully integrating can take time and, in many cases, the non-biological parent never feels fully assimilated. An adolescent's sense of belonging is derived from warm, caring interactions with their biological parent and stepparent, parental attention, feeling listened to and understood, and participation in family activities. Family inclusion (belonging) in a stepfamily is an important component for healthy functioning.

Some mothers take their new spouse's last name while the children keep their fathers' name, creating an obvious but unintentional message about family belonging. Other mothers have kept their ex-husbands last name for the children's sake. Others may resume use of their maiden name. Different family last names are no longer unusual in our society, but last names still give a message of belonging to a specific family.

Studies have indicated that the mother–child relationship has the strongest association with a teen's sense of belonging and that a close relationship with the stepparent is also an important factor.[10] Couples should work together to help all family members feel connected. Interestingly, the quality of the marital relationship was not a significant factor in adolescents' feelings of inclusion and in their adjustment to the new family system.[11] Healthy marital interactions can support a teen's adjustment but does not guarantee a teen's sense of belonging to the new family. Over time, and with the development of emotional connections, a stepparent can become more of an everyday parent and the household will find its own unique sense of family.

Change and Loss

Remarriage or cohabitation bring change, sometimes very little and other times extensive. When the biological mother remarries and her new spouse moves into the household, lifestyle changes experienced by the adolescents may be kept to a minimum. Few divorced parents with teenage children marry a spouse that has not been previously married or does not have children. The children of the new stepparent will also end up making some adjustments. Weekends with dad can now become weekends with dad, his new wife, and her kids.

While parents may be excited about the changes and the beginning of a new marital relationship, teens perceive this life event as a loss of their family as they knew it. This loss can be that of their original family or the single-parent family that developed following the divorce. There is also the end of any hope for parental reconciliation. Teens may be surprised by how living with new family members can result in their having to share their belongings or readjust many of their habits. Who controls the television or computer, dinner protocols, use of the bathroom, curfews, and the ability to freely walk into mom's room are all subject to change. Often the delicate balance achieved after the divorce is upended.

When the new family includes children from both partners moving to a new home and a different school, the transitions are often overwhelming. The addition of stepsiblings increases the changes and perceived losses. A new residence and sharing a bedroom or bathroom may be required to accommodate additional family members. Various family members may live together full-time or on periodic weekends, summers, and holidays. Stepsiblings may be similar in age but differ considerably in personality. The birth order of children in a family will also change as new siblings join the family unit. Suddenly the first born is not the oldest or the only daughter is now one of several girls in the family. Older teens may end up with "annoying" younger stepsiblings that they are asked to help out with. Family traditions, even simple ones, such as pizza and movie Fridays, are subject to change. Even with the best efforts to blend families with care and forethought, the potential for loss of what was is inevitable.

Family Roles

As new stepfamilies form, the issue arises of what roles and responsibilities the new stepparent should take. Roles for all of these possible permutations are complicated and subject to change over time. As the majority of stepfamilies are a biological mother, her children, and a new partner, this section will explore the issue of family roles from the perspective of a stepfather joining the home, although most of the same issues apply to father-lead custodial homes with a new stepmother and to same-sex households. Everyone in the family plays a part in the development of family roles.

Most initial stepfamily roles are ambiguous. In LGBTQ (lesbian, gay, bisexual, transgender, queer or questioning) families, the role definitions may be more complicated but ultimately result in similar patterns and dynamics as heterosexual couples. Roles are negotiated early in the new family. There are the roles the biological parent hopes for or expects, those that the new spouse is open to assuming, and the role that the teens are willing for the stepparent to have.

Most family members are comfortable with the new stepparent assuming the role of provider. New stepparents are well received when their addition to the family provides a better socioeconomic lifestyle. Helping with household tasks and providing needed transportation for teen activities are typically welcomed by the family. Functioning as mom's emotional support is usually an acceptable role for stepfathers. However, the stepparent's interactions and input about the teen's social life, activities, and behavior are difficult to negotiate.

One of the most difficult roles in the newly established household is disciplinarian. When a stepparent has children from a previous marriage, their parenting style may already be established and second nature in his parent–teen interactions. Even when a couple have discussed parenting issues, actual everyday interactions may stimulate conflict and require negotiation. Parents and teens may have different ideas of acceptable behavior at home. Issues can arise concerning noise levels (music, video games, or TV), table manners, and sibling interactions (roughhousing, teasing, and fighting). Respect for a parent's authority is often a highly debated issue in new stepfamilies.

The fact that the children in the family are teenagers usually assures that a new family disciplinarian is not readily accepted. Teens are accepting of a stepfather's help with activities, schoolwork, and transportation, but rarely as a rule enforcer. Mothers are often divided about whether a new spouse should have disciplinary authority with their teens. Most parents prefer to maintain their authority role but welcome help with supervision and as an emotional support in their family interactions. Some mothers, as in the case mentioned previously with Brian and David, encourage the new partner to take control of the teenagers, particularly when the mother believes she is not capable of controlling her teenage children. Often stepfathers prefer not to be involved in setting rules and providing consequences, as they are aware that this is a hard role to assume with adolescents.

As stepfamilies evolve, adults naturally provide care and supervision. When life had been chaotic or their biological father has disengaged, teens may appreciate a caring adult in their lives. Most teens, especially younger ones, look to the adults for direction, advice, and role modeling. The most successful form of parenting is the authoritative style (not to be confused with authoritarian, which is overly controlling). This type of parenting involves supervision combined with a high level of attention and caring. In my book, *The Parent Effect* (2011), I identify these parents as easygoing parents and report that "They often approach parenting in a relaxed, confident, and flexible manner. They do not expect to be perfect or have all the answers. These parents adapt to the needs of the teen and the situation" (p.104).[12] This parenting style works well with teens. When a stepparent moves slowly and gently into this style of parenting, there is a greater chance of acceptance.

Some stepfathers expect that marriage gives them parental rights that were not of issue while dating. Fathers with their own teenage children may have a hard time being hands-off with the mother's children. There is frequently a period of teen limit testing as new roles are established. Rebellious adolescents are more likely to reject a stepfathers' involvement in parenting. Difficult teens may provoke a stepfather to react with a more demanding and controlling style or to disengage. Teen–stepfather conflict early in the stepfamily formation can result in a dysfunctional family system in which arguments develop among various family members. Even when a single parent has established a home with a healthy balance of rules and consequences coupled with attention and caring, a new parent can disrupt the family harmony. Some families cannot manage the changing parental roles and may ultimately not succeed or limp along with underlying tensions for years.

Mothers, whether biological or step, take on many roles in the family that are crucial to the family's functioning. According to Weaver and Coleman (2010):

> When a woman with children remarries, her roles expand in number and complexity. She becomes not only a wife or partner, but also a mediator, an organizer, a co-parent, and, if her new husband has children, a stepparent. She assumes the responsibility of meeting the needs of her children, her partner, and perhaps her partner's children. She may also have to coordinate her children's relationships with their father and his extended family and, very likely, will have employment duties outside the home. (p. 308)[13]

Stepmothers married to fathers with custody have complex responsibilities. Often society and the father expect a woman to naturally assume a lot of the household and childcare responsibilities. When a woman without children marries into a family with teenagers, the role of instant mom will be fraught with problems. Replacing a mother who does not have custody assumes that the biological mother has issues that prevent her from caring for her children on a daily basis. These teens may be more in need of a maternal figure than those whose mothers have custody. It may also create a competition for attention with the biological mother. Non-residential mothers often remain involved in their children's lives and this makes acceptance of a stepmother less likely.[14] Women who marry non-custodial fathers may assume an adult friend or big sister role rather than trying to be a mother figure. More about stepmothers later in this chapter.

Other roles form as the family develops. Some stepparents seek to be the teen's friend or confidant. These roles can cross important adult–teen boundaries. Participating in parties or providing alcohol or drugs as a means of winning a teenager's acceptance is problematic and unacceptable. In some newly formed families, teens may assume the role of confidant for a stepparent or as the caretaker for younger stepchildren. As stepfamilies evolve, different roles may be tried on, then assumed or rejected. Healthy stepfamilies allow for age-appropriate responsibilities. The most important role for a teenager is to continue to be the kid and to work on their healthy transition to adulthood.

Family Culture and Traditions

Do you open presents on Christmas Eve or Christmas morning? Dinner on Sundays at grandmother's? Miracle Whip or mayonnaise? TV shows about zombies or documentaries? Vacation at the beach or visits with extended family?

No one joins another family without running into a number of differences. Daily rituals and habits built into an established family are all subject to change. These habits, traditions, preferences, and life attitudes make a family connected and comfortable. Teens, as much as they believe they are independent and open-minded, often become upset with changes to their family traditions and habits. Opening presents on Christmas Eve is unacceptable! Vacations are always at the beach!

It would be helpful if families could pre-decide any differences but most come as a surprise. There is also the possibility that teens will reject any change simply as a reaction to the new family member. Adults and adolescents are more likely to accommodate different habits or rituals when the couple are just dating; there is more at stake when it might become a permanent change. Possible differences include religion, handling money, discipline, and issues with extended family. Other significant adjustments center on traditions, holiday celebrations, vacation plans, and even gift-giving. Smaller changes can be related to everyday activities, such as healthy versus junk food, watching *Wheel of Fortune* during dinner, curfews, and other assorted topics.

The hardest issues to work out are those connected to family culture, religion, values, and money. New stepparents may hope to involve their newly acquired stepfamily in their religious services or add a cultural component to the family. Managing finances is often a topic that requires negotiation between couples, even when they keep their finances separate. Changes take time and compromise. Additionally, non-residential parents will often have an opinion about major life decisions that impact their children, adding a layer of complication to the family's adjustment.

Sayir, 40, and Penny, 42, met through work and started dating one year after Penny's divorce. Sayir is from India but went to college in the United States and is employed as an engineer in Houston, Texas. Penny was a receptionist at the same company. Sayir had never been married. Penny had joint custody, with her two teenage daughters switching residences every two weeks. The couple had only dated for six months before getting married in a small civil ceremony. Penny appreciated his attention and the financial security he provided. Sayir reported that he had focused on his career instead of dating. He also shared that his parents (living in India) had hoped to arrange a marriage for him but that he preferred to find his own wife.

Soon after the couple married, conflicts started between Sayir and Penny's daughters, pulling Penny into the middle. Sayir felt the girls were loud, disrespectful, and dressed inappropriately. Penny had been a rather relaxed, permissive parent and struggled to manage the conflict escalating between her children and her new spouse. Penny was torn between supporting her spouse and protecting her daughters.

A year after the wedding, Sayir's parents came to stay for an extended visit. The daughters were asked to share a room so the new step-grandparents could have a room. Shortly after arriving, Sayir's parents started criticizing Penny's parenting style and housekeeping. They also voiced criticism of the girls. Penny's daughters felt that their mother was not supporting them and started staying with their father beyond his usual two weeks. To complicate matters, Sayir stated that he expected that his parents would move to America within the next few years and that he wanted them to move in with the couple, as was his cultural tradition. The parents went home to India and the couple tried to work out their differences. However, when the parents stated that they would be coming for another extended visit with their son, Penny moved out.

Differences in religious beliefs surface as the stepfamily develops a family identity. Religious traditions and beliefs often become more of an issue after a marriage or commitment has been made. Stepparents may encourage and even pressure the family into joining their church, even if the issue was not addressed during dating. Adolescents active in their church-based social groups may be critical of stepparents who do not attend religious services. Changes in religious beliefs may be met with resistance from the non-residential parent.

Another significant issue is how money is managed. Many step-couples keep separate financial accounts, others may have a household account but individual savings or investments. Household expenditures are often a topic of negotiation. Spending on the teenagers in the family can be source of contention. Teens are expensive and their wants feel like necessities to them. When a family has two sets of children to support, different ideas about expenses or allowances can surface after the wedding. When a father focuses more on supporting a new family, his own children can resent the perceived financial inequities, especially when their mother complains about any changes. Inheritance can become a major point of conflict between biological and stepsiblings. Religion, culture, and money are central to a family's identity and need to be addressed early in the development of a stepfamily. All too often these get a quick pass over during the exciting period of dating.

Holidays, birthdays, weddings, graduations, and funerals are all family-based activities that are filled with activities, styles, and attitudes. Extended family brings established traditions to a new stepfamily. Thanksgiving for one parent may involve formal dinners with extended family while others' family traditions include chicken wings and football games. Christmas or Hanukkah can be complicated holidays for stepfamilies. Adolescents are often expected to be a part of two or more family holiday celebrations. Add extended family celebrations and these events feel more like a burden of having to shuffle between activities so that all family members have their allotted time. These time-sharing agreements may be in the parent's best interest but not always the teenagers. Old conflicts between ex-spouses can be renewed as new stepfamilies struggle with sharing holidays. Many adolescents prefer to spend their holidays at home or with friends.

On the positive side, Holiday celebrations have the potential to create new family rituals that add a positive dimension and connection to the family identity. Adding enjoyable and meaningful traditions and celebrations with the new stepfamily help teenagers adjust. Driving to the forest to cut down a Christmas tree for their first holiday as a family can become a new tradition. Birthday cake from scratch together can become a new tradition. Mixing different family styles into a new but familiar activity can help a family bond.

Everyday habits, interactions, and personal preferences are central to a sense of family. It is the everyday interactions that can be the most surprising. Food choices, TV watching, morning schedules, household tasks and expectations (no wet towels on the floor, dishes in dishwasher not sink), and even personal word choices can differ. Is it okay for siblings to tease each other? Are the terms sir and ma'am required when speaking to an adult? What are acceptable voices levels in the home? What is a reasonable curfew? These differences, no matter how small, require negotiation and compromise.

Barbara, with two young teenagers, married a co-worker after a year-long courtship. The stepfather went to bed early and expected the house to be quiet after 9 p.m. This translated into no TV, no cell phones, and no loud conversations. Within several months, the household expectations from the stepfather became a source of heated arguments between the teenagers and stepfather. The mother supported her new spouse's need for sleep but intervened for her kids and their need to enjoy their nighttime activities. The family learned to compromise and adjustments included a white noise machine for the stepfather and a new TV in the kids' room. The stepfather also pushed his bedtime a half-hour later and made a point of watching an evening TV show with the teens as a way of connecting. The family realized that despite dating for almost a year, the couple had never spent the night together and the family's nightly habits were relatively unknown.

What needs to be worked out is who has the final say in these differences, the mother, stepfather, or teenager. Actually, everyone needs to have a voice in the changes. It is important for parents to remember that this household has been the teen's home long before the new spouse moved in. Allowing everyone's preferences to be addressed, even those as trivial as mayo or Miracle Whip, can help a family connect. Blending styles and allowing differences can help a home feel comfortable for everyone. Stepfamilies need to create new interactional patterns that respect everyone. Stepfamilies are unique and need not adhere to traditional family norms.

The Other Parent

The last challenge identified by Dr. Papernow is the involvement of the teenager's other parent. According to Papernow (2013), "By definition, stepfamilies include at least one other parent, alive or dead, outside the household, who is an inextricable part of the new family" (p. 102).[15]

Ex-spouses are still biological parents and most parents have a distinct reaction to a new adult in their children's lives. Parents usually want to meet the new adult prior to the wedding and will openly or unconsciously pass judgement on their acceptability as a "parent" for their children. Many stepfamilies become complicated and interconnected as marriages occur. Teens whose parents divorced when they were 13 might find themselves with a new stepparent (or two) by the time they are 16. It takes time for a new single-parent family to settle in to a comfortable routine and for both ex-spouses to find a balance in their parenting responsibilities.

This can change when a parent decides to cohabitate or remarry. Even when the divorce was amiable and the new stepparent is well received, the presence of the other parent changes things. The amount of involvement of the other parent can be a function of the custody arrangement or the cooperative parenting plan agreed upon by the ex-spouses. The presence of a critical ex-spouse or a teen's protection of their other parent's place in their family can impact a new stepfamily's functioning. Ex-spouses can be supportive, critical, manipulative, or vengeful. From everyday parenting activities to major events, the lives of the teenagers are entwined in the adults' (biological, step, grandparents) lives.

Remarriage can precipitate the re-emergence of earlier conflicts. Some parents have continued to clash and when one or both remarry, as the sources of conflict are multiplied. Anger at a former-spouse usually extends to their new partner. Competition between the biological parent and stepparent surfaces. Jealousy over ex-spouses and the teen's attention and affection are possible. "I don't want you but I don't want someone else to have you either." "My son is my business, not yours!" I am taking my daughter to get her prom dress, not you!"

Over the years, I have worked with many stepfamilies that become entrenched in conflict with the teenagers caught in the middle. Teens are expected to take sides and carry messages. For many teens, their needs and issues are secondary to the issues between the warring families.

Cooperative or parallel parenting assumes the involvement of both parents in a range of activities and decisions. Often shared parenting allows ongoing access and involvement by both parents and any new spouses. Regular ex-spouse conversations about teen's activities may be beneficial for parents of teens but can start to irritate a new spouse. These families can find themselves sitting on the same bleachers during sport games or band performances. Picture taking before homecoming and prom can result in a crowded front hall. Even when both families strive to be friendly, the ongoing togetherness can become irritating to a new spouse. These events can highlight the insider/outsider positions mentioned previously. The appropriate seating arrangement at special events (graduation, weddings) is a stressful for most teens and young adults.

Antagonistic ex-spouses can create problems for the adjustment of stepfamilies. When a new spouse enters the picture, old conflicts flare. Parents may actively reject the new adult who is, in essence, taking their place in the family. Encouraging the rejection of the new parent figure can disrupt the adjustment of the stepfather–teen relationship. Even when the non-residential parent's animosity is subtle, the teen picks up on the message that getting along with the new stepparent is an act of disloyalty. Adolescents may feel less of a need to become close to the non-custodial parent's new spouse. Visits are brief and interactions can be civil. Most teens do not spend a lot of their visitation interacting with parents; they are involved in activities or on their phone with friends. Younger adolescents and residential stepparents are more likely to develop a close relationship as they spend more time together.

Stepfamily Relationships

Even though divorce and remarriage no longer carry any stigma, stepmothers and stepfathers are still surrounded with negative connotations. In reality, most stepparents come into the family with a sincere desire to love and care for a family. Adolescents often have a more difficult time making the adjustment to a new stepparent than younger children. Stepsiblings are also a possibility with the teen acquiring younger or older stepbrothers or stepsisters. In some families, the siblings can be from both parents' remarriage. A new half-sibling may also become part of the teen's nuclear family. Step-grandparents, step-aunts, step-uncles, and even step-cousins can enter the picture almost overnight. All of these relationships are complex and everyone's adjustment to the new family system is interdependent. Individual personalities and the willingness to accept a new family member are important components. Judgments about new family relationships should be allowed sufficient time for growth and acceptance. Many step-relationships that start out rocky end up finding ways to connect and function well together.

Stepfathers

Adolescents' reactions to a new stepfather may differ from those of younger children. Additionally, stepfathers may have a harder time connecting with an adolescent. Younger children may be more accepting and respectful of a new adult in the home. They are less likely to push back against an adult's parental role, especially when their mother supports her new partner's involvement and authority. For some new stepfathers, the wife's children may be part of the package and not necessarily a highly desired addition to their lives. After all, who wants to take on a teenager, especially when the adolescent is in the process of separating and is moody and rebellious.

Teenagers, in the process of making peer connections, are not always open to developing an emotional bond with another adult. Some may resent another stepping in as a replacement for their biological parent. "You are not my father" is an oft-used phrase in newly developed stepfamilies. Adolescents, like younger children, may perceive the new spouse as competing with them for a parent's attention. Teens, naturally judgmental about parents and adults, can be very critical of the new family member. Seeking to protect their mother from any heartache, some teens may be hyper-alert to any conflict and readily blame the new spouse for any perceived problems. Often stepfathers need to meet the stringent hypothetical criteria that the teen has established as to what constitutes an acceptable new spouse and family member.

Parental authority is always a question in stepfamilies. Coming into the home and trying to establish a position of authority is often met with resistance. Creating a friendly and supportive relationship and leaving the behavior management to the biological parent makes for a smoother transition.

Authoritative parenting works best with teenagers and a new stepfather should focus on the caring and interest components. Stepfathers integrate better when they offer social support to the teens, enjoy family-based activities, and provide financial and emotional support for the mother. A good relationship between mother and teen is a significant factor in the successful integration of a new stepfather.[16] Teens are more open to a new stepfather when they perceive that their mother is happy and that acceptance of the new spouse is encouraged by the mother.

The title afforded a stepparent is often indicative of the newcomer's acceptance. A study about the labeling of stepfathers by Thorsen and King (2016) indicates that:

> How teens navigate the process of defining who this person is who lives in their household, whether their "stepfather" or their "mother's husband" is shaped by their relationships with their biological parents as well as different aspects of the stepfamily environment. (p. 846)[17]

The term stepfather is descriptive and rarely used as a moniker. The title of dad or father is often reserved for biological fathers. Most teens call their stepfather by his first name, as they have already established a relationship using his given name. As the stepfather becomes more accepted in the family, teens will often refer to their mother and stepfather as "my parents." When the stepfather has been a stable part of a teen's family for a number of years, some teens refer to my dad or even call him dad in certain situations or when talking about his family to others. Calling a stepparent by their first name and referring to them as "my stepfather" does not always specify the degree of connection but usually indicates an acceptance of the stepfather's inclusion in the family. One client of mine felt close to and respected her stepfather, but felt like dad was not appropriate at her age (15) and stepdad felt too standoffish, so she ended up calling him "Stad."

Use of the term "my mother's husband" may be out of a sense of loyalty to their biological father or can indicate that the teen is not completely accepting of the new stepparent. When a teen rejects or resents the stepfather's addition to the family, the title does not matter as much as the attitude behind the moniker. Teens can make any title sound disrespectful. Older teens and young adults may not feel the need to add a stepfather to their family system but accept that their mother is remarried. As teens age and the stepparent integrates well into the family, the title afforded the stepfather or stepmother may change to indicate the developing bond and respect for the stepparent.

Biological fathers can have mixed reactions to a new man joining his children's family. Stepfathers are stepping into the role previously held by the biological father. They can feel that they have been replaced, are no longer needed, or that they will have to compete for their adolescent's attention and love. However, a (2009) study on family ties found that a close and ongoing relationship with a teen's non-residential father does not preclude the acceptance of a stepfather and does not disrupt the father–teen bond.[18]

Some fathers welcome another adult in their teen's lives. Some even develop a type of friendship with them based on their teenagers and any shared interests. Biological fathers often appreciate when stepfathers provide financial and emotional stability to their teenagers' lives. Remarriage of an ex-spouse can eliminate spousal support and reduce some of the animosity in a divorced couples' interactions. However, fathers who suspect the new stepfather of mistreating his children will often intervene and old issues between the parents may surface. Conflicts between the teen and stepfather can even result in the father seeking changes in custody. Stepfathers should show respect for the biological father's bond with their adolescents. Support by the mother and that of the non-residential father can encourage youth to accept and appreciate their new stepfather.

Stepmothers

A stepmother may be the woman who marries (or cohabitates with) a father (or same-sex partner) who has primary custody of his children, regular visitation, or one who lives away from his children and only sees them on holidays and summer vacations. The stepmother may have custodial children of their own; these women are full-time mothers and part-time stepmothers. The combination of various family situations makes their roles ambiguous and complicated. There are two myths that plague stepmothers in our society: that women are naturally caretakers and housekeepers and that stepmothers are wicked or cruel. Our society often expects stepmothers to fulfill the maternal role in the family more often than men are viewed as paternal figures.

Stepmothers have a bad reputation due to Disney movies such as *Cinderella* and *Snow White*. The reality is that most stepmothers join the family with a sincere desire to provide love and care to a family. When joining a family with teenagers, this is a difficult undertaking. The incoming stepmothers and the adolescents may all enter the relationship with misconceptions. Cheri Burns, in *Stepmotherhood* (2001), states that:

> Stepmothers-to-be usually have one of three popular preconceptions about stepmothering: (1) Our stepchildren won't really be a part of our marriage and lives: (2) our relationship with our stepchildren will be close and familial—like one big happy family; (3) we will

> love our stepchildren as though they were our own children. With a little experience we realize that all three beliefs are unrealistic. (p. 10)[19]

These three misconceptions are true for women joining families with adolescents: (1) Teens may not spend every other weekend with dad doing fun activities but they will come and go, making their presence known. (2) Families with teenagers are rarely one big happy family. (3) Loving an outspoken, moody teenager is not automatic. It rarely takes very long for stepmothers and adolescents to encounter some interactional road bumps.

Adolescents often have a difficult time accepting a new stepmother in their lives. They also struggle with having a new woman in their father's life. By adolescence, the mother-child bond is firmly established, even when the biological mother has not been ideal. Fathers often have custody of their teenagers when the mother has significant emotional or drug and alcohol issues, is unable to financially care for the adolescents, or is unwilling or unable to be the primary custodial parent. Difficult adolescents often end up living with their father when their behavior is too problematic for their mother to handle. Bringing a new "mother" into the home is often met with apprehension or even hostility. In some families, adolescents can appreciate the addition of a supportive and kind adult.

It is difficult to replace a mother in a family. There is often a hope that she will get her life together and be the mom again. Teens who struggle with inadequate or disengaged parenting from their biological mother may vent their unconscious anger at the new stepmother. These women end up taking on issues that they were not responsible for creating. Teens usually push back when they sense that the new stepmom is trying to replace their mother. Being a mother figure to these teens is rarely met with acceptance and gratitude. The non-residential mother's sanction of the new wife can help teens adjust to the stepmother's role in the family. As with stepfathers, stepmothers need to respect the mother's connection with their children.

In time, most stepmothers achieve a role that is comfortable for everyone. Creating a harmonious family life takes time, lots of energy, and patience. Stepmothers may find that the teens' expectations are that their father's new wife will provide housekeeping services and meals but not discipline. Adolescents prefer a parental figure that provides support and guidance without coming on too strong. Stepdaughters may find their stepmother is someone who they can confide in about the emotional issues common to adolescence. Stepsons may appreciate a woman's touch in the home. Stepmothers may also moderate conflicts between teens and their biological father or mother.

15-year-old Megan came to live with her father and stepmother at her request. Her parents' divorce was contentious and her mother continued to badmouth her dad, even though both parents were remarried. Megan had been living with her mother, stepfather, and older sister on a small farm in the country since her parents' divorce when she was 10. Visitation with her father was every other weekend and a month in the summer. Megan was struggling in her relationship with her mother whom she believed preferred her older sister. She also felt her stepfather was critical and often sided with her mother in their conflicts. Megan admitted to missing her dad and reported feeling more accepted at his house. She begged her dad to let her live with him following her summer visit before her sophomore year in high school. Megan stated she wanted to spend more time with her dad, liked the idea of a bigger and more urban school, and was tired of the fighting with her mom. The parents finally agreed to a temporary change in custody.

Megan's stepmother, Barbara, was an intelligent, soft-spoken woman who worked at an oil company in the human relations department. She had been married previously but had no children of her own. The couple had been married for three years and the relationship between the girls and their stepmother was amiable. From early on, Barbara had stayed out of the conflict between her husband and his ex-wife and allowed him to provide the rules and consequences when his girls visited.

Megan found that the adjustment at her dad's was not as easy as she expected. Going to a new school and making new friends was a struggle and her dad had high expectations for her grades and household chores. Additionally, her mother continued to criticize her father and pressure her to return home. Throughout her adjustment period and amidst her adolescent angst, her stepmother proved to be her biggest ally. Barbara helped Megan negotiate her conflicts with her dad, encouraged her to join activities and make new friends, and listened patiently to her struggles with her mother. When Megan left for college, it was her stepmother that she called regularly to share her experiences and ask for advice.

Women may find themselves being a mother and stepmother simultaneously. Complex stepfamilies afford the most complicated roles for women to balance. Women who are full-time mothers and part-time stepmothers walk a fine line. When both sets of children are with the family, the expectations for each are often different.

More likely, it is a complicated situation where two biological parents are parenting their own kids in the same home while "hosting" the other family. The step-couple's interactions should provide support to the various connections without competing with each other or overstepping boundaries. Stepsibling interplay can help or impede a harmonious family environment. When the father's teenagers visit a family with no other children, the stepmother's role is difficult to determine. They may provide support for the father, meals for the family, and perhaps an ear to listen with some helpful advice. Stepmothers will plan holidays and celebrate birthdays. There is often a sincere effort to provide their step-teens with affection and caring. Feelings may be hurt when the stepmothers' efforts do not result in reciprocal feelings and the stepmom finds herself struggling to love children who treat her like the hired help.

Stepsiblings

Imagine that you're a teenager living with either your mom or your dad and your siblings after your parent's divorce. Everything seems to have settled down and your parents are getting along most of the time. Then your dad gets remarried and his new wife has three kids who are now going to be living with your dad. Or your mother gets remarried and her new husband has children. Remarriage or cohabitation of both parents may result in teens having two sets of stepsiblings, those of their mother's new husband and those of the biological father's new wife. Suddenly, you have stepsiblings! These new siblings may be older or younger and the same or the opposite sex. Your recently married parent expects you to consider them your siblings.

These changes can be unsettling. The bedrooms are now their rooms, the meals are what they like, and the bathroom is full of their stuff. Suddenly, you are the outsider in your non-residential parent's house. In your primary residence, you are being asked to share your space and belongings with new stepsiblings. Additionally, the new family expects you to change your usual weekends so the newlyweds can have weekends alone. Complicated and emotionally challenging is an understatement.

In complex stepfamilies, the biological children of both spouses live with the new couple and become an instant family. The couple have been dating for a while, are in love, and have a lot of commonality that bonds them together; this is not the case for the children, who may only superficially know each other. The adjustment of teenagers to instant siblings is complicated. Teens may be close in age but have very different personalities and interests. The snobby girl who looks down at you may be your new sister, the jock you have been in competition with is your new brother, and the opposite-sex sibling is attractive. Some teens find that there is a good age fit and connection between the siblings and the new family dynamics seem exciting. Older teens may find themselves with younger siblings who look up to them. New stepsiblings may initially bond over their reaction to the marriage of their parents. Even when siblings initially get along, some conflict will be inevitable. Loyalty issues and other rivalries may develop and will need to be negotiated.

While younger children may welcome new playmates into their lives, teens may feel very differently. Peer connections are carefully developed during adolescence and being asked to accept peers as sudden siblings can be met with apprehension and resistance. Teens may compete for limited resources, such as parental attention, money, and belongings. Older or stronger personality youth may influence the behaviors of younger teens. A need to be accepted may result in actions that are not typical for the teen. Teasing and bullying is possible and parents may look the other way or assume that the kids will work it out among themselves. New stepsiblings can cause a change or rift in previously established sibling relationships.

A complex development occurs when two opposite sex teens find themselves attracted to each other. Barbara LeBey in *Remarried with Children* (2004) acknowledges that:

> Kids thrown together in the same house during the years of awakening sexuality need to be watched very carefully for seductive behavior. ... The notion that new stepsiblings of the opposite sex will have attractions for each is not unlike any unrelated boy and girl having these feelings. (p. 207)[20]

Adding to the attraction between stepsiblings is that the newly wed parents are role modeling affection and sexual activity. In this situation, the parents need to monitor the stepsibling relationship and intervene when necessary.

Remarriage may result in the birth of a new child, who is a half-sibling on both sides of the family. A mother's pregnancy can be uncomfortable for teenagers, especially in front of their peers. When the child is that of one's biological mother, teenagers may feel more connected to the new baby and take on a protective and caring role. Younger teens worry about being replaced by the child. Non-residential adolescents may be concerned that the new child will pull their biological parent away from them. Jealousy is a possibility, as babies naturally require more time and attention. In many families, this new half-sibling will help solidify the family bond and provide the stepsiblings on both sides with more of a connection. According to Hetherington and Kelly (2002):

> We found in adolescence, increasingly in young adulthood, biological relatedness influenced the quality of sibling relationships. There is not only more engagement and support between biologically related siblings but also more rivalry, especially in half-siblings, than is present in stepsiblings. ... The involvement of biologically related siblings is just more emotionally intense and sustaining. (p.238)[21]

Stepsiblings and half-siblings who see each only on weekend visits may develop a friendly but superficial relationship that may not continue into adulthood. Stepsibling relationships that begin during the adolescent years can become more of a friendship in adulthood. Parental support and monitoring of the developing stepsibling relationships will help these new family members develop enjoyable and appropriate connections.

Adolescent Adjustment

After divorce, many teens' primary residence stabilizes and they settle into a comfortable balance at home and in their relationship with each parent. Other teens may continue to experience turmoil in their family. Remarriage of one or both parents brings a new challenge and the adolescent's reactions to a new adult (and possibly new stepsiblings) is rarely simple. Teen adjustment to these stepfamilies is dependent upon a number of factors. As Julie Gosselin (2010) in an article on adolescent adjustment states:

> Each stepfamily member adjustment is the result of both factors shared by all respondents (such as the quality of communication, the presence of conflict and custody arrangements) and factors unique to their position in the stepfamily (role and boundary ambiguity, triangulations, psychological distress). (p.120)[22]

Stepfamily formation does not affect all teens in the same way. Adjustment is dependent upon the adolescent's personality and strengths, the parent-teen relationship, and the style of parenting.

Relationships

Stepfamily relationships develop over time and the initial settling-in depends on the interactions among family members. A remarriage may upset the established parent-teen relationship. It requires teens to accept a new family member and may add other children to the family system. This is difficult for teens struggling to develop individuation and peer relationships. Many aspects of a teen's life are at stake in the new family situation. The new home may not feel as safe or as consistent as that of their childhood family. Even in high-conflict homes, children feel bonded to their parents.

The step-couple relationship can act as a role model for a healthy, committed marriage. After a divorce, teens may benefit from witnessing a happy, successful marital relationship. They may learn to believe in love again and be more willing to take a chance on their own intimate connections. As stepfamilies adjust, normal conflicts within the marital relationship may develop and these arguments, no matter how minor, can reactivate fears and emotions experienced during the divorce. Parents who work through these difficulties help teach teens good communication styles and constructive problem-solving skills. Communication that is open, sensitive, and respectful is critical to a teen's adjustment. Healthy families allow all members to appropriately express their opinions. Happy homes make teens feel safe and allow them to move into adulthood with a family that they want to come back home to for support and connection.

Adolescent well-being in stepfamilies is usually connected to their interpersonal relationships with their primary custodial parent, stepparent, their non-residential parent, and their newly acquired stepsiblings. These connections work both ways; parents' and stepparents' treatment of the teenager and the teen's attitudes are interconnected. A close bond with a stepparent provides for more well-adjusted teenagers. In return, adolescents who are friendly and respectful are easier for a stepparent to bond with.[23] How the adults treat each other is also critical to family harmony.

Emotional Well-being

A parent's remarriage during one's adolescent years can create emotional ambiguity. Parents who thought their teens could handle a divorce may also assume that these teens will easily adjust to a new stepfamily. Perhaps they will, however adjustment is never straight forward or simple. Younger teens still require attention, supervision, and connection with their parents in order to work on their important developmental tasks. Older adolescents may seem independent but family stability is still critical for their development. Changing family roles can be confusing and impact adolescent identity development. Stepfamilies that balance their attention among family members and provide affection and supervision allow for better teen adjustment.

It is difficult for many adolescents to predict how they will react to a new adult in their home. Teens may struggle having to live with newlyweds and feel left out when their parent focuses on their new partner. Receiving less attention can cause a teen to become moody and act-out their insecurity. Limit-testing with the new adult may increase teen rebellion. Some respond by becoming withdrawn and choose not to voice any of their opinions about the household changes. Teens wanting to support their parent may not feel comfortable complaining about the new stepparent. Fear of push back from the new adult can keep teen concerns suppressed.

Mature teens realize that adjustment takes time and thus avoid quick judgements of the new stepparent. Many accept and approve of the new stepparent but may still encounter issues requiring accommodation. Some teens voice approval, but this may not actually be the case. Adolescent behaviors can be clues to unconscious responses to the restructured family system. Parents and stepparents should take note of any changes in emotions or behaviors and help the teen talk about what is going on with them as it pertains to the new family.

Living in a stepfamily does not automatically result in problems for adolescent emotional well-being, but the transitions and presence of new family members may make the developmental stages harder to work through. Asking a teen to bond with a new family member while they are working on individuating from family adds a level of complication.

Family forms the basis for a teen's adult identity. "I am a Jones, I am a Catholic, I am Irish." Therefore, it may be harder to form one's identity while changing from a single-parent family to a stepfamily. This home-based upheaval can disrupt a teen's school work and their emotional well-being.

According to a report by Jensen et al. (2018), "Findings from nationally representative studies and meta-analysis indicate that children in stepfamilies are at an elevated risk of experiencing maladjustment in terms of academic, social, behavioral, and psychological well-being" (p. 478).[24] Even when youth in stepfamilies have shown poorer academic, emotional, and behavioral outcomes compared to those in intact families, this difference is small. For many teens in stepfamilies, the socioeconomic struggles, the stability of the family structure, and the parent–teen bonds are the primary factors that influence well-being. Transitions during the adolescent developmental period can complicate the normal teenage angst, but a stable stepfamily can help a teen emerge successfully.

Stepsiblings

As teenagers are in the process of developing peer choices that reflect their identity and emotional needs, the addition of stepsiblings has mixed reactions. Stepsiblings may live with the family full-time, part-time, or during irregular visits. These new configurations include children of different sexes, ages, and personalities and can create adjustment issues. New adolescent-age family members may influence teen attitudes and behaviors. A stepsibling who is acting out may influence the other children in the family toward more risky behaviors. Older peer siblings can elicit emulation of actions such as drinking, mischievous behavior, or being disrespectful to other family members.

On the flip side, teens may be positive role models for behavior and activities. Teens struggling with school may get encouragement and support from stepsiblings to succeed academically. Stepsiblings may introduce teens to new activities, such as sports or video gaming. In complex stepfamilies, adjustment to multiple family members with different alliances and loyalties can complicate the adjustment. Living with similar-aged peers may result in interactions that are compatible or competitive. Sibling rivalry may occur as teens vie for parental attention and family resources.

Mary was 12 and her sister, Jill, was 10 when her parents divorced. There were conflicting stories as to the reasons for the divorce, with both parents insisting that the other parent had cheated during the marriage. Mother had primary custody and her father had regular visitation. Her father remarried within a year and the new stepmother had a son aged 13 and two daughters aged 12 and 10. Mom remarried the following year to a man with five children ranging in age from 14 to 25. Mom's new spouse had shared custody of his children.

Prior to their mother's remarriage, the family had lived in the same neighborhood as their paternal grandparents, with whom the girls were very close. After the wedding, the family moved into the stepdad's home near his other children, where he kept his recreational boat. The house was not designed for a family. Jill's room was a converted fishing equipment closet. The change meant a relocation to a low-income neighborhood and a change of schools for both girls.

After their dad's remarriage, he built a house with his new wife, which was to include room for all the kids. This turned out not to be the case, so during their limited visitation the girls slept in a downstairs storage area. The father's second marriage lasted less than three years. According to one of the stepsiblings, the new house was never intended to include Mary and Jill as her stepmother did not want her family to include the girls. Dad eventually remarried a third time and added two more kids, one a new half-sibling to the family dynamics.

Within five years of her parent's divorce, Mary and Jill ended up with eight then eventually nine stepsiblings plus a half-sibling. Adjustment was difficult. Her stepmom's son, one year her senior, had an issue with anger and would "play" wrestle with her. Stepmom excused his behavior as he was "frustrated because his dad was an alcoholic." Mary learned to avoid him.

When Mary was 17, her older stepsister (21) got her a fake ID and took her to bars. Not wanting to disappoint her older stepsibling, Mary engaged in a number of behaviors that she was admittedly not ready for. Mary also wondered why her mother allowed her to go out with her stepsibling who was known to be involved with drinking and drugs. Later, this particular sibling told Mary that none of the siblings really liked her and this comment hurt terribly, as Mary had thought she had good relationships with them. Their parents are still married, but the stepsibling connections are strained. In discussing her family history, Mary states "I feel a bit like my sister and I have been erased from the family history, I guess because the folks have all moved on and our section of history is something neither parent wants to discuss."

Gender

Studies have found that girls may have a harder time adjusting to stepfathers, but may adapt better to stepsiblings and half-siblings.[25] Girls may feel that their mother's new spouse is interfering with their mother–daughter connection. Also, girls tend to be more socially inclined and empathic. They may connect with siblings who are also struggling with experiencing the new family situation. Girls internalize their feelings and seek out peer support to deal with the changes. Adolescent males, on the other hand, are more likely to compete, even if only friendly competition, and are less willing to share their feelings. Boys typically spend more time in peer-based activities and express themselves through externalizing behaviors. Ultimately, adolescents are resilient and often make a healthy or at least adequate adjustment to new siblings in the family. Stepfamilies who are aware of the importance of the various relationships at play can help develop healthy interactions and connections.

Summary

Parental divorce is difficult for teens to navigate. Remarriage after the divorce adds layers of issues that must be addressed. Acceptance of the stepparent as a family member may take time and effort by all involved. Problems develop during the initial coming together due to the developmental period of adolescence and the lack of clarity about family roles. Close parent–teen ties, even with the non-residential parent, have been shown to help the teen adapt to the family restructuring. Stepmothers and stepfathers must often overcome unwarranted bias. Stepfamilies need to find their own unique identities.

Stepfamily development is difficult and complex. The level of closeness, honesty, respect, and participation are all on the line and will ultimately be negotiated. Some blend well and a new, stable family identity is formed. Some remain fractured with occasional superficial closeness. Others accept and respect but don't really connect, becoming more like roommates than family. Teens function best when they feel that they are living in a safe, connected, and loving family unit.

6.

I Didn't Ask for This!

Tips for Helping Parents and Adolescents Cope

Every word we say to our children, good or bad, positive or negative, shapes their future. Choose wisely.
—Christina McGhee, *Parenting Apart*[1]

Parental divorce is a drawn-out process that impacts the emotional well-being of all family members. It is not a brief shift in living arrangements, it is a redefining of a family's identity. The various stages of divorce will create different emotions and behavioral reactions. Parents cognizant of their own emotional responses can manage their divorce in a manner that allows for the family's healthy adjustment.

Adolescence is a developmental period characterized by changes in a teen's physical, cognitive, emotional, and social life. Parental separation and divorce during adolescence can create a disruption in their personal development. Adolescents will benefit from awareness of their more obvious and also their unconscious responses to their parent's divorce. Parents' handling of their divorce is directly correlated to their teenager's responses. Teens need support and guidance from parents, extended family, and friends to adjust to the family changes. Both parents need to remain actively involved in their teen's daily lives.

Adult Responses and Behaviors

Decision and Implementation

The choice to end a marriage is a difficult one for any adult. When an adult begins to question the viability of continuing in their relationship, several important steps should be taken in order to make an informed decision. These suggestions are not necessarily taken in any specific order but are a guide to help the adult consider their options.

- Be realistic about the marital problems and issues.
- Don't get caught up in negative thinking and rumination.
- Consider where you are in your life.
- Try to view the issues from your spouses' perspective.
- Talk over the situation with a trusted friend or therapist.
- Consider couples' therapy. If the divorce occurs, you will have support for the implementation.
- Be realistic about possible options before jumping into a divorce.
- Consider a trial separation.
- Gather your strength.
- Make a realistic plan with your children as a priority.
- Assess your financial situation and develop a plan for managing your expenses.
- Give minimal, realistic, and age-appropriate information to your children.

There are times in any marriage when the relationship is strained or problems seem insurmountable. Some life events create stress on a relationship. Perhaps a job loss or change, caring for an aging parent, or the difficulty of dealing with a rebellious adolescent has strained the marriage. Changes in one's life create personal unhappiness that seems indicative of a failing relationship. We often expect our partners to make us happy and may blame them when life becomes unsatisfying. Marriage cannot always protect an individual from feeling overwhelmed or lonely. Be realistic as to the source of unhappiness. Additionally, the discovery of a perceived betrayal (perhaps a brief affair) does not always mean that a divorce is necessary.

Many relationships overcome significant problems. Putting the marital problems in perspective can help with possible options for resolution of the issues. Deciding too quickly that a divorce is the only option starts a path that is difficult to pull back from.

Focusing primarily on the negative aspects of a relationship or dwelling on the other person's flaws often lead to even more critical thoughts or perceptions about the relationship. In the same way that focusing on physical pain can increase the sensation of discomfort, problems can be blown out of proportion and lead to finding other sources of unhappiness in a marriage. One client kept a running tally of her grievances against her husband and by doing so found it harder for her to see any of the positives in the relationship. Dissatisfaction and anger with a spouse often develop slowly over time and fueling these negative emotions erodes at the stability of the marriage. Try to balance relationship perceptions by considering the positive aspects of the marriage and your spouse's qualities. Remember the reasons you married or the important life challenges you have faced together. Marriages are rarely a 50-50 relationship. There are tremendous fluctuations in how much give and take occurs at any given time or life stage. Don't rush to leave when time may allow issues to subside, and the functionality of a marriage may later shift in a more positive direction.

When experiencing marital differences, it is helpful to consider both spouses position and concerns. This cannot be stressed enough. Objectively understanding your spouse's thoughts and feelings about the marital problems can help with developing solutions that prevent divorce. Being angry over having to handle a lot of the childcare may be offset by considering how stressful your spouse's job may be for them. Even when a couple opt to divorce, being aware and respectful of the other spouse's feelings or concerns can help create an atmosphere conducive to a reasonable divorce agreement. Co-parenting plans are easier to implement when considering the needs of the soon to be ex-spouse. Remember, this individual is still the parent of your children.

Before making a major decision that will seriously affect your family, consider talking over the issues with someone who will help you be objective and realistic. Do not seek out a friend or family member who is already predisposed to a negative opinion about your spouse or marriage. A recently divorced and still bitter co-worker is not a good option. A therapist can provide guidance in assessing the issues and making the best decision. They will often provide support to all family members in coping with the changes inherent in the divorce process. A good therapist can save couples thousands of dollars in attorney fees and hours of emotional pain.

Selecting the right therapist is important. Seek out a licensed therapist experienced in family therapy. Therapists should be objective and offer guidance not personal opinions. Some Christian counselors have negative biases against divorce. Look for someone who can consider the needs of both partners. They should also be concerned with the impact of the divorce on the children. Some therapists work with both spouses and will respect the confidentiality of individual sessions. If two therapists are working with the family, they should work together (with appropriate releases) to help the couple deal respectfully with each other. Have an initial session with a therapist to gage your level of comfort. Do not be afraid to meet with several different therapists to find one that feels like a good fit for you and the family. Avoid therapists that appear to have a bias or agenda that is evident in their initial questions or advice.

It is never a good idea to rush into implementing any decision. Immediately filing for divorce is not the only option to a problematic relationship. Consider a trial separation which may give some relief from the tension but also allow opportunities to work on the problems. Time apart will help couples find ways to work through their issues or begin to understand what divorced life will be like. Knowing that a reconciliation may occur, encourages adults to behave in a more civil manner toward each other. Often a therapist can help a couple set up a realistic plan for separation. If a divorce is decided upon, some of the preliminary changes may help make the transitions easier for everyone. Separation may also help a teen accept the changes in their family. Remember, teens will need to continue their relationship with both parents.

Sometimes, divorce is a reasonable and viable decision. Many decisions to divorce come about following an incident that highlights the longstanding problems in the marriage. When this defining interaction occurs, often one partner takes the initial steps to begin the process of separation. In other situations, the decision is the result of a well thought out plan following years of unhappiness. Careful thought should be given to how to implement this life choice. Do not decide impulsively to leave or to kick out your spouse. Plans should be made with awareness of to the realities of separation and divorce. There are many considerations to plan for: financial, housing, children, and safety. Parents should always consider the impact of their decision on their children.

Maria was married for 16 years with two children. Her spouse was a physician and Maria managed his practice. Her husband started exhibiting episodes of rage early in the marriage. Rarely were the outbursts physically directed at her or the children but property destruction was common. Maria learned to manage these temper outbursts by placating him or withdrawing from the situation. Maria's life was focused on raising her children and keeping the family business afloat. While she was worried about the impact of her husband's temper on her children, she hoped that her parenting offset and protected her children. While there were many times in which Maria thought about leaving, the steps needed to leave seemed overwhelming.

One evening, her daughter (15) had a friend over when the rage started. The girl contacted her father who came over and took both girls to his home. On the way out, he told Maria, "I will come back for you and your son (age 12)" and he did. At that point, Maria realized that there would be friends who supported her and that her carefully kept family situation was not as much of a secret as she thought. The next day, she contacted a realtor and found a rental house that she (and her children) moved into within the month. Maria found someone to manage the medical practice and went to work at a local hospital using her administrative skills. She finally accepted that she was not going to change his behavior. It was several years later that her ex-husband finally sought treatment for his temper.

Divorce has significant financial repercussions. Finances are always a point of contention and some vindictive spouses use money as a weapon in the divorce battle. Consider the changes in income when two homes will need to be maintained. Set up a separate account if there is concern of financial problems, especially if you are not the primary breadwinner. Do not drain the family account. Save for attorney fees or related expenses.

Living and custody arrangements are an important consideration. Both spouses may want to remain in the family home but costs may be prohibitive. If remaining in the family home is unworkable, consider options for alternative residence. Staying in their current school is extremely important to teenagers. Suddenly moving out of state to be near your mother may benefit you but will not be in the best interest of your teenagers. Temporary housing may be necessary until final divorce agreements are made.

The request for a divorce may escalate a controlling or abusive spouse. These situations require preplanning. Consider where you will go if your home is unsafe and you need to leave quickly. Contact a trusted friend or family member, local shelters are also available in some locations. Place a hidden set of keys to the house and car that can be easily accessed. Set aside some emergency cash. Don't be afraid to call the police if needed. If possible, have the kids out of the house when you inform your spouse of your intent to leave. Meet in a public place to minimize the emotional reactions. Be realistic about the possibility of danger when informing a volatile spouse about the decision to divorce.

Before starting the process of divorce, consider your emotional and physical health. Start making healthy choices for eating, exercise, and emotional health. Learn some relaxation techniques. Preparing emotionally will help make the transition easier. Develop and make use of a good support system. Talking over your issues with a therapist can help develop your emotional strength. Consider joining a divorce support group.

Before either parent moves out, talk with your teens about the fact that the marriage is experiencing problems and may be headed for divorce. Talking with teens together is advisable if you can present a calm and united front. At the very least, decide ahead of time what you will tell the kids. Do not get into blame or unnecessary detail. Teens will often be cognizant that problems exist and need realistic information that will help them understand what is happening to their family. More about talking to teens will be addressed later in this chapter.

Emotions and Adjustment

Divorce is a roller coaster ride of emotions. Emotions often get played out through behaviors and decisions. Managing the emotions and being careful to behave responsibly is difficult but important to one's adjustments and future relationships. Over reactions create additional problems and rarely relieve the pain or anger. Also hiding feelings behind a stoic face or excessive activities will eventually fall out of you like a broken dam, sweeping you away. When asked how you are doing, be honest, "I am not okay but I am trying." Share only what and with whom you choose. Be selective. You do not need people gossiping, only supporting. The most common feelings that will need to be addressed include denial, fear, guilt, sadness, anger, and relief.

In dealing with any feeling several steps occur and being cognizant of this process helps manage the emotions in a healthy manner. First a feeling is created in response to an event, thought, or person. It is important at this point to acknowledge and appropriately label the feeling. Are you scared or angry, sad or lonely? Often emotions are mislabeled; just in the same way that the source of physical ailments does not always correspond directly with where the sensation is felt. Use your body clues to help identify the feeling. Feeling cold and shaky is anxiety or fear. Place a value or level of distress on the feeling. Is it minor, fleeting, acute, chronic, or significant? Feelings are meant to be transient. Don't ruminate.

Finally decide how you want to express this feeling. Try not to overreact or repress the feeling. Your choice of response may provide relief or can intensifying the emotion. Screaming may only escalate an angry emotion. Think about the damage done by road rage. Impulsive reactions rarely work well. An appropriate response does not always have to be overt. You might opt to let it go or turn to humor to deflate the situation. We all know that laughing at yourself can help alleviate embarrassment, likewise humor offsets other intense emotions. Hurt may be helped by crying or giving yourself an alternative interpretation as to the reason for the pain. For example, teens may say hurtful things to parents when the real issue is with a peer. After you decide on how you want to express the feeling, allow yourself to be satisfied with your handling of the situation. Finally, recover and move on. While this process of managing feeling seems complicated, it can easily occur in a few minutes or even seconds once you learn more about yourself. For your own health, opt for responses that reduce intense feelings rather than aggravate them.

The early stages of the divorce find adults dealing with denial, guilt, and fear. Managing these feelings often set the stage for future acceptance and adjustment. Most start with a bit of denial that this life change is actually happening. Beginning to accept that your partner is asking for a divorce may take some conscious effort on your part. Seek to understand why they are requesting such a significant change, even when your need is to deny what they are saying. Ask yourself if the relationship has been deteriorating and if you have been avoiding the developing tension or unhappiness. Review recent events that may have been indicative of the problems. Many spouses report that efforts to convey their unhappiness have been ignored by their spouse.

Trying saying out loud "my spouse wants a divorce" or "I have decided that I want out of this marriage." (Do not say this out loud with your teens within earshot). Share the possibility with a trusted friend. Ask your spouse for some time to deal with the request. No need to move out immediately. If possible, have one spouse move into the guest room temporarily. Tell the kids before taking any actions. They will notice the atmospheric and literal change in their parent's dynamics.

Even after years of unhappiness or conflict, the thought of change is scary. Denial is often mixed with fear. Fear of what being divorced means. Concerns about being alone and fear of the unknown are often front and center. How will you deal with your new identity as a single person? What will your financial security look like? Will you be able to stay involved in your teen's everyday life? Dealing with these feelings may require stepping back and looking at the situation objectively and realistically. Denial and fear create worse-case scenarios in our imagination. Making a list of changes that divorce entails helps develop a realistic view. As Fisher and Alberti (2016) state in *Rebuilding When Your Relationship Ends*:

> Fear can be paralyzing until you're able to recognize it as a part of you that is your friend. Fear then becomes a motivator and a way to learn more about yourself. Fears are a major part of the feelings you experience when you are in the pits of divorce. (p. 43)[2]

Relaxation exercises or physical activities can help you deal with your fear and anxiety. Don't ruminate on the fears or imagine worse-case scenarios. Be downright absurd about how terrible it could be. "I will end up living on the street, playing my guitar for pocket change." Not true! Take any negative statements and create a positive alternative. Start a journal. Seek out support system that will listen and help calm your fears without being critical. While many fears will surface during all of the changes, perspective and a belief in your ability to overcome challenges will help to decrease the power of the fear. It helps to remember that courage is doing something even when you are afraid.

Guilt is a powerful feeling and often experienced without valid and realistic reasons. Deciding to end your marriage, for whatever reason, often evokes powerful feelings of guilt. "I am being selfish." "I am harming our children." "How can I abandon my vows?" Guilt may also be felt by the parent who does not want the divorce but may feel they have not done enough to keep the marriage viable. Guilt is another feeling that requires perspective. Guilt is often derived from past experiences. Children who are shamed as children may often feel guilt unnecessarily. Childhood guilt comes roaring back when faced with taking steps to make yourself happier in your life. "I should honor my vows." "I am breaking up the family." "I will embarrass my family by becoming a divorced woman." Some families and religious denominations still consider divorce a sin or a dishonor.

Feeling guilty can be appropriate and even helpful in managing our behavior. Acting in a way that is knowingly hurtful to another should evoke some degree of guilt however, asking to end a dysfunctional relationship should not invoke guilt. It can be a viable solution to continuing in a situation that is harmful to all family members. Leaving in an angry and vindictive manner should create moral discomfort that encourages one to be more reasonable in one's actions and responses. Guilt may persuade you from emptying bank accounts or destroying property.

Take stock of your degree of guilt and try to be realistic about its value as a feeling in a particular situation. Get a friend to give you honest feedback about the validity of your feelings. Find other emotional labels to identify what you are feeling. Perhaps you feel empathy with the pain your spouse is dealing with. You may be concerned with providing your teens with a healthy home environment. Remorse, sadness, or responsibility are more manageable feelings than guilt. Forgive yourself if you think your choices are making others unhappy, especially when your reasons are valid. Avoid guilt; it is an overused and damages self-worth. Therapy is often useful in separating and dealing with guilt that emanates from previous life experiences.

Sadness comes in various forms and levels of intensity. Unhappiness, loneliness, hopelessness, and a sense of being disconnected are emotional states related to sadness. Grief and depression are common reactions to the losses that accompany divorce. Sadness is a normal and healing emotion. Experiencing these feelings can help one accept and get past the hurt. Pain may be expressed and channeled in various ways, many of which are healthy. Talk to a friend, write in a private journal, take a long walk, listen to sad music, watch tearjerker movies. Feel sorry for yourself (within reason). Acknowledge your losses. Write a long letter saying goodbye to your old life. Be kind to yourself and don't expect to manage all your changes well. Let some little things go. Excuse some of your shortcomings. Let the laundry pile up for another week. Sad feelings combined with negative thoughts lead down a dark hole. Seek a balance in your thoughts. Break emotions into workable periods of time. Make use of your support system to help alleviate the sadness.

Allowing yourself to cry and connect with your sadness helps drain the emotions. Be careful not to let your tears overrun your strength. Place a limit on your reactions; set a timer, have a good cry, and then go do something, anything else. Take a walk, watch a TV show, call a friend, do a puzzle. Break the cycle. It is also not healthy to avoid shedding tears. You have the right to be sad! Be careful not to upset your children with uncontrolled wailing. The client who cried hysterically in her room bemoaning the responsibility of her children may have benefited herself but not her children. Teens can understand tears and may view them as permission to experience their own sadness but they should not have to manage a hysterical adult. Keep a handle on your feelings. Cry when the kids aren't home. Scream alone in your car. Cry in the shower. Don't let it overwhelm you. Get support if you can't get a handle on your emotions.

Grief is a part of the divorce experience. According to John Schneider (as quoted in *This Thing Called Grief (2006))* "Grief is a natural process of discovering what is lost, what is left, and what is possible" (p. xiii).[3] There are so many losses in the divorce process. Loss of the primary relationship, family identity, extended family, and future dreams. Financial and household changes occur in most families. Change involves some form of loss and impacts adults and teens alike.

Grief is often associated with the stages identified by Dr. Elisabeth Kubler-Ross (1926-2004) which are Denial, Anger, Bargaining, Depression, and Acceptance. While initially developed in the context of loss by a death, the stages are very applicable to divorce. As stated by Kathleen Gay (2014) in *Divorce: The Ultimate Teen Guide*, "For divorce, experts say, that there are anywhere from five to seven stages of grief ... These stages can include Shock or Disbelief, Denial, Anger, Bargaining, Guilt, Depression, Acceptance, and Hope" (p. 51).[4] Some hope to skip some of the stages but this rarely occurs. Denial is often the initial response, but reality usually kicks in pretty quickly for most. Denial does not stop the process but may slow it down temporarily.

Anger is the most difficult stage and causes the most damage. It is also the emotion up front and center in parent's interactions. Management of these emotions are critical to moving past the pain. Anger never brings love back; it only erodes past memories and sets up future negative interactions. Getting stuck at this stage is detrimental.

The stage of Bargaining is different during divorce than with the death of a partner. Letting go of a marriage can involve actual efforts to change a partner's decision, negotiating new interactional patterns, a reassessment of the marriage, and changes in personal identity. Depression is the prolonged and deep experience of the pain that loss brings. Left unattended it can lead to additional problems and issues. Each stage leads toward a resolution of the hurt and anger felt during divorce. The stage of acceptance brings the most hope and comfort. All the feelings, actions, and changes brought on by divorce will eventually led to acceptance. The individuals involved have a direct effect on the ways each step is handled. Take stock of your process as it unfolds. Be aware of getting stuck. Some divorces last longer than the marriage. Grief or divorce support groups help with the process.

Depression develops when sadness, grief, or even anger is not addressed and managed. Painful feelings that settle in and don't evolve or resolve may lead to clinical depression. Be aware of the symptoms of depression and take steps to get help. Symptoms include ongoing sadness, feelings of helplessness, fatigue, excessive crying, sleepiness or insomnia, lack of interest in everyday activities, difficulty concentrating, and negative thoughts. As depression continues, suicidal thoughts and even attempts may occur. There are several types of depressive clinical conditions. There is often a genetic or biological component.

Depression should be treated by a mental health professional. Start with your general practitioner or find a licensed psychotherapist. Many companies offer mental health referrals.

Depression can be treated by medication and therapy, but a combination is usually most effective.

In dealing with depression, many of the techniques used in dealing with sadness, anger, and grief are valuable tools to reduce the intensity of emotions. Physical health should also be addressed including healthy eating, exercise, regular sleep, and avoiding alcohol. Alcohol is a depressant and should not be used in connection with medication. Adding new activities and connections can help alleviate depression as the symptoms are associated with the loss, rejection, and uncertainty divorce creates. Contradict negative thoughts with positive statements about situations, future, and self. Write things down to clarify the extent of the negative thoughts. Be realistic but positive. "I am unlovable" can be restated as "I have many loveable qualities." "My kids blame me for the divorce" to "my kids are capable of understanding why I left, it may just take them some time." Wait to start a new romantic relationship until the divorce emotions are resolved.

Anger is an inevitable emotion during divorce. Even when couples mutually agree on separating, tension develops. However, anger can be extremely harmful and destructive. According to Fisher and Alberti (2016) "Divorce anger is extreme. Rage, vindictiveness, and overpowering bitterness are common feeling among people when a love relationship is ending. It is a special kind of anger that most of us have never experienced before" (p. 112).[5]

While an amiable divorce is possible, feeling a sense of anger about the changes and losses is inevitable. Rejection is contradicted by emotionally dismissing and denigrating the other partner. "I hate you, please don't leave me" becomes "you don't want me, I hate you." Dealing with all the configurations of anger takes effort. Some may think that divorce gives one permission to be vindictive in their pursuit of a settlement. After all, many "good divorce attorneys" are chosen based on their ability to be ruthless. Ongoing interparental conflict is known to be connected to significant problems for the couple and their children.

Anger, more than any other emotion, needs to be managed. Doing so is difficult, as anger is such a basic and often raw emotion. Often as children, we are taught to hide our rage rather than find ways to express it appropriately. Anger serves many functions in a divorce process. It may be controlling, a means of denying pain, a way to intimidate, a tactical position, and a means of strength. Anger helps us gain strength and let go. As with any emotion, dealing with our anger starts with acknowledging the feeling and its possible sources. Exploding or burying the emotions is not helpful. Repressing anger takes a toll on emotional and physical health. Expressing unpleasant feelings can be done in healthy ways.

Suggestions on handling anger include:

- Identify the feeling and consider what is behind it. Don't rage when the actual feeling is one of pain. Cry instead.
- Sometimes ignoring behavior is the best way to extinguish it. Ignore your ex-spouse's petty behaviors or hostility.
- Try writing your feelings down. Expression does not need to be verbal.
- Draw your anger into a representative picture.
- Evaluate your feelings. Is the anger really worth your time and energy?

- Talk to a friend. It's okay to be little snarky but don't go on and on. It will make your friends uncomfortable.
- Take a walk or drive and focus on the activity. Enjoy the view.
- Learn and practice relaxation exercises.
- Count to 10, several times if needed.
- Create an anger range. Label it as to degree from mild irritation to total rage. In reality, total rage is not a rational or appropriate response to something your ex is doing. Aim for a middle ground or less in your level and response.
- Write a letter, you don't need to send it. Read it three days later and take out any unnecessary rage. Send only if you think it will help.
- Let your lawyer handle it.
- See a therapist.
- Decide on a way to express your feeling that lets it out but does not intensify your pain or frustration. Make an action plan for dealing with your anger at your ex-spouse.
- Solve the problems or issues causing you to be angry. Isn't that why you're getting a divorce?
- Let it go by choice, not fear or lack of self-worth.
- Share your feeling simply and directly.
- Use your anger to speak up and set boundaries. Don't accept mistreatment or an unfair settlement.
- Avoid name calling. It is childish and results in names being hurled back.
- Scream alone in your car. Do not engage in road rage!

- Go ahead and do something petty but not over the top. Throw away his favorite golf shirt—don't scratch his car.
- Consider anger management classes
- Anger don'ts: don't strike out physically, destroy property, attack verbally, call names, curse, involve the kids, or seek revenge.

When the divorce provides a break in the ongoing conflict, a sense of relief occurs. Tensions may abate and a degree of calm develops knowing that a decision has been made. The family will stabilize, the conflict is over, the pain subsided. While there are many emotions that arise with this changing life situation, hope is possible. Relief and even happiness may not occur immediately, but many find that the resolution or ending of an unhappy marriage improves their emotional and physical well-being. Learn to let go of past hurt and forgive your ex-spouse. Holding grudges keeps you tied up in an unhappy past. Be careful not to forget that the children may still view the changes as a loss. Respect their need to grieve and adjust.

It's okay to celebrate new beginnings. Embrace the new possibilities by making changes, even minor ones, to signify moving on and developing a new normal. Rearrange your living room. Eat dinner at a different time. Start a pizza and movie Friday. Buy new sheets and comforter. Join a club or support group. Get a new job. Volunteer during your free time. Write that novel. During the later stages of divorce, the pieces can begin to fall into place. Feelings that were once overwhelming subside, often replaced with hope and an openness to new experiences. Life goes on and the family continues with a new kind of balance and stability. In *To Take Away the Hurt* (2001), the authors write:

> Whatever degree of failure in her marriage she had felt earlier had faded away and was being replaced by a strength coming from where emptiness once had been. Freedom had replaced the feelings of unfairness she had once harbored. She began to see that change was what she had feared most, and yet when the pieces of change were put together, they became growth. (p. 59)[6]

Custody Arrangements and Parenting Plans

Divorce is a legal agreement that divides assets and establishes custody of minor children. State statutes differ but the basics are similar. Divorce agreements can be established by mediation or by court decrees. Drawn-out custody battles are the most harmful for everyone. Many of the issues between the couple are better addressed by therapists and not attorneys. Aggressive attorneys often escalate the conflict. Many states have collaborative law attorneys that are dedicated to helping couple divorce in a respectful manner. Select your attorney carefully. Never select an attorney that offers to destroy your spouse financially.

Legal battles do not help heal the pain and conflict inherent is a divorce. Mediation is always the gentlest form of divorce adjudication. The couple, sometimes without attorneys, meet with a mediator to work out a settlement of the issues. An agreement is then sent to the court to be signed and filed. Mediators are not always attorneys; they may be therapists or a combination of professionals. Sometimes mediation or, in some states, collaborative law teams include a financial advisor, a parenting coordinator, a therapist, and an attorney. Opt for mediation and be open to compromise.

Unfortunately, some divorces escalate into long-term conflicts. In these cases, a custody evaluation may be requested. Teens will find these evaluations uncomfortable. Encourage them to be open with their feelings and that their statements will be confidential. Do not coach them on what to say, tempting as it may be. Even when your spouse is being unreasonable, try and maintain your dignity. Dragging your children into these conflicts creates emotional problems that your teen will live with for years.

Custodial arrangements in families with teenagers need to be more flexible than with younger children. Standard visitation may be agreed upon in the divorce settlement but parents often work with each other to accommodate their teen's active lives. Set up a parenting plan. Parenting plans are agreements that clarify the teens' residence, their right to spend time with the other parent, who makes major decisions, and financial allocations. Often parenting coordinators are available to help develop workable parenting plans. A good parenting plan will also address issues such as vacations and holidays, visitations with extended family, general behavioral rules, and consequences. Plans should include periodic re-evaluations to meet the changing needs of adolescents. Consider these points when making a parenting plan:

- Remember this is about your being a parent, not a bitter ex-spouse. Manage your emotions and behavior.
- Teenagers have an opinion and will appreciate having some input. Remind them they are not the final decision makers (it is not fair to put that responsibility on them).
- Consider the teenager's school, activity, and social schedules. Teens often have sports, afterschool jobs, and

social gatherings. Parents need to be available for transportation as needed.

- Driving can impact teen schedules and parental visitation. Allow teens to have more flexibility when they can drive.
- Custody should allow a balance of time with both parents. Get creative with division of time and places to spend time together.
- When non-residential parents live too far away to allow regular visitation, build in methods of interaction and regular visitation such as long weekends or holiday visits. Plan on making trips to their hometown to spend time with them.
- Teens should not have to choose who gets to attend their extracurricular events. Sit apart if necessary.
- Communication is extremely important. Both parents (unless contraindicated) should be kept in the loop about major events and pertinent information (medical, educational, legal). Finds ways to share information without sending messages through the teen. Email, text, or private conversations. If needed, some websites or APPS allow for information exchange. Specify which types of formats are best for which types of information. Don't text something best shared in person. Don't call or text constantly with little complaints "Your son won't clean his room." "Your daughter made a C on her algebra test."
- Teens need ongoing communication with both parents. Make sure they have a phone. Split the cost. Do not interfere or restrict phone use with the other parent.
- Schedules should be in writing and balanced. Make a calendar and allow the teen full access. Teens feel more

secure when they know their schedule and can plan for visitation times. Input changes immediately. Last minutes changes or interference with visitation hurts your teen more than your ex-spouse.

- Ask teens to share changes in their schedules so that adjustments can be made.
- Do not interfere with the other parent's relationship with the teen.
- Make a basic set of rules for the teen that stands in either home. Agree to follow through on consequences as appropriate. Do not keep a teen from visiting or talking to the other parent as a punishment. Even if a teen is grounded, parents should keep the visitation agreement.
- If cooperative parenting is problematic, consider parallel parenting. Parallel parenting allows for each home to establish their own rules but show respect for the other household. "Dad lets you keep your phone at night, but at our house we put them on the kitchen counter at 10pm." Strive for basic rules in both homes including rules about drinking, regular school attendance, and reasonable curfews.
- Transitions between homes should be as stress free as possible. This is not the time to argue with your ex. Make the transfer as simple and as consistent as possible.
- If conflicts arise, set up a separate time for negotiation. Enlist a third party if necessary.
- Pay child support on time and consider direct deposit. Don't involve the teens in the financial issues.

- If teens are struggling emotionally, arrange for a therapist and participate as requested by the therapist. Specify that both parents will cooperate with the treatment plan.

Parenting plans do not cover all issues in families with teenagers. If conflicts seem unworkable, seek assistance and amend the plan. Remember that this is for the best interest of your children, not a way to hurt your ex.

Special Situations in Divorced Families

Ongoing interparental conflict, parentification and alienation may stem from the stress of divorce. These situations create short-term issues for teens that may lead to long-term repercussions. Conflict between the parents may have started long before the divorce was initiated and continues unchecked even after the final papers are signed. For some couples, divorce creates anger that becomes the new form of interaction between the couple. The nastier the divorce, the longer and more bitter the divorce.

Parentified teens are usually a response to the changes in the family's needs. When a parent is overwhelmed by the break-up, they may be unable to manage their household responsibilities or need emotional support. Teens may assume many of the roles previously the domain of the adults in the family. Parental alienation is a form of revenge that asks the teen to side with one parent to disrespect and reject the other parent. Alienation disrupts and even destroys a teen's relationship with a parent. Parents must be aware of the potential harm that these situations create for their teens. There are steps that parents can take to recognize and manage these family life and interactional developments.

Interparental conflict ranges in type, amount, and intensity. Too often arguments continue and even intensify even after the couple separate. For some, the breakup creates issues that only serve to maintain the negative feelings. For some, the rage creates a connection to the relationship that no longer exists. Hate can be as strong a bond as love. As ex-spouses seek reasons to be bitter, adolescents often find themselves in the center of that conflict. Continuing hostility is detrimental to adolescent adjustment. Even when they become adults, the bitterness between their parents pervades many of their adult life celebrations and experiences.

Hostile interactions often turn you into a person you do not like or respect. Ask yourself if you would behave that way with anyone else. Parents need to take steps to manage their conflict and consider the needs of their teenagers. If you care about yourself and your children, find a way to stop the fighting. According to Fruzzetti (2006) in *The High Conflict Couple:*

> If defeating your partner is also self-defeating, then stopping the fight is both showing the courage to do what is needed to survive and the courage to engage in self-preservation ... Notice how proud you can be about your self-control. (p. 32)[7]

Suggestions for managing interparental conflict include:

- First and foremost, be cognizant of the fact that you are engaged in an ongoing battle with your ex when you should be interacting as co-parents. Not being able to separate these issues will result in many of your post-divorce conflicts being centered (unfairly) around your teens.

- Try thinking about your interactions in the last month and note how many were anger based. Ask your ex to do the same. (Don't get in an argument about your choice of issues!)
- Take an inventory of the problematic issues. Assess if the issue is valid, which are expressions of old conflicts, and which are born out of pain and bitterness.
- Work toward limiting the interparental hostilities.
- Pay special attention to those issues that relate to your children. These deserve your attention and resolution.
- Issues that are remnants of past conflicts need to be let go. Divorce should signify the end of these old issues.
- Select a few significant problems and make some suggestions as to what changes might help.
- Arrange a meeting (with a mediator or therapist if needed), to address issues. (Keep this meeting teen free).
- Work very hard to keep emotions in check. Feelings often escalate issues. Get a handle on your emotions before interacting with your ex. Act as if a neighbor is watching. Too often your children are unwilling spectators.
- Don't get pulled into a conflict, walk away.
- Do not scream, insult, or become physical.
- Set boundaries where needed. "I think we need to talk about this at another time."
- Specify the issues in behavioral or objective manner. "There seems to be difficulty with having a consistent time for picking up the kids on Friday evenings."

- Use "I" statements and avoid "you" complaints. "I need the kids picked up on time as I have plans with friends on those nights."
- Keep focus on the present not the past.
- Ask nicely for their view on the problem and any ideas they have for resolution or compromise.
- Always remember that the goal is a blending of needs and not a victory.
- When it seems impossible to interact civilly, find alternative ways to exchange kids or work on issues. Meet in a nearby shopping center and have both parents stay in the car.
- Try appreciation or kindness with your ex. It can be disarming. "Thank you for being such a concerned dad, I am also worried about the kids attending after game parties." You don't have to like someone to be a person who treats others with respect.
- Find ways to validate your ex-partners concerns. This does not mean you agree, only that you are acknowledging their opinions.
- Teens may complain about a parent's decision. Don't jump on the bandwagon and disrespect your ex-spouse. However, there are times when a parent needs to take a teen's concerns seriously. Listen openly if your teen is afraid or if they are unsure how to handle a situation.
- Don't let yourself be drawn into arguments, if needed, calmly walk away.
- Practice different ways to end a conversation before it gets too escalated.

- Establish a communication system and use it. Do not use the teens as messengers.
- As interactions become more comfortable and civil, many of the old issues will drop away.

Parentification is a redistribution of family roles in which the adolescent assumes the household tasks or responsibility for the parent's emotional well-being. While teens may be capable, they should not be asked to assume most of the household chores. Meet with teens to assess the tasks that need to be accomplished and allot carefully. Chores should be age appropriate. Parents should always carry more of the load. Rebalance monthly as needed. Make tasks joint efforts as working together helps teens feel needed and responsible but not overwhelmed. Care for younger siblings may be necessary at times but always back up teens' efforts with support and gratitude.

Emotional parentification is never in the teen's best interest. If your teen is spending Friday nights with you instead of friends, reassess your expectations and the emotions you are putting out. Teens should never become a parent's confidant or companion. It will create long-term psychological issues for your teen. Also, you are not your teen's friend, nor should you be partying with teenagers. Find you own friends! Find ways to spend time alone. It can be refreshing and healing.

Parental Alienation is a concerted effort to turn a child against the other parent or, at the very least, to diminish that parent in their teen's eyes. Far too often, ex- spouses need others, including their children, to feel as angry and vindictive toward the ex-spouse as they do. Despite their level of awareness and independence, teens are vulnerable to alienation. The level of alienation that can develop between divorced parents is frightening in its intensity. Often in its extreme cases, the alienating parent is so bitter that they do not fully realize how destructive their actions are. Alienation may require the help of a therapist and an attorney. Many alienated families are referred by the courts for interventional services.

Owen and Nina were high school sweethearts and married shortly after graduating. Nina came from a very religious family. The couple quickly started a family. By age 25, the couple had three small children. Nina's days were spent caring for her children and volunteering at her church. Owen worked long hours as a mechanic. The couple fought often and Owen started staying away from home, drinking at a local bar with his friends. By the time the children were teenagers, Owen was an alcoholic and the conflicts between the couple had become daily occurrences. Owen finally acknowledged his unhappiness and the role alcohol was playing in his life. He moved out of the family home and shortly thereafter entered a 30-day treatment program. Owen was committed to staying sober. He also decided that he wanted a divorce and requested joint custody.

Nina had not been supportive of Owen's treatment program, insisting that he should overcome his problems through prayer and service to the church. She refused to allow the children to see him while he was in treatment. During his absence Nina repeatedly told the kids that he had abandoned them and broken his wedding vows. As the divorce progressed, Nina became more bitter and actively denigrated him to the children. She insisted he was a sinner in the eyes of God and an unfit parent.

All attempts by Owen to visit their teenagers was sabotaged by Nina. She had her oldest hide liquor bottles in his back seat and then insist to the courts that he was drinking and driving the kids while intoxicated. Nina found a church-based counselor to work with the kids. Unfortunately, the counselor only consulted with Nina and subsequently reinforced the teen's anger and disrespect for their father. The divorce evolved into a bitter custody battle. Owen eventually received joint custody but Nina continued to badmouth him. The teens reluctantly saw their father as ordered by the court. They often acted as messengers for their mother's bitterness.

Don't think you are alienating your children? Any form of badmouthing, criticizing, or sharing negative information can be a form of alienation. Even if you don't see yourself as an active alienator, following the suggestions below can help your teens stay connected to both parents. This is not to say that there are not some parents who are unfit, however protecting your teens is not the same as alienating them. Parents often hide behind the mistaken belief that their teens are making their own choices and that they are only sharing the "truth about their father/mother." It helps to consider the possibility that lousy spouses can be good parents. Separate the two roles in your portrayal of your ex-partner.

Recommendations for alienating parents:

- If the mere thought of your ex makes you angry, you may be portraying them in a negative manner to your children. Rethink your recent conversations with your teens.

- Never create false accusations against your ex-spouse. Your teen will suffer more than anyone else.
- Be realistic about your reasons for sharing any negative information about your ex-spouse.
- Consider the emotional consequences on your teen of your negative comments.
- Watch for your teen's reactions to your disparaging remarks. They may not say anything but they will get quiet, look uncomfortable, or join in your anger.
- If your teens are expressing anger, disrespect, or hatred toward your ex, ask yourself what role are you playing in this?
- Refusing to talk or visit with a parent is a red flag that something is wrong. It may be that teens are feeling alienated from a parent. Find out more about their reasons and be open to your role in this situation.
- Teens often complain about a parent's decision. Don't jump on the bandwagon and disrespect your ex-spouse.
- Question teens' reasons for their anger at their parent. There are times when a parent needs to take a teen's concerns seriously. Listen openly if your teen is afraid or sad. If they are unsure how to handle a situation, offer support.
- Do not interfere is your teen's phone calls or visitation.
- Keep transitions between homes civil. This is not the time to argue. If adults can't be civil, don't interact. Drop and go.
- Even when frustrated with your ex keep the issues between the two of you. Don't share information in a

way that will make teens uncomfortable or disrespect their other parent. "We can't buy new shoes, your dad is late with the child support again!"

- When teens ask for information, answer questions honestly and fairly but without disrespect. "Yes, sometimes your father drinks too much but we hope in time he will get some help with it. Please feel free to call me if you feel concerned or afraid."
- Love your children more than you hate your ex-partner. Consider your emotions when talking to your teens about their other parent.

Suggestions for alienated parents:

- If you think your teens are being alienated from you, review information carefully: What part is your ex playing, how are your actions contributing to the situation, what issues does your teen have with you?
- Avoid badmouthing the alienating parent. It often leads to the teen taking sides or defending their parent.
- Do not stop calling, attending events, or visiting your teen even during stressful times.
- Seek outside help such as a therapist or by legal means.
- When dealing with false or negative information being offered by an alienating parent, talk with your teens calmly and give them alternative facts that counter some of the negative information.
- Encourage your children to look at the information objectively. "I know your mom is really angry with me but I have always been there for you and our

relationship is important to me." "I know your mom told you that I had an affair before our separation but that is not true."

- Reminisce with teens about your relationship history. Tell stories about the good times you had together. Remind them that you will always be there for them.
- Develop your thick skin. Don't let your ex get to you. Rise above.
- Don't retaliate. Your goal is to take care of your kids, not get revenge on your ex-spouse.
- Keep records of alienation behaviors. Report facts, do not editorialize.
- Do not abandon your teens in order to avoid your ex. Fight for them, not over them.
- Try not to get angry at your teens, they are the victims as are you.
- Don't be manipulated into buying your teen's love.

Helping Adolescents Cope

Adolescents will struggle with the divorce of their parents. It is not simply a matter of one parent moving out. The changes often feel monumental and frightening to an adolescent that is already experiencing a lot of personal changes. Home is suddenly no longer a safe haven. In a young adult novel by Dressen (2011), she poignantly writes:

> In the real world, you couldn't really just split a family down the middle, mom on one side, dad the other, with the child divided equally between. It was like when you ripped a piece of paper in two: no matter how hard you

> tried, the seams never fit exactly right again. It was what you couldn't see, those tiniest of pieces, that were lost in the severing, and their absence kept everything from being complete. (P. 165)[8]

It is the parents' responsibility to help their teens understand and adjust to the many changes. In order to cope, teenagers need some basic things from their parents:

- First and foremost, they need love and attention. Divorce can zap a parent's energy and teens may be unknowingly neglected.
- Access to and right to love both parents and extended family.
- Allow them personal space in both homes and respect their need for privacy.
- Supervision of their activities by both parents. Know their activities and their friends.
- Clearly established rules and appropriate consequences. Basic rules should be agreed upon and be upheld by both parents.
- Opportunity to express and validation for their feelings
- Allowed to have both parents at their extracurricular events and celebrations.
- Parents should not expose teens to their conflicts. In particular, avoid arguments during periods of transition.
- Grieve the loss of their family.
- Opportunity to continue their developmental journey.
- Teens need a way to still believe in love.

Teens and Communication

Talking with your teenagers about divorce takes forethought and respect for their experience. Teens need information as soon as the possibility of divorce is a viable option for the couple. Do not tell them on a Friday and then have a parent move out on Saturday. Abruptly leaving the family home by a parent can be very traumatizing for an adolescent.

Before meeting with your teens, discuss what you will be telling your children about the separation. If you can remain civil, talk to your teens together. Present a cooperative parental front. If not, at least agree to what you will say and meet with them individually. Both parents still need to talk separately with their teens about the upcoming changes. Make your conversation information based, brief, and without blame. Adolescents will want to know how this will affect them. Who is leaving the family home, where will they live, how will they get to see their other parent? Ask your teen if they have any questions. Answer them as clearly as possible without pulling them into the issues between you and your ex-spouse. Help them with ways to tell their friends about the separation.

Make sure that you stress that the problems are within the marital relationship and not their fault. Tell them the marriage is ending, not the family. If they have been witnesses to the conflicts, explain that the fighting is part of the couple's problems but not a good form of conflict resolution. Let them know that they do not need to take sides or mediate conflicts. Do not blame or badmouth the other parent as this brings them into your issues. They are your children, not weapons in your divorce war.

Expect a variety of reactions. Anger, denial, tears, storming to their room. Don't set limits on their reactions. Give them time to absorb the information. Reassure them that you will be checking in with them regularly. Do not assume they are fine even if they tell you they are. Find opportunities to talk with your teens about the family disruption. Sharing some of your emotional reactions (don't overwhelm them) will help them feel safe with sharing their own.

Talking with your teenager is tricky. They will often downplay their feelings and try to avoid talking about the divorce. It is important to check in with your teen regularly, not just in the beginning. Find appropriate times and ways to communicate. A suggestion by Dr. Emory (2016) in *Two Homes, One Childhood:*

> If you really want to talk to your teenager, try taking her on a long drive. Why? You don't need to make eye contact. There are plenty of little distractions but no big ones—just make sure that you leave both of your cell phones at home. And as long as you are moving, she cannot run away. (p. 235)

Another important component of communication is finding opportunities to talk. Conversations do not need to be about the divorce or even anything serious, just talk, share, and listen. Interpersonal communication exists at three levels. The first level is the basic communication that is required to live together; what time do you need to be picked up? Have you finished your homework? Set the table for dinner.

The second level is social interaction, which involve discussing experiences, ideas, and opinions. Sharing your day, talking about school or work, asking about activities. Dinner conversations or talking on the way to school are chances for type of relaxed communication. This level does not ask anything of the other person except interpersonal sharing.

The third is communication that occurs on a deeper level. It is about personal opinions, experiences, and emotions. Discussions with teens (or anyone) is easier and more comfortable when the second level has provided a connection and flow of conversation. Have friendly conversations with your teen and they will be more likely to talk with you about their feelings and struggles. If the majority of your communication with your teen are directives (level one), they are less likely to share their feelings with you.

Find opportunities to talk and check in. Sometimes sharing some of your struggles will encourage them to talk about their emotions. Validate their feelings even if you don't understand them. Ask questions that are open ended, not yes or no questions. How have you been handling the changes between your dad and I, not are you doing okay? When they do talk, allow them time to fashion their thoughts. Don't jump in too soon or finish their sentence.

If your teen is struggling to find the right words, offer a few words to prompt their thoughts. Help teens understand what is happening and what they may be feeling. Listen with your whole self. Do not check your phone, it indicates disinterest. Make eye contact, use body language to engage, show facial expressions. If your teen seems uncomfortable with sharing her feelings, try relaxing your stance and eye contact. Offer simple touch, perhaps a hug. Boys may be more uncomfortable with physical affection but it can be given in small ways. Touch their shoulder or pat a knee. Some appreciate a hug. Make suggestions to help them cope. Get them therapy if they are struggling and especially if they ask for it.

A message to teens: communicating with parents about what you are feeling or questions you may have is not always easy. Parents may seem preoccupied with all the changes they are trying to manage. Other parents are shut down or angry and approaching them feels uncomfortable. When a parent is distraught, you may not want to add to their distress. However, most parents want to be there for their children and will respond with concern if you make the effort to talk with them. If you having been telling them you are okay, they may not realize how hard all of the changes are on you. Take a chance and ask to talk about the divorce. Ask questions, share feelings, have opinions. Sometimes it won't make a big difference but silence doesn't help either. If it is easier, send a text or write a letter. This can start a conversation. If parents do not respond to your need to talk, find an adult that will. This may be a school counselor, a friend's parent, or relative. Ask directly to see a therapist. Many schools or churches have groups for teens with divorced parents. There are online support groups or websites that help.

Managing Their Feelings

Emotions that arise during the process of parental divorce that may be confusing and overwhelming for adolescents. Many teens may find themselves experiencing feelings that are new and frightening in their intensity. Teens often do not have enough life experience to help them to know how to deal with these feelings or that they will lessen over time. The most common feelings are denial, confusion, fear, sadness, and anger. Some find a sense of relief when the family conflict is decreased. Teens may develop a sense of self-worth and accomplishment when they successfully manage the family changes.

Denial is often the first reaction for teens. Even when they witnessed parental conflicts and observed their parents making efforts to work it out, disbelief may follow the announcement. Parents should not expect that one conversation will be sufficient. Teens often need time to process the reality of a parental divorce.

It is also unsettling when parents threaten divorce repeatedly without taking any actions. A parent moving out often forces a teen to accept the reality. Parents should help teens process the information by proceeding slowly, being direct about the upcoming changes, and engaging in several conversations that allow teens to react and ask questions. It is okay to admit that you don't have all the answers yet but will keep them informed. Some teens handle the news better if parents have previously shared that they are having problems and are working on options. Teens who were witnesses to marital arguments and unhappiness may find it easier to understand the decision to separate. When conflict was quieter or more hidden, teens may be surprised and confused. Help teens deal with the changes by clarifying how this separation will affect them. When denial is replaced by awareness, many additional feelings develop.

Fear is a natural reaction to being faced with the unknown. Fear may be expressed in a number of ways: irritability, withdrawal, or acting out behaviors. Parents should address this feeling directly as teens may not recognize the source of their fears or are afraid to say them out loud. Will I still get to see my dad/mom? Will we have to move? What will my friends think of me? Explain that fear is a common reaction and even adults have them in this kind of a situation. Reassure them that many of these concerns will work out in time. Ask teens to help develop solutions or ways to be reassured concerning their fears. Perhaps a weekly update about the family changes will help. Ask teens to participate in some of the decision making, such as visitation, ways to keep in touch, or household rules. As fears create anxiety, teens need to learn how to manage this feeling. Eat, exercise and sleep regularly, learn relaxation or meditation, talk about these feelings with a friend, parent, or adult.

Anger is a common emotion that surfaces during adolescence. Negative reactions to a parent's decision to divorce include anger at parent's inability to make their marriage work, frustration over the family changes, and fears about their future's stability. Teens often cover their fears and sadness with anger. Expression of these feelings can range from general irritability to out of control rages. When teens are afraid to express their anger, they may withdraw, become tearful, or even self-harm. Parents need to watch for signs of anger and help their teens manage these intense and scary feelings.

Suggestions for helping teens manage their anger-based emotions and behaviors include:

- Recognize subtle signs of anger. Withdrawal, sarcasm, refusing to comply with requests.
- Pay attention to your modeling of anger. Parental conflict styles teach anger expression.
- Talk about anger in general to help educate teens about ways that anger is felt or expressed.
- Gently point out some of the behaviors you see that indicate that your teen may be feeling angry about the divorce. Ask teens directly to talk about their anger.

- Discuss different levels of anger. Help them label their level of anger 1 (mild) to 5 (extreme). Help them realize that very little in life is really a level 5. Label each level with possible situations. Match their reactions to their level. When they are upset, ask them to give it a level. What will help it become less stressful?
- Let them know it's okay to be angry but not to hurt others, property, or themselves.
- Allow them to be angry (respectfully) at you. After all, you just rearranged their whole world.
- Help them find appropriate ways to manage their negative emotions. Tell someone why they are angry, hit a pillow, write it down, draw their emotions symbolically, listen to music, take a long walk. Take a walk with them.
- Yell, if it helps, but do not scream at other people.
- Teach them how to be assertive not aggressive.
- Problem-solving and negotiation skills are taught not instinctive.
- Let them win some of the normal parent-teen battles. It helps them develop a sense of control. "Okay, color your hair green."
- If they need to blow off a little steam, give them space to do so.
- Let some things slide. They didn't clean their room as requested, let it go. Pick your battles.
- If a conflict arises, help them find a way to back away from their anger. Don't get into ultimatums.
- Use humor and teach them to do the same.
- Some sibling skirmishes help teach anger management. Let them work it out.

- Never allow one child to bully another.
- Agree to rules about anger. Remind them the rules are for safety and to help them calm down. It is not of issue of parental control.
- If your teen cannot handle their anger, get them professional help.

Thomas was 14 when his parents informed him that they were getting a divorce. Their marriage had been fraught with conflict and they decided to separate after his older sister left for college out of state. When informed, Thomas yelled "why can't you just get along!" and stormed into his room. Dad moved out the following week. For financial reasons, they opted to sell the family home and mom moved to a smaller apartment which required a school change for Thomas. Dad moved closer to his work (a 45-minute drive from the mother's apartment). Dad initially came every weekend to bring Thomas to his apartment for the weekend. Both parents checked in with him during the first few months but he assured them "it was no big deal."

Over the next couple of months, Thomas' grades started to fall, he was irritable and disrespectful to his mother, and started spending more time on video games. Mom also noticed that Thomas was hanging out with new friends but was glad he was meeting kids at his new school. Six months after the separation, Thomas's anger outbursts intensified. His rudeness turned into screaming rages directed at his mother. Several times he stormed into his room and punched a hole in the wall. His parents consulted the school counselor who recommended a therapist for the family. Within a year, Thomas grades were better, he resumed regular visitation with his dad, (who moved closer to his mom's apartment), and he was managing his anger.

He was able to talk about his anger and hurt over his parent's divorce, his history of living in their conflicted marriage, and his sense of being abandoned by his sister who dealt with the divorce by staying at college except for holidays.

Teens who are overwhelmed by their parent's divorce may express their feelings through various acting out behaviors. Becoming argumentative, refusing to follow rules, anger outbursts, skipping school, minor mischief, and using alcohol and drugs are some of these behaviors. New, but questionable peer associations may be indicative of teen's struggle to deal with the family disruption. Parents should pay special attention to negative teen behavior that occurs shortly after the parental separation.

Parents need to take several steps to deal with their teen's acting out responses. First, notice when your teens' attitudes, reactions, and behaviors are becoming more negative in nature. Have a direct conversation about the changes you are noticing and express your concern. Set up some rules that are aimed at providing structure and supervision. Set a curfew and check in with them after they are out at night. Don't be afraid to ask questions about activities and check for possible intoxication. If signs of drug use are evident, investigate further and if necessary, get a drug screen. If you suspect they may be sneaking out at night, check in on them in the middle of the night. Help them get involved in activities that will provide healthy outlets. Give extra attention and love.

Sadness is part of the grief process and a normal reaction to the losses sustained in a divorce. Daily family interactions are altered by parental separation and parents may have less time or energy to spend with their teens. The non-residential parent (often the father) may become disengaged (degree varies) due to relocation, limited visitation opportunities, or in order to deal with their own pain. For those teens who move or change schools, the loss is even more profound. Unhappiness may be seen through tearfulness, irritability, spending time alone, or being withdrawn

Helping a teen address their sadness is critical to their moving past the divorce. Many of the techniques utilized in dealing with anger also apply to sadness. Outlets are needed which express the emotional responses to loss. Talk to someone, find a way to express the feelings including writing, drawing, listen to music, cry (briefly). It is also beneficial to help the teen realize that although divorce brings loss, there are many elements of their life that stay the same. Make a list of the aspects of their life that are not changing. They still have two caring parents and their school, friends and home will stay the same. Their tastes in food, music, and tv shows are rarely disrupted. For those elements that will change, develop some options for managing them.

When an adolescent is struggling to manage their sadness along with all the other stresses inherent in the teenage years, depression may develop. Signs of depression include persistent sadness, inability to keep up with everyday activities, trouble sleeping, irritability, and suicidal ideation. Teens may cope with these feelings by withdrawing into themselves, becoming irritable, or using alcohol or drugs. If you notice these changes in your teen, talk openly about what they are experiencing. Get them help as needed. They may resist, but most teens respond well to the therapy process. Make sure both parents are aware of the situation and participate in their teen's treatment. This is no time for petty arguments. Depression is a frightening experience for teens and requires parental intervention.

For many teenagers, the changes of divorce bring about relief from the parental conflict and the development of various positive characteristics. Remind them that change will bring new experiences and help develop inner strength. Skills that can come from divorce are resilience, empathy, responsibility, courage, and ability to adapt to changes. Parents can help develop these strengths:

- Help teens express their emotions appropriately. Show support, not judgement.
- Teach problem solving and negotiation skills.
- Be a role model in and outside of the home.
- Keep your promises. It teaches integrity and commitment.
- Stay active in the teen's life. Show up for visitation and extracurricular events.
- Give them additional responsibilities and privileges that are age appropriate.
- Offer encouragement, praise, and rewards for their efforts in school and at home.
- Know and be accepting of their friends. Help teens deal with peer pressure.
- Encourage their social and fun activities. Let them be teenagers.
- Explain that even though their parents' marriage didn't last, love and commitment are possible and worth pursuing in life.

Helping Stepfamilies Succeed

Following divorce, families often take several years to stabilize. This process is complicated by the addition of new family members to the family system. Parents may date, cohabitate, or remarry, often within a few years of the divorce. Stepfamilies come into existence when parents marry or even just live together. Individual family members suddenly find themselves sharing their lives homes with relative strangers. This process will only succeed if parents take care with how this process unfolds and respects all the different needs of the involved individuals.

Parental Dating

Adults may think that what they need to move on is to find a new romantic partner. However, adolescents need time to adjust to the new family system that develops after parental divorce. Teens find parental dating an awkward development. Parents also find that introducing a new person to their teenagers is rarely met with unconditional acceptance.

Before entering the dating world consider what you are looking for. Are you needing companionship for social reasons, looking to heal a broken heart, want someone to help pay the bills? Others date as a form of revenge against their ex, to fill the lonely nights, or as a chance to correct the mistakes that led to the failure of the marriage. The answer to that question will help you decide if you are really in the right place to begin dating. Beware of well-meaning friends pushing you to "put yourself out there" or setting you up with one of their single cousins. Also consider whether or not your teens are ready to handle your dating. Resistance from your teens will make dating complicated. Spending a bit more time stabilizing your newly formed single parent family can go a long way in having a future romantic partnership succeed.

Dating with a teen at home is tricky and requires some forethought about how to combine these two aspects of your life. Take it slow. Dating too soon will only complicate a family's stabilization. Residential parents may find it more difficult to date under the wire. Teens will quickly notice if your actions indicate you are starting to date. Consider having initial dates when your teens are at the other parent's home.

Tell teens upfront that you are considering dating and some of the reasons why. A simple explanation is that you would enjoy some adult social interaction. Teens may say they are accepting of your decision but watch for actions that indicate otherwise. If they seem ambivalent, have several conversations over time to help them process what this will mean for you and for them. Don't ask them to become too involved, they may feel uncomfortable helping you set up your online profile or choosing an outfit for your first date. Additionally, remember teens need you to remain a parent to them. Teens may be independent but they still want and need your attention. Teens can find a parent's dating to be competition for their attention. Also, there is no need to introduce every date, even if you do need to meet all their new friends.

When starting to date consider setting up some rules for yourself. Always date with safety in mind. Meet for the first time at a public area and drive your own car. Be upfront about your divorce status and that you have teenagers (some will run but that's okay). Never have a date stay the night before your relationship is a committed one and your teens have had the opportunity to know them outside of their home.

When a dating situation is progressing into a more committed relationship, share more detailed information about your children with them. Gauge their level of interest in getting to know and interacting with your kids on a regular basis. Discuss expectations for future relationships. Some adults may prefer limited time with your kids which may be problematic going forward. When a potential life partner is interacting with your teenagers, be aware of any of their behavior you don't feel is appropriate. Don't allow an adult to bully, tease, or make sexual comments to your teen. These are red flags that the relationship will have significant issues in the future.

When a relationship becomes serious, you need to introduce them to your children. Set up the initial meeting during a short, relaxed activity. Give your teens a little background information and why you enjoy spending time with this individual. Explain that they don't need to like your friend (yes they know they are more than just a friend) but must behave respectfully. Remind them that they expect you to treat their friends with kindness and acceptance. After the first meeting, ask teens to share their perceptions with you. Don't underestimate your teen's "spidey sense" about your new love interest. Most of the time they will be critical or superficial. "They laugh too loud, they seem boring" "I guess he's okay." Remember this new person will be seen as competition for your attention or a replacement for their other parent. Teens often find it hard to be excited for your new relationship even if they want you to be happy. Give them time.

When a new companion has met your kids, consider introducing them to your ex-spouse, especially when the co-parenting relationship is cordial. If you are the one meeting a new a partner, be friendly. Being jealous is normal but should not be permission to be snarky to the new adult in your ex's life. If your ex marries this person, they will become part of your children's family. Make a good first impression and future interactions will go smoother.

Stepfamilies

Creating a stepfamily is a complex undertaking. Adding a single stepparent with no children of their own is the simplest form. The marriage of both parents, within a few years of each other, all with biological children is obviously the most complicated. Couples get caught up in the romantic aspects of the upcoming nuptials and may fail to adequately prepare for the realities of blending two families. Successful family development takes planning and a lot of reality checks.

Couples deciding to marry (or cohabitate) need to inform their children and allow time for the kids to react, process, and hopefully accept. Some kids enter a stepfamily kicking and screaming. Have discussions with each family member and all the subgroups. Explore some of the possible changes, develop rules and norms for interaction, and create realistic plans for sharing space. All family members need their own private space. Rules for use of personal items and general family items should be discussed. Talk openly and candidly about shifting roles, especially in terms of parenting responsibilities. Ask for and listen openly to teen input. Give stepsiblings time to get to know one another. Assure them that instant connection is not required but respect is.

Couples need to interact with their new stepchildren individually to start making connections. It may be helpful to ask your kids for ideas to help you get to know the new teenager. Just because you have teenagers doesn't mean you know how to engage with other teens who are suddenly having to accept you in their life. Try and think ahead of how this new life will really function.

The wedding may be a small affair or a larger ceremony. Share plans with your children first. Include all the stepkids as equally as possible, no matter what the final living situation will be. If a teen is resistant to being involved, allow them to take on any role they feel comfortable with, even if it is only as a guest. Leave the option open to join in at a different degree as they become more comfortable. Weddings create stepfamilies, not just a marriage.

A stepfamily can be created that works well and meets the needs of all family members. Do not expect too much too soon. As Michael Riera (2012) points out:

> You should not gauge the success of the transition by its immediate results—these transitions are usually somewhat awkward, reserved, tense, and messy, no matter how much you intend otherwise. The results of a successful transition are, however, evident down the road. Time and thought invested on the front end of this transition are well-rewarded over the life of the new family. (p. 191)[9]

Suggestions for a smoother transition into a family are:

- Make space for everyone, including a room, place at the table, and role in the family.
- Accept and nurture individuality.
- Create basic rules for interaction.

- Don't remove pictures, memorabilia, or other objects that have meaning for an individual without asking. For example, don't remove old family photos, add new ones.
- Discourage comparisons between family members or about the child's other parent. "My mom is a better cook than your mom" "your dad's car is a piece of junk"
- Model appropriate behavior including showing affection, active listening, problem solving, using humor not sarcasm, and sharing.
- Develop family traditions that are new but merged with the old ones.
- Respect individuality while creating a family identity.
- Adults should have individual time with their biological children. Also 1:1 time between stepparent and stepchild is helpful for making connections.
- Encourage stepsiblings to spend some time together without parents. Don't push.
- Biological parents need to be responsible for discipline. Stepparents take a supportive adult role. Roles may evolve as family progresses over time.
- Don't demand an authoritarian role just because you are an adult.
- Take time to be a couple. Consider regular date nights or adult vacations.
- Communication is key to family development. Ask for input, encourage opinions, respect feelings. Differences are not a bad thing—it makes your family unique.
- Validate everyone's experience in the family. It may differ from person to person. Everyone has a place.

- Do not denigrate the teenager's other parent or other stepfamily. Kids may need to find a way to be a part of two distinct families. Help teens deal with their loyalty dilemmas.
- Treat the teen's other parent with respect. Do not engage in petty battles. Do not join forces with your new spouse against the other parent. Did you marry for love or to have someone join in your hatred of your ex. If the other parent is being difficult, take the high road. The teens will notice (eventually).
- Be aware that parents will always be closer to their biological children but try not to show preferences in everyday life.
- Being a "step" is easy, earning the role of parent takes more time.
- Acknowledge and try to blend parenting styles in shared homes. Two different sets of rules and parenting styles can create all kinds of problems. Authoritarian parenting is the best for all concerned.
- Stepparents support parents and parents respect the stepparent's concerns.
- Don't expect instant love. Affection comes in time as interactions are enjoyable, nurturing, and validating.
- Expect family holidays to be confusing the first few years. Traditions are ingrained in family systems. Negotiate changes slowly. Expect some ideas to fall through. Some holidays may initially need to be spent apart with celebrations occurring on a different day or time.

Walt, was a widower with two teenage children and Victoria, divorced with three teenagers. They met through their church affiliation. The children all went to the same high school but were not friends. After dating for a little over a year, they married. The teens were all involved as either bridesmaids or grooms. Even though the divorce had been somewhat contentious, Victoria and her ex eventually developed a workable parenting relationship. He was invited to the ceremony which he attended with his girlfriend.

Before the wedding, the couple bought a larger home in the same school district and had it remodeled to allow each teen to have their own bedroom. The couple arranged numerous activities to allow the teens to get to know each other. The couple also held monthly family meeting to coordinate activities, assign household chores, and talk about any problems. The hardest negotiations for the couple were adapting their parenting styles and responsibilities. Victoria's children had a father who was actively involved in their lives with regular weekends at his house. Walt's children were more open to Victoria taking on a mother role as their mother had died several years prior. What they did struggle with was sharing their dad's attention. Weekends when Victoria's kids were at their dad's, Walt had special alone time with his children. There were some initial sibling conflicts which settled out pretty quickly. Overall, the family adjusted well.

The relationship between a teenager and stepparent can be fraught with problems from the very beginning. However, in most families these difficulties are overcome with time and through positive experiences. The hardest times are when teenagers are being hateful and rejecting (yes, it happens). Stepparents can find these teens to be hard to like and accept. While teens need to be held accountable for their actions, it is the adult's primary responsibility to handle negative interactions in a mature manner. When confronted with a teen's disrespect, see if you can find out more about their reasons for their anger. Ask questions, validate feelings, be empathetic. Ask nicely but firmly for respect.

Awkward questions need answers even if they are stated rudely. "Did you marry my dad for his money?" "Why do you hate my mom?" Teens will eventually be won over. Many adults will tell you how they hated their stepparent at first but learned to care about them. Most report that the relationship grew when the stepparent was open to making a connection and showed concern for the teenager.

Biological parents need to be open to the stepparent's issues or concerns but conversations should be between the couple privately. Parents can help by encouraging the teen to give the stepparent a chance or explaining their spouse's motivations. Parents should also protect their teens from words or actions that are hurtful. Again, have discussions privately. If any type of mistreatment is taking place, step in immediately. Never let a stepparent verbally or physically abuse your children. Remember the case study of the mom's boyfriend who attacked the son at mom's encouragement. The mother lost her son's respect and her weekend visitation. Stepparents need to expect some pushback from teens but need to remain hopeful. Sometimes kids just need to know you are not going to reject them or try to change them. Beware of the other parent's role in the rebellion. Teens may be more difficult following time with their other parent. Loyalty issues and changing affections can be hard for teens to navigate.

Parents and the same-sex stepparent can become important allies in the stabilization of a family. A remarriage can create an extended family that includes ex- spouses who are still primary parents. Teens are most damaged when both families engage in warfare. Friendly interactions at teen events or during shared holidays take the sting out of having two families to contend with. An occasional friendly meeting with all parents to discuss the best interests of the children can be helpful tool in preventing misunderstandings, conflicts, and teen manipulation. Get a mediator if necessary.

Sometimes stepparents may try and develop a relationship with their stepchild as a friend or ally. It is important to keep adult/child boundaries in place. Some important rules for stepparents:

- Never offer alcohol or drugs to your stepteens or their friends. If you suspect or know about drug use, inform the parent.
- Do not keep secrets from their biological parent. This is different from confidences. A confidence may be that your stepdaughter likes a boy in her class. A secret is that she is sneaking out at night to see him.
- Don't side with a teen against their biological parent.
- Don't undermine the biological parent's discipline.
- Don't snoop in the teen's room.
- Don't ridicule a teen's fashion, hair, or weight.
- Don't let a teen manipulate in you exchange for acceptance.

There are times when a stepparent can be a useful ally or confidant. Stepmothers can help a girl deal with her physical changes or needs. Stepfathers may help a boy understand his feelings about his sexual needs. Be careful not to usurp a biological parent's role. Stepparents can be helpful in developing a teen's self-worth. Compliments or encouragement from a stepparent can mean a lot (teens know parents have to say that). Stepparents can be mentors or teach teens new skills or interests. There are many ways in which an adult and teen can find common interests or enjoy time together. Make the stepparent position a gain not a loss.

Stepsiblings come from parental remarriage and can be different ages and sex. Some stepsiblings live in the same households while others only interact on weekends or holidays. Many initially get along well as they are in the same situation and often more focused on the new stepparent relationship. As Papernow (2013) points out:

> Some stepsibling relationships become intimate and nourishing. Others add more stress to the challenge for children. "We are family now" may be the adults wish but not the child's reality. If stepsiblings don't like each other or rub each other the wrong way, help them maintain some space from each other. (p. 58)[10]

Teens may struggle more when their stepsiblings live full time with their non-residential parent. There is a sense of competition for their parent's attention. Non-residential parents need to build in alone time with their visiting children. Custodial parents need to help new teens feel welcome. All parents should be cognizant of sibling interactions. Help mediate conflicts. Other issues to look out for are bullying or sexual attraction. Intervene without taking sides. Protecting a biological child is natural but may not be helpful to their adjustment. Give stepsiblings time to negotiate their own relationship.

Summary

Divorce during one's adolescence creates a myriad of emotional and behavioral reactions. Parents are key to an adolescent's adjustment. Management of the parents own divorce reactions are helpful in the family's adjustment. Consideration of the adolescent's needs are tantamount to a workable custody arrangement and parenting plans. Always allow for adjustments as adolescents age and their needs change. Teens will need parental support in dealing with difficult and often scary emotions.

Creating a stepfamily takes time, patience, and planning. Start slow and think about all the individuals involved. Respect individuality, make room for everyone, and create new family traditions. Allow everyone to have a role and value in the family.

Stepfamily relationships should be flexible and allow for growth and change. Don't get tied up in stereotypes about stepparents. Forget the need to be like any other family. Find your own unique identity as a family. Make the wedding a joining of family members not just the couple. However, don't forget to be a couple and spend time on the marital relationship.

As stepparents, be respectful of roles and responsibilities. Sometimes closeness doesn't become easy until the teen becomes an adult. Allow stepsiblings to develop a relationship in their own ways. Don't give up too soon. Many stepfamilies take years to stabilize. Most are worth the effort.

7.

Why Am I Still Dealing with This?

Impact on Adult Adjustment

It wasn't until I was struggling through my own personal attachments as an adult that the fallout from my parent's breakup began to become apparent.

—Stephanie Staal, *The Love They Lost*[1]

The numerous studies on the long-term impact of parental divorce show conflicting results. Adults from divorced families do not differ significantly from their non-divorced peers.[2] When differences are detected they usually relate to psychological well-being and attitudes toward marriage. All life experiences, particularly those during the adolescent years, impact the development of adult personality. Parental divorce is a traumatic process that unfolds over several years, and the stresses associated with the process directly affect development.

The type and degree of this impact depends on a number of factors: interparental conflict before and after the separation, style of parenting, socioeconomic changes, the parent–teen relationship, an individual's temperament, and degree of social support. Areas of impact seen in adulthood include educational attainment, career choices, financial attitudes, social adjustment, attitudes toward love and commitment, family relationships, and emotional well-being. Many teenagers "believe that the negative effects of divorce on adolescents are underestimated" (p.325).[3] Most adults, when asked about their parents' divorce, will share their pain and anger about their experience; very few feel they came away unscathed.

Adult Choices

Academics and Career

The middle and high school years (ages 12-18) are complicated and challenging. Classes are less personal with a myriad of academic expectations. Divorce during adolescence has been shown to result in lower grades, lower standardized test scores, and a higher dropout rate.[4]

One possible reason for this is parental involvement; divorcing adults have less time and energy available for supervising and encouraging schoolwork. Time constraints can also limit a single parent's direct involvement with their teen's school (parent conferences, school events, graduation planning) and extracurricular activities. Adolescents, especially younger ones, still need homework supervision and help with more difficult papers and school projects. Studying for a test while parents are fighting isn't easy. Completing projects when time and resources are split between two households is challenging. One teenage client with feuding parents stated that his father would not allow him to do any schoolwork while he was at his home. He reported that his father complained that homework took away his son's visitation time and that he could do his homework after returning to his mother's house on Sunday night.

For older teens, a decline in family stability can impact not only grades but also the steps necessary for getting into college and making career choices.

The instability and emotional turmoil of divorce can interfere with a teenager's attitudes toward and interest in school and college. Preparation for college begins in the junior year with SAT testing, college visits, and scholarship applications. These activities need parental involvement and financial support. A 2018 study by Devor, Stewart, and Dorius found that young adults from divorced families were less likely to obtain a college degree and even less likely to obtain a post-baccalaureate degree.[5] This finding held true even when taking into account a variety of factors such as parental encouragement and financial support. It can be surmised that the stress of parental divorce has a negative correlation with college attendance for many adolescents.

What is known is that parental involvement and post-divorce family stability can be positive factors in the teen's academic accomplishments and future career choices.[6] Parents who emotionally and financially support college attendance are more likely to have adolescents who achieve success in this arena.

For some divorced families, financial means for college are in question. Previously earmarked college funds may be needed elsewhere and non-custodial parents may be unwilling to help pay for college. In some states there is the possibility of financial support past age 18, but most states still do not include this in divorce agreements. A strained non-residential parent–teen relationship can preclude financial assistance for college. Even with scholarships and part-time jobs, college is an expensive undertaking that is easier with some parental assistance.

College provides adolescents with an opportunity to thrive outside of the family drama. The social and educational experiences allow a young adult to develop emotionally without assuming all of the complex adult responsibilities that will eventually follow. Older teens may struggle with college when part of their focus is still on their family difficulties. Divorce during the early adolescent years allows an opportunity for the restructured family to stabilize, making the adjustment to college easier. A close, positive relationship with one or both parents is important to the teen's college adjustment. On the positive side, teens from chaotic homes may be better at staying focused and studying despite the noise and activities going on around them. Dealing with changing residences on a regular basis can help a teen learn to be prepared and organized, traits that are helpful in adulthood. While students with divorced parents may handle the educational aspects of college well, issues may surface in other areas.

Beth and Amy were college freshmen at a college approximately three hours from their homes. Both girls came from families whose parents had divorced during their early adolescence. Beth lived with her mother, had younger siblings, and had irregular visitation with her father. Beth's parents had a contentious relationship and divorce. During the week, Beth's mother called frequently to complain about her unhappiness and anger at her ex-spouse. Beth went home over the weekends to spend time with her mother and siblings. Beth's grades began to drop, and she started going home earlier on Fridays and not returning until her first class on Monday morning. She could not stop worrying about her mother and being angry at her father. By the second year, Beth had dropped out to return home, stating that her mother needed her. She got a job at Macy's and moved back into her mother's home, paying rent.

Amy's parents were less conflicted and made more of an effort to leave their kids out of their disagreements. They shared custody, with Amy feeling free to spend time with both parents. Initially, Amy went home on the weekends but her parents reassured her that they were doing well and encouraged her to get socially involved at school. Amy joined the school newspaper and started to make new friends. She soon started staying at school several weekends a month and spent the other weekends equally between her parents. Amy thrived academically and socially.

The differences between the girls were their family situations and their own personal strengths. Beth's family could not let her disengage from the family dynamics and, in essence, sabotaged her success at school. Beth did not focus on her own needs and interests, letting her family situation override her college life. Amy continued to stay connected to her family but had their support to get involved in campus life and pursue her educational ambitions. Amy found independence and a sense of achievement through her college experiences.

College is not the only path to life satisfaction and a sense of achievement. Acquiring a job or studying a trade can be stabilizing and satisfying for teens who have struggled with their parent's divorce. Joining the armed forces may be a good choice for some teens. Being in the military provides financial security, self-discipline, a sense of belonging, educational opportunities, and career options. For families with lower socioeconomic status, teens may forgo college for immediate job acquisition and financial stability. Older teens may bypass college, as they want to be independent of the family as soon as possible. Some teens are encouraged to move out after high school for financial or other reasons. Parental support for a stable job, training for a trade, or being in the military allows young adults to find their sense of accomplishment.

Career choices are the culmination of a teen's interests and talents, parental encouragement and support, and financial ability to pursue their choices. Adolescents may be lacking in awareness of possible career choices and opportunities. Parents are instrumental in a teen's choice of occupation when they provide information, encouragement, and support. Disapproval of certain career choices can interfere with a teen's occupational interests. Parents and relatives may be role models for occupational choices. In some cases, adolescents opt for a career that they believe brings them the love and approval of their primary or even an estranged parent. A stay-at-home mother may enter the work force and her new career presents her children with a role model for working and succeeding. A helpful teacher or therapist may spark an interest in that career field. Other teens may avoid certain careers as their experience during the divorce left them with a distaste for a particular career, perhaps the lawyer they believed mistreated their mother. Another possibility is that parentified teens may seek a career that allows them to remain in the caregiver role. Careers such as physician, social worker, or childcare worker allow an adult to continue in the caretaker role that they assumed in their family.

Divorce may limit the amount of time and monetary support a parent can provide after high school. Adolescents who found that divorce resulted in family financial deficits may opt for a career that provides a stable and regular paycheck. Some teens may feel the need to help support their financially-strapped parent. Some teens may leave home as soon as possible to find a job that pays well, foregoing their career dreams. While parental divorce may alter or delay an individual's career options or choice, most adults go on to establish themselves in their respective occupations. The experience of divorce can teach important work skills such as determination, flexibility, problem-solving, negotiation skills, self-reliance, and organizational skills.

Financial Attitudes

Financial adjustments are a component of divorce. Families may need to shift their lifestyles and spending habits. Single parents may not be able to provide funds for electronics, cars, or the latest fashions. Conflict between parents over money rarely goes unnoticed by teens. Non-residential parents may use money as a means of connecting to and even manipulating the teen's affections. For many adult children of divorce, there is a direct line between their financial experiences in their divorced families and their own attitudes toward money. Some will spend excessively as a way of denying the money issues that caused their family pain. Others are frugal, as they learned during the divorce that money is important to stability and happiness. There are entitled young adults who come to equate love with money and then come to expect their job, friends, and romantic partners to pamper them and provide monetary support. These spoiled adults are easily dissatisfied with their jobs and relationships, as money does not equal love or happiness.

Adults in relationships may end up dealing with conflicts over money that resemble those witnessed in their families of origin.

Children of divorce often feel they need to have separate financial accounts. Some adults have trouble trusting a partner with their finances. Watching a non-custodial parent spend lavishly on themselves or their second family while their custodial parent struggles financially may result in teens seeing money as a luxury to be enjoyed or as a source of fear and insecurity. Adolescents who witnessed battles over child support may end up feeling that they were a burden or unworthy. This feeling can create a need to be financially independent so that no one else has to pay their way. They may also struggle with spending money as they watched a parent carefully allot so much per month for necessities. These adults may have difficulty accepting gifts or spending anything extra on themselves. Saving for a rainy day (or a divorce) is a necessity for many adult children of divorce. In *The Love They Lost (2000)*, Staal writes:

> After growing up in an uncertain world of broken promises, fallible parents, and economic ambiguity, money offers the best bet for security. Money we can depend on in a way that we can't rely on people; money we can see and touch; money makes us independent. (pp. 92-93)[7]

Adult Characteristics

Adult characteristics and personality are developed from the innate temperament of an individual, life experiences, and specific choices. During adolescence, characteristics are developed, tried out, stabilized, and eventually ingrained into the adult personality. When a family upheaval occurs during this time, changes in the adult developmental trajectory are inevitable. It is not possible to elucidate all of the possible ways divorce can impact a teenager's future personality development. Some of the negative characteristics seen in young adulthood may persist into later adulthood.

Other adults develop more of their own strengths as they move away from the divorce effects to experience their own life events. Many adolescents are able to manage the changes in their families with little disruption to their individuation and identity development. Adult life experiences can diminish or intensify the effects of trauma experienced during high-conflict parental divorce. Recognition of possible divorce impacts can help adult children of divorce make choices that offset the negative outcomes.

Negative Characteristics

Negative characteristics that can evolve from difficult divorces include self-centeredness, entitlement, low self-worth, aggressiveness, and cynicism. Adult children of divorce may become overly emotional or stilted. Some lack depth and engage only superficially with others. Others need to manipulate or control situations and people. Most of the negative characteristics are the result of interparental conflict, changes in residences and lifestyles, and loss of closeness with a parent. Negative adult emotions and characteristics may develop as a protection from difficult emotions.

Anger is often front and center in the process of divorce. Interparental conflict can result in increased anxiety and anger in adolescent family members. Residual teenage anger can evolve into an adult characteristic in several ways. An angry teenager is not unusual, but an angry adult is a different situation.

Angry adults are judgmental, confrontational, cynical, negative, and volatile. Their anger can play out with spouses, children, co-workers, friends, and even strangers. Adults may be unaware of the reasons behind their anger; many believe they have moved past their family's divorce issues. Yet the underlying anger that pervades their interactions stays with them. Many of the men who have carried their adolescent anger into adulthood believe they are "tough guys" who simply don't allow anyone to take advantage of them. Like the childhood bully whose aggression masks their pain and insecurities, these adults unconsciously protect themselves.

Witnessing or being drawn into the ongoing conflict between parents can result in a tendency to think cynically. Generalized negative thinking may develop during the stressful changes inherent in divorce. "Life isn't fair." "You can't trust people." "Why go, I won't have fun." "No one at work will like my idea." "This relationship won't work out." These adults often expect the worse. They may feel the need to manipulate or control people and situations in order for their life to remain predictable and to protect themselves from hurt. This thinking can pervade an adult's life and keep them from taking a chance on opportunities and experiences.

Loners and Avoiders

Social behaviors and attitudes that begin in adolescence often extend into adulthood. When an adolescent finds the feelings associated with parental divorce intense and overwhelming, emotions may be downplayed or suppressed. High-conflict interactions between ex-spouses can be frightening, even for teenagers. Teens may respond by denying feelings, isolating in their room, or staying away from home. This tendency in adolescence can become an ingrained response in adulthood. Believing that unacknowledged feelings are less painful or easier to deal with, these adults become stoic and unemotional.

Some adults look easygoing or laid-back, but still waters run deep. Unexpressed feelings can surface as physical manifestations or depression. Others hold on to their emotions until they overflow and explode with out-of-character reactions. Many of these adults may avoid emotion-laden experiences and relationships, becoming loners. Loners find a quiet predictable life safer than the chaos they lived with in their family of origin.

In some situations, being aware and empathetic of another's emotional state can become problematic; a need to recognize and avoid conflict can make for overly cautious interactions and a tendency to please others. Poor resolution skills and conflict avoidance may be learned in response to interparental disagreements. These adults lack the ability to compromise or negotiate effectively when differences arise with co-workers, friends, and significant others. Watching parents denigrate each other can create adult disrespect for authority and give tacit approval for being rude or dismissive with others. Social interactions with peers and co-workers require understanding, tact, and socially-responsible behavior.

Mental Health Issues

Lack of a social support system, repression of emotion, and unresolved childhood issues can result in adult psychological disorders. In a 2019 meta-analysis on the long-term consequences of parental divorce the authors found that "A significant association between parental divorce and every aspect of mental health was found" (p. 107).[8]

Mental health issues that can arise during adulthood, with possible links to earlier adolescent issues, include depression, generalized anxiety disorders, and adjustment disorders. Younger adolescents may have experienced more life transitions, had difficulty maintaining closeness with their non-residential parent, and had fewer coping mechanisms to protect them from the psychological distress brought on by divorce. Older adolescents spend fewer years dealing directly with the family's problematic changes and conflicts. They may have been more individuated, had a stronger social support system, and had a variety of coping skills.

However, it is not only the number of stress-laden years that impact adolescents but also the intensity of the family conflicts. Higher conflict divorces that continue beyond the separation are more likely to impact adult personality development. Young adults dealing with combative parents may have more difficulty separating their own lives from that of their families. The possibility of remarried parents can create additional issues for adults, such as which parent to spend Christmas with or where to sit divorced parents at their wedding, may create loyalty issues and stress.

Emotional well-being may be established in adolescence and extend into adulthood. According to a 2019 study by Schaan et al.:

> There was an increased risk for depression in adults of divorced parents compared to non-divorced parents … Young adults of divorced parents reported more overall chronic stress (especially more social isolation, chronic worrying and work discontent), more loneliness, and

> attachment anxiety and avoidance during their everyday life. (p. 96)[9]

Depression is a genetic, chemical, social, and psychological condition marked by sadness, fatigue, hopelessness, and irritability. Loss of interest in everyday activities, trouble sleeping, and suicidal ideation are also indicators of depression. Research has indicated that during adolescence, living with parental conflict and having a parent with depression were predictive of adult depressive episodes.[10] Lack of effective coping skills can interfere with individuation and healthy emotional development. An older woman I worked with struggled with depression for years. During one of her sessions, she started sobbing: "I can't believe that here I am at 65 crying over my parents' divorce."

Even for adolescents who struggled with contentious parents, mental health issues are not inevitable. There are protective factors that are linked to better psychological health in adulthood: a close relationship with one or both parents, a social support system, and the individual's ability to adapt and cope with change. Emotional well-being in adulthood is possible when adults make a concerted effort to create a balanced and healthy life for themselves. Dealing with issues related to their parents' divorce, perhaps in therapy, is beneficial in moving past the impacts.

Adult alcohol and substance abuse is often associated with earlier use in adolescence. Divorce is a stressor that can lead to use of alcohol and drugs by teenagers. Parental use of substances in order to cope are models for adult use. A 2008 study by Thompson Jr. et al. found that "adolescents who experience parental divorce/separation may be more vulnerable to developing alcohol dependence than those from intact households, and that this vulnerability may be increased when parental alcohol problems are present as well" (p. 268).[11] Not all teenage use of substances continues into adulthood, some actually develop healthy drinking attitudes or avoid all use of substances.

Problematic behavior that started as a response or coping mechanism, for example, joining a gang or criminal mischief, in adolescence may extend into adulthood in the form of criminal activity or connection with negative social groups. Teens struggling with family discord may be vulnerable to negative peer influences. Delinquent activities may be short-term expressions of anger or insecurity. Negative or inappropriate adolescent behaviors may not continue into adulthood and may instead encourage a young adult to "pull it together" and create a life for themselves that is more emotionally healthy and satisfying than their life during their parents' tumultuous marriage.

Self-perception

Self-worth, self-esteem, and self-efficacy are parts of individual temperament that have their beginnings in childhood and are tested in adolescence. Adulthood finds shifts in an individual's perception of self, but many of the roots are established earlier. Teenagers are often noted for their fluctuating moods and self-perceptions. Adolescents continually judge themselves against parental and peer expectations. Shifts in day-to-day self-esteem may occur but self-worth usually remains fairly stable. A positive self-perception is developed through achievements, parental accolades, and peer approval. A stable home life is a key component of self-worth.

Negative self-perceptions are more likely in highly contentious family situations in which teens feel rejected or criticized. When a family is fraught with conflict, upheaval, and loss, a teen's self-esteem and self-worth are impacted. When teens (in particular younger teens) are drawn into their parents' conflicts, there is a distinct possibility that their self-concept will suffer. These teens feel less capable and feel caught between their parents. They may see themselves as judged by their peers for being children of a broken home. Young adults drawn into parental loyalty conflicts without the ability to make constructive changes feel frustrated and inadequate. As adults, they may carry feelings of abandonment and insecurity, and struggle with self-worth. Adults may incorporate these negative self-perceptions throughout life, even seeking out relationships and situations that validate this negative belief about self.

The relationship between a teen and their non-residential parent is an important aspect of self-worth that can extend into their adult sense of self. Despite the appearance of independence, teens need attention and acceptance from both parents. When a parent distances themselves emotionally or physically, their adolescent feels unlovable and worthless. These young adults may suffer from insecurity about their abilities and their value to others. As adults, they may come to expect the same reactions from others in their life, even when confronted with statements to the contrary.

Positive Characteristics

Adolescents who manage these significant life changes while maintaining a positive self-image ultimately become more confident, independent, and self-assured. Many strengths developed during adolescence will be carried into adulthood. Positive outcomes can include becoming resilient, empathetic, self-sufficient, and organized.

Resilience and independence are two characteristics that many adults will identify as a positive outcome of working through a family divorce. Adults gain independence when they are able to separate their parent's marital issues from their own relationships and accomplishments. Healthy adults develop their own sense of identity separate from their parents' expectations.

Unfortunately, some young adults' identities are a form of defensive reaction to parental demands. Achieving a healthy sense of self in spite of parental criticism is a laudable accomplishment. For some adults, the additional responsibilities (housework, care for siblings, self-care) associated with their parents' divorce allowed them to feel needed, capable, and independent. Positive parental support for the teen's ability to manage the changes can be incorporated into their adult self-perceptions. "I can handle life's changes." "I am good at being organized." "I am an important member of my family." "I can make good decisions for myself." School achievement or extracurricular activities may have been satisfying outlets for teens and can create a focus and drive to succeed in adulthood. Traits such as determination, ambition, creativity, and self-efficacy are possible in adulthood and success in careers and relationships equates with self-worth.

Overall, adult children of divorce develop in ways that are heathy and satisfying. It is more difficult when parents are unable to separate their problems and unhappiness from their adult children's lives. In some families, the adult child becomes the more mature and reasonable person and establishes interactional norms that provides for more amiable family gatherings. Healthy adults often set ground rules for family interactions that sidesteps the earlier family drama. When parents accept the limits set by their adult children, these adults feel empowered. It may take time and a little effort, but a successful, fulfilling, and happy adult life is possible for all adult children of divorce.

Family Ties

Family is forever but the intergenerational relationships shift, rebalance, or dissipate over time. There may be ongoing family issues associated with the divorce. One of the primary goals of young adulthood is to achieve independence from family. The transition to adulthood brings a number of changes to the parent–child relationship. Some adolescents only spend a few years with divorced parents before leaving for college or out on their own. Others delay moving out, believing that they are needed at home. Parents, especially after the loss of a spouse from divorce, may struggle with letting their teen differentiate. Some teens find themselves having to pull away through anger or indifference. Others feel compelled to stay out of loyalty to a distressed parent. Some may move into adulthood kicking and screaming, as past issues can create tight bonds. Eventually adulthood is achieved.

Opinions and Choices

One important right of adulthood is the opportunity to develop one's own opinions and choices. Often young adults begin to look more objectively at their parent's failed relationship. They may request more information about the problems that led to the divorce. They may be critical of their parents' choice to divorce, especially when the reasons were not obvious to them.

However, as adults, they are better able to understand relationship struggles, allowing for more acceptance of their parents' choices. Some may continue vilifying one parent and protecting the other. As young adults live through their own joys and struggles, they can process their parents' actions in a more mature, insightful way. Even if they continue to struggle with their parents' choices, as an adult they can develop relationships in ways that sidesteps their earlier family drama. They may realize that their parents could have been a lousy spouse but a still be a good parent. These changes in perception can be instrumental in establishing their adult relationships with their peers, parents, and siblings.

Another important skill in adulthood is learning how to handle ongoing interparental conflict. Just because an adolescent is maturing doesn't mean that the parents will become more reasonable. Some parents hold on to anger and need for their children to do so as well. When parental alienation has occurred, a shift in family relationships may be met with anger and an escalation of conflict between parents and between parent and young adult. Alienating parents need their children's attention and for them to share in their anger. Young adults may choose to reconnect with their non-residential parent, pushing their alienating parent to feel abandoned, similar to the emotions created by the divorce. This can trigger tremendous conflicts and shifts within the established family system. Custodial parents may have a hard time letting go of their older adolescents and will struggle to maintain control. In these situations, young adults may need to assert their autonomy and set limits with parents.

Since Deanne's parents divorced when she was 13 she had lived primarily with her mother with only sporadic visits with her father. The divorce was contentious with ongoing interparental conflict, both parents sending hateful messages through Deanne. The relationship between mother and daughter was complicated. The mother was critical and demanding, and Deanne was understandably rebellious. At 18, Deanne moved out, living with several roommates and working full-time. Her mother remained overly involved, often calling and criticizing Deanne's life choices.

At 19, Deanne informed her mother she was moving in with her boyfriend, who was seven years older. Mom exploded. Conversations about Deanne's decision ended up with screaming and slammed phones. Finally, Deanne refused to answer her mother's calls and instead sent an email stating: "I know that you have been calling but, I will not be answering or calling back. I have thought long and hard about our relationship and cannot allow you to repeatedly mistreat me, call me names and ridicule my choices. I am also no longer willing to side with you against my father. I will not argue with you about my feelings, my relationships, or my decisions. I love you as my mother but cannot deal with our relationship as it is. I am an adult and deserve to be treated with respect as an adult and as your daughter. If you feel you can communicate without trying to control or criticize me, please let me know." Bringing this note with her, Deanne's mother came into therapy to address her relationship with her daughter and to finally resolve her anger at her ex-husband.

Adult Individuation

Individuation is the process of establishing a life independent of parental control. Healing from the stress of parental divorce is an integral part of the maturation process young adults go through on the road to adulthood. As young adults establish their own separate lives, relationships with parents change. However, family connections continue to be a central part of an adult's life.

In reality, very few adults sever ties with their parents. Young adults who felt loved and supported leave home with a better chance of adult well-being and success. Adults who were close to their parents usually remain positively connected and develop appropriate relationships, which may become even closer when grandchildren enter the picture. There is also a greater chance for ongoing connection to extended family. Relationships with the non-residential parent (usually the father) that have become distant may evolve into a mutually respectful, warm connection.

Divorce during the teenage years create changes in parent–teen interactions. When the relationship was contentious, problems may continue even as the teen moves into adulthood. When the teen was a parent's major source of companionship and support, their individuation may not be achieved without parental pushback. Parentified teens may become attached to the caretaker role and continue, as adults, to take care of their parent. Some parent–child relationships remain stagnated and daughters, in particular, feel obligated to continue seeking and following "mother's advice." The classic mother-in-law issues stem from this need of the mother to be involved and stay in control. Some adults remain interdependent with their parents.

Young adults can choose how much contact to have with either parent. Efforts may be made to repair some of the family estrangements that were a by-product of the divorce. Young adults begin to set limits with parents and require parents to behave civilly. These issues are most prominent when planning family activities including holidays, graduations and weddings. There will always be parents who refuse to be in the same room with their ex-spouse or the ex's new spouse. Over the years, I have worked with many young adults who have agonized over planning their graduation or wedding due to the inability of their parents to behave maturely during shared family events. Some young adults cave to the parent's demands, while others stand up for themselves. These limits set by adult children may bring a new sense of peace within the entire family system.

Relationships with parents and extended family are typically lifelong and many of the issues from the divorce resolve over time. When divorced parents are able to behave in a friendly, or at least in a civil, manner the potential for healthy parent–adult relationships are more likely. According to Dr. Ahrons (2007), "The ability of divorced parents to establish a supportive, low-conflict parental unit reverberates throughout the family even some 20 years later" (p 60).[12] Parents usually want their adult children to escape the legacy of their own failed relationship.

Fathers

The parent-teen relationships that established around the separation and divorce have long-term implications. Research has found that the father–child (especially non-custodial) connections suffer the most following divorce and on into future interactions.[13] Fathers who did not remain actively involved may find that their adult children are disconnected from them. This disengagement can lead to an adult relationship that is superficial at best. Unacknowledged tension often lingers in these interactions. Adults have less of a need to include their father in their lives. When the father was perceived as the initiator or the cause for the divorce, he is more likely to remain in a negative light. To offset these perceptions, the father needs to actively pursue a connection with his kids. Unfortunately, some fathers resign themselves to remaining on the periphery of their adult children's lives. Distant parents may be included in life events but remain somewhat on the sidelines. Adults who remain only minimally involved with their father may also spend less time with paternal grandparents and extended family members.

Adolescent and adult relationships with one's father may be different for daughters than sons. Daughters are typically closer to their custodial mothers than their fathers. Additionally, female young adults may find a satisfying male relationship which decreases their need to be close to their fathers. Anger at their father for the divorce or as a protection of their mother may preclude closeness. According to Nielsen (2011) in a review of research on divorced fathers and daughters: "Even years after their parents' divorce, when they get married or have children, daughters are less likely than sons to reconcile or become closer to their dads" (p.79).[14]

Parents who have made a point of staying connected (even with underlying tension between exes) are more likely to enjoy a relationship with their adult children and their families. Some fathers became more involved post-divorce (often due to shared parenting arrangements) and see their efforts rewarded in their adult relationships with their children and grandchildren. Adults disengaged from their fathers due to parental conflict, distance, or remarriage may be open to re-establishing a connection. Maturing perceptions, ability to forgive past mistakes, desire for a connection, and ease of access allow for improved relationships. Sometimes this reconnection takes years and many important moments or events are missed. Adulthood brings opportunities to improve the father bond. However, this renewed relationship requires effort on both sides. Extended family and stepfamily will benefit from these renewed connections as well.

Stepfamilies

Remarriage of a parent may affect family connections. According to research, most families experience the remarriage of one or both of their parents within 20 years of the divorce and children struggle most with their father's remarriage, especially when he remarries within the first few years.[15] Fathers who remarry are less likely to have close relationships with their adult children. These men have created new lives and families for themselves and may not make enough of an effort to stay connected to their adult children. Remarriage of a custodial parent allows for more connection with a stepparent and any stepsiblings. In any stepfamily, relationships can be friendly or strained.

In adulthood, stepparent interactions can be more relaxed, equal, and respectful when the issues of authority or loyalty do not come into play. My father's wife is easier to accept than my stepmother. Some stepparents disengage from the children of a previous marriage. When reconnection does occur, it is often due to the effort of the father, the maturity of the adult child, and the support of the mother. Mother's encouragement and acceptance of a close father–child bond goes a long way toward a healthy relationship with the father and stepfamily.

Aaron's mother had become pregnant at an early age and did not marry his biological father. When Aaron was five, she married Lionel and he assumed the role of father for Aaron. Aaron was 17 when his parents divorced. The divorce was amiable and Aaron was allowed open access to both parents. He denied having any strong issues with the divorce and continued doing well in school and socializing with his close friends. One year after the divorce, his dad started dating and was married within nine months. During Aaron's freshman year at college, Lionel had another son with his second wife. Aaron expressed excitement and came to visit during his school holidays.

Over the course of the next few years, Aaron's visits and phone contact declined. Following his graduation, Aaron distanced himself even further from his father. Eventually, Aaron stopped all contact with his father and his new family, despite their efforts to reach out to him. Aaron's mother also had limited contact with her son. After 10 years, in which Aaron traveled and tried out different careers, he re-contacted his father. The absence was not directly addressed and the current relationship is comfortable and close. It seems likely that Aaron was unaware of the extent of the loss he felt about his father's remarriage and the birth of a biological son. As Aaron got older, he was able to appreciate the circumstances of his parent's divorce and was able to reconnect with his father.

Siblings

Siblings can be best friends, biggest rivals, or worst enemies. In families who divorce during a child's adolescent years, the bond between siblings has been established and the children in the family weather the changes together. Siblings have one important shared experience: what it was like to go through a parents' divorce. This creates a unique bond that allows for mutual understanding and support. Simple rivalries and conflicts over the computer or bathroom use become less important when your family feels like it is falling apart. Siblings may perceive and experience their parents' struggles in very different ways and this can alter previously established relationship patterns. They may become divided by the changes and loyalty issues that arise during divorce. There is also the possibility of competition for parental attention.

Also, siblings may take on different roles within the family. Teenagers may provide care and support for younger brothers and sisters. When older siblings leave home to escape the divorce drama, the younger ones may resent being left behind to manage the situation alone. Custodial agreements may have children living in different homes. When teens reside with different parents, their loyalties are strained and their closeness is diminished.

The patterns of sibling interaction created during family upheaval can extend into adulthood. In most families, adult siblings naturally drift apart as college, jobs, and peer relationships become priorities. Holidays, family reunions, and periodic phone calls become the point of contact. It may be that the time between visits or phone calls does not negate the connections. "We are family and our ties will always bind us together." Siblings may continue to be a support system for each other through adulthood. When parents remarry, become ill, or need physical care due to aging, this support system can make these life issues easier to handle. Ultimately, no one else understands how difficult it can be to deal with parents and two separate households over issues such as holiday visits, wedding plans, or aging parents.

Unfortunately, the same issues that create sibling bonds can result in a distant or contentious relationship in adulthood. Without being aware of the reasons, siblings can develop conflict styles similar to what they witnessed in their parents' fights. These conflict styles can contribute to difficulties in adult sibling interactions. Even small issues can cause a resurfacing of sibling rivalry. Younger siblings may expect their older ones to continue taking care of mom or dad, as these roles were established during the divorce.

It is common for sibling conflicts to reignite when elderly parents become ill or questions of inheritance come into play. Who bears the biggest responsibly for mom's care or has to help dad when he doesn't want any help? Sibling (including stepsibling) conflict during the illness or funeral of a parent have been the topic of a number of Hollywood movies: *The Family Stone, Knives Out, This is Where I Leave You,* and *Death at a Funeral,* to name a few. Where old conflicts resurface, distancing and superficiality are more likely to occur than family solidarity. However, some sibling relationships weather the stresses of divorce, and their family ties are solid and enduring.

Stepsiblings may come into play as parents remarry. Stepsibling relationships vary based on many factors, such as relationship with stepparent, age and sex of the children, and reaction of biological parent to the new spouse. Sometimes remarriage occurs while the adolescent is still living at home. The addition of new family members is rarely welcomed. When the parent married the person that they were involved with before the divorce, the new stepparent and their children may be initially rejected. For some, time allows for a less hostile response to the new family members. Usually, when stepsiblings enter each other's lives as adults, the interactions are cordial and even friendly.

Family gatherings may bring adult children together, and the sense of family develops over time. Stepsiblings may form friendships based on shared experiences and shared relatives. More often than not, adults think of stepparents as their mother's or father's spouse and stepsiblings are family by way of marriage, not biological family. Half-siblings are frequently considered as biological family. There is more of a likelihood that a sibling bond will form with half-siblings. Children born of one's biological mother usually results in a stronger connection. The adults' relationship with their half-sibling may also depend on the quality of the relationship with the stepmother (the child's mother). In any situation, the interactions between siblings, whether biological, half, or step depend on the attitudes and behaviors of the parents. Another source of potential conflict between stepsiblings is money (support or inheritance). It is difficult to balance all the relationships and issues in blended families.

Love and Marriage

Our early perceptions of love, commitment, and marriage come from observing the interactions in our home and those of extended family members. Numerous studies have connected family experiences during childhood and adolescence with future relationship attitudes and behaviors. Parental divorce during the teenage years is particularly impactful as this is the developmental period in which peer romantic connections begin to take the place of family relationships. According to a study by Doucet and Aseltine (2003), "Troubled family relations in childhood beget troubled adolescent dating relationships, which are linked with less satisfying and more conflictual marital relationships, thus reflecting a great deal of continuity in intimate relationships over the life course" (p. 837).[16]

Many factors go into the development of adult relationships. Attitudes about love, commitment, marriage, and divorce are learned from family interactions. How love is expressed is conveyed by parental statements and examples. Parental conversations teach communications styles. Problem solving and conflict resolutions skills are modeled during parental arguments. Peers, especially during the teenage years, are also powerful sources of information about love and commitment.

Adolescent Relationships

Dating during adolescence is the precursor to adult relationships. Not all teenagers date, but all interact with peers at some level. Heifetz et al. (2010) noted that: "adolescents move in a sequence from same-gender friendships to mixed-gender affiliations, to casual dating, and finally, to a dyadic romantic relationship" (p. 367).[17] The shifts in peer relationships may be hastened or delayed due to changes in a family's dynamics. Adolescent dating experiences coupled with witnessing parental interactions become the blueprints for adult relationship attitudes, values, and interpersonal skills.

Teens need and want to believe in love and marriage. Young love is rarely deterred by parental divorce, as teens are often optimistic about their own chances at love. Adolescents, even when faced with intense parental arguments, believe that they can have a relationship that is better than that of their parents. The initial infatuation in a new relationship can provide temporary excitement and healing from family pain and loss. Adolescents do not simply accept the messages about love and marriage from parents, they question and form their own perceptions. Teens will form judgements about their parent's actions and may learn from their mistakes. Some may become cynical about love. Still, love is often blind when it comes to teenagers and romance.

Lessons learned from family interactions can replicate in adult relationships. When parental conflict was front and center, the insights were not always positive. Teens may be frightened by the prospect of a relationship, while others escape into early dating and sexual activity. Peer connections become a substitute for family attention and affection. Older teenagers may rush into marriage or cohabitation, perhaps as a replacement family for their own fractured one. Sexual behavior may be a means of feeling wanted and cared about. Adolescents can become cynical about love and seek out superficial interactions and sexual activity without true commitment (i.e., friends with benefits).

Teenage males who witnessed father aggression may become controlling and physical with their girlfriends. Females may become compliant in order to avoid conflict. Absent or disengaged fathers can create a void in a daughter's life that a male peer (especially an older one) can temporarily fill. Overwhelmed by the family dysfunction, some teens may withdraw from peers and find other activities, (academics, video games, or sports) that are easier to focus on and do not require emotional attachment.

This is not to say that healthy teen relationships are not possible, but when one's parents are continually fighting, love seems more like hurt than joy. Teens and young adults witnessing parental conflict while experiencing young love are living with conflicting life messages. Parents fight, then make-up. "I hate you" is often followed by "don't leave me." Adolescents may try to work through a difficult family experience is by creating their own relationship in which the outcome is happier and the control is theirs.

Attitudes and Expectations

Young adulthood (18 to late 30s) is an important period in the development of independence and interpersonal relationships Establishing a career path, becoming financially independent, and finding a life partner all take place during this time. The choices and decisions made at this juncture are critical to one's life satisfaction. Establishing a romantic relationship is complicated; emotional needs, attitudes about marriage and divorce, and communication styles are all aspects of this decision. High-conflict parental interactions may create difficulties in adult relationships. Low-conflict exchanges model healthy conflict resolution techniques, even if the couple opt to divorce. Most adults engage in a number of relationships before making a major commitment of marriage or cohabitation. Ideally, these early connections provide lessons that help an adult find a long-term relationship that is healthy and enduring.

Most adolescents move into adulthood believing that they will find love. However, messages gleaned from parental conflict and divorce can derail adults in their search. Factors that are salient to adult relationships include beliefs about commitment, ability to trust, communication styles, conflict resolution, and partner choice. Some of the struggles faced by adults is poignantly written by Staal (2000):

> I have built up walls, rarely letting anyone in. I have trouble living in the moment, and often find myself wondering how things will end, even as they start. I feel like the rug could be pulled out from underneath me at

> any time. I constantly set up tests, forcing people to prove their love to me. I have a hard time trusting. I am scared of being abandoned. (p. 6.)[18]

Young adults may not trust their own ability to commit to a long-term relationship and may instead experience a number of short-lived encounters. These adults will step away as soon as conflict develops, believing that most problems are unresolvable. Other young adults rush into commitment, as they need and want the stability that they lost with their family's breakup. Early marriages, often borne out of the need to escape family conflicts, may not hold up over time. Life brings stress, such as job loss, health issues, and children. It can be difficult to work through difficult situations while maintaining a close connection.

Adult children of divorce love with caution and are quick to identify weaknesses or flaws in others. Disagreements, even minor ones, can lead to the breakup of a relationship with the belief that worsening conflicts are inevitable. Adult children of divorce may become hypervigilant in relationships. They are able to discern problem areas early, but perhaps too easily. They are often critical of other's flaws and end up overreacting to small issues. They may question the possibility of love and are slow to say I love you. They lack trust in others and easily become insecure for no apparent reason. If infidelity was an issue in their parent's marriage, they may be jealous and irrational. Others may need constant reassurance of their value.

> *Fran (45) and George (50) married after a nine-month courtship. Both had previously married young and were recently divorced. Fran had two daughters, ages 22 and 27, and*

George had a son, age 30, and a daughter, 27. All the children were out of the home and established in their own lives. The couple came into therapy two months after getting married. The request for therapy came from George who had been in therapy with his ex-wife and found the process helpful. Fran had never seen a therapist.

George felt that the couple had a regular and satisfying sexual relationship. However, in the last month, as their sex life started to slow down from its initial frequency, Fran became quite upset if George did not want to have sex. George insisted that he was still attracted to his wife but did not feel a need to make love as often as Fran. George acknowledged: "I am getting older and sometimes I just want to come home from work, eat, and watch TV." The more George declined sex, the more upset Fran became, to the point of becoming hysterical. Fran felt that George's loss of interest in sex meant he was no longer in love with her. At some level Fran understood that her fears and reactions were irrational, but she worried that George was pulling away from her, even worse, having an affair. George insisted that neither were true.

In discussing their backgrounds, Fran shared that her parents had divorced when she was 14, after her mother discovered that her father had been having an affair. The divorce was contentious and Fran's mother repeatedly badmouthed her father and his "destruction of their lives" due to his infidelity. Her father married his girlfriend and Fran saw very little of him following the divorce. Fran also acknowledged that her first marriage was the result of her pregnancy at age 18, and that she and her husband stayed together for the sake of the children. Her first marriage felt safe but lacked emotional and sexual connection. Fran was afraid of feeling abandoned in her current marriage. For her, sex was proof of love.

When divorce was unexpected, adults may live with the fear that any issue, no matter how small, might lead to divorce. Many adult children of divorce doubt their lovability. Romantic relationships offer the opportunity to feel cared about, the chance for stability, and a way to avoid loneliness. Adult children of divorce can be cautious and selective in their choice of partners, hoping to avoid the mistakes their parents made. They may be attracted to partners who come from stable families, appear established in their careers, and are sound financially. These adults may enter into love with a sense of caution but also one of hope. They may strive to have a committed relationship that solves the issues that their parents could not overcome. If parents dealt with their conflicts in a reasonable and respectful manner, their children are more capable of managing disagreements in a healthy manner. Unfortunately, most divorcing couples are unable to be reasonable when so much is at stake.

Adults may learn from what they perceived to be their parent's problematic behaviors and consciously engage in actions that support a good relationship. Listening more, limiting criticism, allowing each other space, showing affection, and sharing housework are just some of the techniques that support a healthy relationship. Many of these issues may have been the source of conflict in their family of origin. Wanting to avoid the same sources of unhappiness can help adults identify negative relationship behaviors and avoid some of the problems that led to their parent's divorce.

Attitudes about Marriage and Divorce

Prior to their parent's decision to separate, most teenagers gave very little thought to the issues of commitment, marriage, and divorce. Perceptions of these issues surface as young adults begin to develop their own romantic relationships. Young adulthood, from age 18 to late 30s, is the time when individuals select careers, become economically independent, and engage in significant peer relationships. There is a natural draw toward romantic encounters. Even when adolescents witnessed the breakup of their parents, they enter adulthood with the hope of finding a satisfying romantic connection. Adult children of divorce (ACD) may be aware of the problems that can result in failed marriages but still believe in love. According to Miles and Servaty-Seib (2010), "Most researchers have found that ACD have similar expectations to have marriages that are high quality … and enduring" (p. 211).[19]

High-conflict parental interactions and contentious divorces can create biases against marriage but do not preclude young adults from entering into relationships. Some may balk at marriage, especially in their 20s, when their parents' divorce is a fairly recent and vivid memory. Some end up in committed monogamous relationships or cohabitate, as this feels safer than marriage. Others marry early with a belief that their love is stronger than that of their parents. Others marry as a way of denying or disproving the messages learned from their parents' failed marriage.

As teens were observers of their parents' marital interactions, they are also paying attention when their divorced parents date or remarry. In a research article by Collardeau and Ehrenberg (2016), they reported that:

> Parent's romantic experiences after parental divorce could be more influential to children than the biological parent's romantic relationship: highly successful second marriages could restore beliefs in lasting romantic relationships, while successive divorces could potentially reinforce negative attitudes toward marriage. (p.25)[20]

Often children do not pay attention to the marital aspects of their family's interactions. Separation or divorce brings those issues into the forefront for adolescents, thus they are more likely to observe and examine parent's post-divorce romantic encounters. Healthy, loving relationship modeling can be reaffirming for young adults, allowing them to believe it was not love or marriage at fault but a mismatch of personalities between their biological parents.

Despite a societal perception that adult children of divorce are more likely to divorce themselves, the research is contradictory at best. Society no longer considers divorce as shameful or a response of last resort. When divorce provides a family with relief from the stress of fighting parents, it is seen as a viable option to serious or unresolvable marital problems. Young adults are often optimistic about their own marriage, but also more willing to consider divorce as an option. At times, this tendency to view divorce as a viable solution to a couple's issues may preclude couples from making a concerted effort at resolving issues. When in doubt—leave, is not always the best option for couples and families.

Children of divorce may want to avoid and protect their own children from the trauma of a contentious, protracted divorce.

Often memories of difficulties witnessed during the divorce of one's parents create a lifelong fear of re-creating the same experiences in one's own marriage. Trepidation surrounding divorce trauma can push some adults to stay and make it work, perhaps waiting till the kids are out of the house to separate. Others leave at the first sign of problems and before having children. High-conflict divorces can lead to the children later repeating the same patterns. Mistakes that are not acknowledged are often destined to be repeated. Sadly, some adults employ some of the same negative tactics in their own marital breakups, especially if they perceived them as successful. Hiding assets, refusing to compromise, badmouthing the ex-spouse, and hiring high-priced, aggressive attorneys are all learned tactics in divorce.

Divorce can be a viable solution when relationships encounter problems that are unresolvable, particularly in marriages where physical abuse or ongoing substance abuse is occurring. Adults who decide to terminate the relationship may handle the divorce in a healthier manner that avoids many of the problematic behaviors seen in their parents' divorce. Contentious parental divorces teach the children in the family what to avoid and how to get through a breakup with civility and dignity.

Partner Choice

Parental divorce can have an impact on why someone chooses a particular partner. Children of divorce may seek out a partner who will care for them and provide the stability that was disrupted in their adolescence. They may avoid individuals who appear too needy, as they do not wish to take on the responsibility of another distressed adult (as they did with their parent). Some adults believe they are not capable of taking care of others, as they were overwhelmed by the responsibilities placed on them as teenagers. Parentified adolescents may seek out a partner who allows them to continue in their caretaker role. Individuals resembling the parent that the young adult holds responsible for the divorce are avoided. Others may seek out a replacement for a parent who became distant. Many adult children of divorce want a partner who will help them create a stable, loving, and long-lasting relationship. Hopefully, one's adult partner choice breaks the intergenerational transmission of divorce. It is not being a child of divorce that creates problematic and ultimately failed marriages but the interactions and commitment between the couple.

Relationship Skills

Relationship skills, also referred to as interpersonal skills, are the ways in which people communicate, resolve differences, express emotion, and share themselves. Many relationship skills are learned in childhood and adolescence, as family interactions are models. Open communication, empathy, active listening, caring, responsiveness, affection, validation, and honesty are all skills vital to the development and maintenance of a relationship, whether with friends, coworkers, or significant others.

Good communication skills include honesty and active listening and should allow for open sharing of thoughts and ideas. Conflict resolution skills include respect for different opinions, ability to disagree about an issue, and compromise. Conversations should avoid attacking the other person. All of these skills are particularly salient to healthy romantic relationships. Problem-solving and conflict resolution skills may have been poorly represented in one's family of origin. Negative conflict skills that may be learned from parental discord are verbal abuse, disrespect, withdrawal of affection, and refusing to discuss issues.

Men and women from divorced parents may have acquired different relationship skills while observing parental interactions and conflicts. In adolescence, modeling of interaction styles may occur between father and son or mother and daughter. In a 2002 study with college students, differences in male and female communication styles affecting marital stability and longevity were found. Mullett and Stolberg (2002) reported that in relationships in which the woman came from a divorced home, the couple reported significantly lower levels of intimacy, more problematic communication styles, and mutual avoidance of conflict.[21]

The same did not hold true when the male was from a divorced family or when both were from intact families. It may be that teenage girls are more sensitive to parental discord and carry the learned behaviors into their adult relations. It may also be the case that female communication and conflict styles dominate the couple's relationship interactions. Males are more likely to withdraw from persistent conflicts or complaints. Recognition of communication and conflict styles help couples navigate issues that surface in the course of a long-term relationship.

Relationship skills provide the basis for a healthy marriage and many children of divorce actively work on developing their relationship techniques after having witnessed poor interpersonal skills in their family of origin. Some adults may need life experiences to learn what skills are necessary for healthy adult connections, be it with friends, co-workers, or spouses. Over the years, I have worked with many adults from divorced families who experienced a brief marriage in their late teens to early 20s and then went on to have successful marriages. Partner choice is an important component in long-term happy relationships. Often older adults have been able to work through their family's divorce issues, learn from their mistakes, and form loving and enduring relationships. Just as some adults go through several job changes until finding a career that is satisfying, the right choice in life partner may take time. Adulthood brings the opportunity to create a relationship that is inherently different from that of feuding parents. Marriage and parenthood are major responsibilities and should be entered into with maturity and the reasonable expectation that it will take work to maintain a successful partnership.

Summary

When adolescents move into adulthood, they bring certain ideas, attitudes, interests, and dreams. Some of these dreams may have been tainted by the drama of their parents' divorce. Children of divorce may tackle adulthood with a bit of trepidation. Many young adults are resilient and make their own way in the world. They go to school, obtain a job, and develop a career. They become financially independent and move out on their own. They make friends and learn new ways of interacting and loving. They seek out new adventures and social experiences. Peer connections can lead to lifelong relationships. They may love with caution, but they do love and make commitments to share their lives with another. Healthy communication and conflict management skills are developed. When relationships do not work out, the partners can leave with dignity. Some drag the past out and put it on display but most rewrite the scripts they learned at home. Parental divorce can teach these young adults that a new beginning is possible. These adult children of divorce stay connected to their family of origin but allow themselves to set limits that respect their adult status. Adult children of divorce are resilient. Divorce is not an adults' legacy, but it is a viable choice.

Endnotes

Chapter 1

1. Weedn, F. & Weedn, L. (2001). *To take away the hurt*. San Rafael, CA: Cedco Publishing.
2. Baldwin, B. (2008). A win-win situation. *In Canfield, J., Hansen, M.V., & Hansen, P. (Eds) Chicken soup for the soul. Divorce and recovery: 101 stories about surviving and thriving after divorce (pp 17-19).* Cos Cob CT: Chicken Soup for the Soul Publishing.
3. Ahrons, C. (1994). *The good divorce. Keeping your family together when your marriage comes apart.* New York: Harper-Collins.
4. American Sociological Association. (Aug. 2015). Women are more likely than men to initiate divorce, but not non-marital breakups. *Science Daily*, retrieved from www.sciencedaily.com/releases/2015/08/150822154900.htm.
5. Ahrons, C., (1994).
6. Sbarra, D. A., Emery, R. E., Beam, C. R., & Ocker, B. L. (2014). Marital dissolution and major depression in midlife: A propensity score analysis. *Clinical Psychological Science*, 2 (3), 249-257.
7. Leopold, T. (2018). Gender differences in the consequences of divorce: A study of multiple outcomes. *Demography*, 55(3), 769-797.
8. Wallerstein, J. S., & Blakeslee, S. (2003).*What about the kids: Raising your children before, during, and after divorce.* New York: Hyperion.

Chapter 2

1. Pitzele, S. K. (1991). *Surviving divorce: Daily affirmations*, Deerfield Beach, FL: Health Communications.

2. Nielsen, L. (2014). Shared physical custody: Summary of 40 studies on outcomes for children. *Journal of Divorce and Remarriage*, 55, 613-635.
3. Marquardt, E. (2005). *Between two worlds: The inner lives of children of divorce.* New York: Three Rivers Press
4. Nielsen, L. (2018). Joint versus sole physical custody: Children's outcomes independent of parent-child relationships, income, and conflict in 60 studies. *Journal of Divorce and Remarriage*, retrieved from DOI:10.1080/10502556.2018.1454204.
5. Pearce, L. D., Hayward, G. M., Chassin, L. & Curran, P. J. (2018). The increasing diversity and complexity of family structures for adolescents. *Journal of Research on Adolescence*, 28(3), 591-608.
6. Livingston, G. (April 2018). The changing profile of unmarried parents. *Pew Research Center.*
7. McCutcheon, V.V., Agrawal, A., Kuo, S. I-C., Su, J., Dick, D.M., Meyers, J.L., Edenberg, H. J., Nurnberger, J. I., Kramer, J. R., Kuperman, S., Schuckit, M.A., Hasselbrock, V. M., Brooks, A., Porjesz, B., Bucholz, K. K. (2018). Associations of parental alcohol use disorders and parental separation with offspring initiation of alcohol, cigarette, and cannabis use and sexual debut in high-risk families. *Addiction*, 113 (2), 336-345.
8. Cookston, J.T. (1999). Parental supervision and family structure: Effects on adolescent problem behaviors. *Journal of Divorce and Remarriage*, 32 (1/2), 107-122.
9. Breivik. K., Olweus, D., Endresen, I. (2009). Does the quality of parent-child relationships mediate the increased risk for antisocial behavior and substance use among adolescents in single-mother and single-father families? *Journal of Divorce and Remarriage*, 50, 400-426.
10. Breivik, K., Olweus, D., (2006). Adolescent adjustment in four post-divorce family structure: Single mother, stepfather, joint physical

custody and single father families. *Journal of Divorce and Remarriage*, 44 (3/4), 99-124.

11. Breivik, K., Olweus, D. & Endresen, I. (2009).
12. Nielsen, L. (2011). Shared parenting after divorce: A review of shared residential parenting research. *Journal of Divorce and Remarriage*, 52, 586-609.
13. Ibid.
14. King, V., Sobolewski, J.M. (2006). Nonresident fathers' contributions to adolescent well-being. *Journal of Marriage and Family*. 68, 537-557. King, V., Sobolewski, J.M. (2006).
15. Fosco, G.M., Grych, J.H. (2010). Adolescent triangulation into parental conflicts: Longitudinal implications for appraisals and adolescent-parent relations. *Journal of Marriage and Family*, 7, 254-266.
16. Afifi, T. D., McManus, T., Hutchinson, S., Baker, B. (2007). Inappropriate parental divorce disclosures, the factors that prompt them, and their impact on parent's and adolescents' well-being. *Communication Monographs*, 74 (1), 78-102.
17. Ibid
18. Videon, T.M. (2002). The effects of parent-adolescent relationships and parental adolescent well-being. *Journal of Marriage and Family*, 64, 489-503.
19. Baumrind, D. (1971). Current patterns of parental authority. *Developmental Psychology Monograph*, 4(1), 1-103
20. Maccoby, E. E., & Martin, J. A. (1983). Socialization in the context of the family: Parent-child interaction. In Mussen, P. H. (Ed.), *Handbook of child psychology*, (pp. 1–101). New York: Wiley & Son.
21. Carlson, J. (2011). *The parent effect: How parenting style affects adolescent behavior and personality development*. Washington D.C.: NASW Press.
22. Hetherington, E. M., & Kelly, J. (2002). *For better or for worse: Divorce reconsidered*. New York: W.W. Norton.

23. Ibid.
24. Carlson, J. (2011).
25. Parra, A., Sanchez-Queija, I., Garcia-Mendoza, M.d. C., Coimbra, S., Oliveira, J. E., Diez, M. (2019). Perceived parenting styles and adjustment during emerging adulthood: A cross-national perspective. *International Journal of Environmental Research and Public Health,* 16 (15), retrieved from 10.339-ijerph16152757

Chapter 3

1. Riera, M. (1995). *Uncommon sense for parents with teenagers.* Berkeley, CA : Celestial Arts.
2. Casey, B.J., Jones, J.M. Hare, T.A., (2008) The adolescent brain. *Annals of the New York Academy of Science,* 1124:111-126.
3. Lansford, J. E. (2009). Parental divorce and children's adjustment. *Perspectives on Psychological Science, 4(2), 140-152.*
4. *Ruschena ,E., Prior, M., Sanson, A.,Smart, D. (2005)* A longitudinal study of adolescent adjustment following family transitions. *Journal of Child Psychology and Psychiatry, 46:4, 353-363.*
5. Fear, J. M., Champion, J. E., Reeslund, K. L., Forehand, R., Colletti, C., Roberts, L., Compas, B.E. (2009). Parental depression and interparental conflict: Children and adolescents' self-blame and cooing responses. *Journal of Family Psychology,* 23 (5), 762-766.
6. Wallerstein, J. S., & Blakeslee, S. (2003). *What about the kids: Raising your children before, during, and after divorce.* New York: Hyperion.
7. Booth, A., Amato, P. R. (2001). Parental predivorce relations and offspring postdivorce wellbeing. *Journal of Marriage and Family, 63, 197-212.*
8. Foa, E., Andrews, L.W. (2006). *If your adolescent has an anxiety disorder: An essential resource for parents.* New York: Oxford University Press.

9. Wallerstein, J. S., Lewis, J.M., and Blakeslee, S. (2000). *The Unexpected legacy of divorce: The 25 year landmark study*. New York: Hyperion.
10. (Spring 2004). Divorce can trigger adolescent and teen compulsive buying. *Baylor Business Review*. Retrieved from http:///findarticles.com/p/articles/mi_qa5431/is_200404/ai
11. Menning, C.L, (2008). "I've kept it that way on purpose" Adolescents' management of negative parental relationships traits after divorce and separation. *Journal of Contemporary Ethnography*, 37(5), 586-618.
12. Lansford, J.E. (2009).
13. Mohi, G. W. (2015). Positive outcomes of divorce: A multi-method study of the effects of parental divorce on children. *The University of Central Florida Undergraduate Research Journal*, 7 (2), 49-62.
14. Frisco, M.L., Muller, C., Frank, K. (2007). Parents union dissolution and adolescents school performance: Comparing methodological Approaches. *Journal of Marriage and Family*, 69, 721-741.
15. Lansford. J. E., (2009).
16. Ibid.
17. Ronen, T.,Hamama, L., Rosenbaum, M & Mishely-Yarlap, A. (2016). Subjective well-being in adolescence: The role of self-control, social support, age, gender and familial crisis. *Journal of Happiness Studies*, 17, 81-104 .
18. Sun, Y.& Li, Y. (2007). Racial and ethical differences in experiencing parent's marital disruption during late adolescence. *Journal of Marriage and Family* 69 (3), 742-762.
19. Ibid.
20. Truit, T.S. (2007). *Surviving divorce: Teens talk about what hurts and what helps*. New York: Franklin Watts.

Chapter 4

1. Warshak, Richard A., (2001). *Divorce poison: Protecting the parent-child bond from a vindictive ex. New York: Regan Books.*
2. Emery, R. E. (2016). *Two homes, one childhood: A parenting plan to last a lifetime.* New York: Avery.
3. Black, B. T. and Sleigh, M. J. (2013). Relations among parentification, parenting beliefs, and parenting behaviors. *Journal of Student Research,* 2(1), 52-57.
4. Wallerstein, J. S., Lewis, J. M., & Blackeslee, S. (2000). *The unexpected legacy of divorce: The 25 year landmark study.* New York: Hyperion.
5. Peris, T. S., Goeke-Morey, M.C., Cummings, E. M., & Emery, R. E. (2008). Marital conflict and support seeking by parents in adolescence: Empirical support for the parentification construct. *Journal of Family Psychology,* 22(40), 633-642.
6. Silva, C. S., Calheiros, M.M. & Carvalho, H. (2016). Interparental conflict and adolescents' self-representations: the role of emotional insecurity. *Journal of Adolescence,* 52, 76-88.
7. Stallman, H. M., and Ohan, J. L. (2016). Parenting style, parental adjustment, and co-parental conflict: Differential predictors of child psychosocial adjustment following divorce. *Behavior Change,* 33 (2), 112-126.
8. Miga, E. M., Gdula, J. A. & Allen, J. P. (2012). Fighting fair: Adaptive marital conflict strategies as predictors of future adolescent peer and romantic relationship quality. *Social Development,* 21, (3), 443-460.
9. Stahl, P. (1999). Personality traits of parents and developmental needs of children in high conflict families. *Academy of Certified Family Law Specialists Newsletter,* 3, 8-16.
10. Miga, E. M., Gdula, J.A., & Allen, J. P. (2012).
11. Felder, R. and Victor, B. (2011). *The good divorce: How to walk away financially sound and emotionally happy.* New York: St. Martin's Press.

12. Michael, K. C., Torres, A., & Seeman, E. A., (2007). Adolescent's health habits, coping styles and self-concept are predicted by exposure to interparental conflict. *Journal of Divorce and Remarriage,* 48, (1/2), 155-172.
13. Harold, G T., and Sellers, R. (2018). Annual research review: Interparental conflict and youth psychopathology: An evidence review and practice focused update. *Journal of Child Psychology and Psychiatry,* 59 (4), 374-402.
14. Afifi, T. D., Schrodt, P. (2003). "Feeling caught" as a mediator of adolescents' and young adults' avoidance and satisfaction in divorced and non-divorced households with their parents. *Communication Monographs,* 70, 142-173.
15. Michael, K.C., Torres, A., & Seemann, E.A. (2007).
16. Simon, V. A., and Furman, W. (2010). Interparental conflict and adolescents' romantic relationship conflict. *Journal of Research on Adolescence,* 20(1), 188-209.
17. Godbout, E. and Parent, C. (2012). The life paths and lived experiences of adults who have experienced parental alienation: A retrospective study. *Journal of Divorce and Remarriage,* 53, 34-54.
18. Darnall, D. (1998) *Divorce casualties: Protecting your children from parental alienation*. Lanham, MD: Taylor Trade Publishing.
19. Baker, A. J. L. and Ben-Ami, N. (2011). To turn a child against a parent is to turn a child against himself: The direct and indirect effects of exposure to parental alienation strategies on self-esteem and well-being. *Journal of Divorce and Remarriage,* 52, 472-489.

Chapter 5

1. Papernow, P. L. (2013). *Surviving and thriving in stepfamily relationships: What works and what doesn't.* New York: Routledge.
2. Nueman, M. G. & Romanowski, P. (1998). *Helping your kids cope with divorce the sandcastles way.* New York: Random House.

3. Nielsen, L. (1999). College students with divorced parents: Facts and fiction. *College Student Journal,* 33 (4), 543-572.
4. Raley, R. K. & Sweeney, M. M. (2020). Divorce, repartnering, and stepfamilies: A decade in review. *Journal of Marriage and Family,* 82, 81-99.
5. Manning, W. D. & Lamb, K. A. (2003). Adolescent well-being in cohabitating, married, and single-parent families. *Journal of Marriage and Family,* 65, 876-893.
6. Manning, W. D. (2015). Cohabitation and child wellbeing. *Future Child,* 25(2), 51-66.
7. Jenson, T. M. (2017). Constellations of dyadic relationship quality in stepfamilies: A factor mixture model. *Journal of Family Psychology,* 31, (8), 1051-1062.
8. Papernow, P. l. (2013).
9. Ibid.
10. King, V. & Boyd, L. M. (2016). Factors associated with perceptions of family belonging among adolescents. *Journal of Marriage and Family,* 78, 1114-1130.
11. Jensen, T. M., Lippold, M. A., Mills-Koonce, R. & Fosco, G. M. (2018). Stepfamily relationship quality and children's internalizing and externalizing problems. *Family Process,* 57(2), 477-495.
12. Carlson, J. E. (2011). *The parent effect: How parenting style affects adolescent behavior and personality development.* Washington, D.C.: NASW Press.
13. Weaver, S. E. & Coleman, M. (2010). Caught in the middle: Mothers in stepfamilies. *Journal of Social and Personal Relationships,* 27, (3), 305-326.
14. Gosselin, J. (2010). Individual and family factors related to psychological adjustment in stepmother families with adolescents. *Journal of Divorce and Remarriage,* 51, 108-123.
15. Papernow, P. I. (2013).

16. King, V., Amato, P. R., & Lindstrom, R. (2015). Stepfather-adolescent relationship quality during the first year of transitioning to a stepfamily. *Journal of Marriage and Family*, 77(5), 1179-1189.
17. Thorsen, M. L. & King, V. (2016). My mother's husband: Factors associated with how adolescents label their stepfathers. *Journal of Social and Personal Relationships*, 33(6), 835-851.
18. King, V. (2009). Stepfamily formation: Implications for adolescent ties to mothers, nonresident fathers, and stepfathers. *Journal of Marriage and Family*, 71(4), 954-968.
19. Burns, C. (2001). *Stepmotherhood: How to Survive without feeling frustrated, left out, or wicked*. New York: Three Rivers Press.
20. Lebey, B. (2004*). Remarried with children: Ten secrets for successfully blending and extending your family*. New York: Batam Books.
21. Hetherington, E. M. & Kelly, J. (2002), *For better or for worse: Divorce reconsidered.* New York: W.W. Norton.
22. Gosselin, J. (2010).
23. Amato, P. R., King, V. & Thorsen, M. L. (2016). Parent-child relationships on stepfather families and adolescent adjustment: A latent class analysis. *Journal of Marriage and Family*, 78(2), 482-497.
24. Jensen, T.M., Lippold, M.A., Mills-Koonce, R. & Fosco, G. M. (2018).
25. Cassoni, C. & Caldada, R. HL. (2012). Parenting style and practices in stepfamilies. *Psychology Research and Behavior Management*, 5, 105-111.

Chapter 6

1. McGhee, C. (2010). *Parenting apart: How separated and divorced parents can raise happy and secure kids*. New York: Berkley Books.
2. Fisher, B. & Alberti, R. 2016. *Rebuilding when your relationship ends.* Oakland, CA: Impact Publishers.
3. Ellis, T.M. (2006). *This thing called grief: New understanding of loss.* Minneapolis: Syren Book Company.

4. Gay, K. (2014). *It happened to me: Divorce, the ultimate guide*. Lanham, ML: Rowan and Littlefield.
5. Fisher, B & Alberti, R. (2016).
6. Weedn, F.& Weedn, L. (2001). To take away the hurt. San Rafael, CA: Cedco Publishing.
7. Fruzzetti, A. E. (2006). *The High Conflict Couple: A dialectical behavior therapy guide to finding peace, intimacy and validation*. Oakland, CA: New Harbinger Publications.
8. Dessen, S. (2011) *What happened to goodbye.* New York: Viking.
9. Riera, M. (2014). *Uncommon sense for parents with teenagers*. New York: Ten Speed Press
10. Papernow, P. L. (2013). *Surviving and thriving in stepfamily relationships: What works and what doesn't.* New York: Routledge.

Chapter 7

1. Staal, S. (2000). *The love they lost: Dealing with the legacy of our parents' divorce.* New York: Dell.
2. Kulka, R. A. (2010). The long-term effects of parental divorce in childhood on adult adjustment. *Journal of Social Sciences,* 35(4), 50-78.
3. Gatins, D., Kinlow, C.R., & Dunlap, L.L. (2013). Do the kids think they're okay? Adolescents view on the impact of marriage and divorce. *Journal of Divorce and Remarriage,* 54, 313-328
4. Sun, Y. and Li, Y. (2009). Post divorce family stability and changes in adolescents' academic performance: A growth-curve model. *Journal of Family Issues,* 30(11), 1527-1555.
5. Devor, C. S., Stewart, S.D., & Dorius C. (2018). Parental divorce, social capital, and postbaccalaurate educational attainment among young adults. *Journal of Family Issues,* 39 (10), 2806-2835.
6. Sun, Y. and Li, Y. (2009).
7. Staal. S. (2000).

8. Auersperg, F., Vlask, T., Ponocny, I. & Barth, A. (2019). Long-term effects of parental divorce on mental health: A meta-analysis. *Journal of Psychiatric Research*, 119, 107-115.
9. Schaan, V. K., Schulz, A., Schauchinger, H., & Vogle, C. (2019). Parental divorce is associated with an increased risk to develop mental health disorders in women. *Journal of Affective Disorders* 257, 91-99.
10. Bohman, H., Laftman, S. B., Paaren, A. & Jonsson, U. (2017). Parental separation in childhood as a risk factor for depression in adulthood: A community- based study of adolescents screened for depression and followed up after 15 years. *BMC Psychiatry*, 17, retrieved from https//doi.org/10.1186/s12888-017-1252-z
11. Thompson, R., Lizardi, D., Keyes, K. M., & Hasin, D. S. (2008). Childhood or adolescent parental divorce/separation, parental history of alcohol problems, and offspring lifetime alcohol dependence. *Science Direct*, 98, 264-269.
12. Ahrons, C. R. (2007). Family ties after divorce: Long-term implications for children. *Family Process*, 46(1), 53-65.
13. Ahrons, C. R., and Tanner, J. L. (2003). Adult children and their fathers: Relationship changes 20 years after parental divorce. *Family Relations*, 52, 340-351.
14. Nielsen, L. (2011). Divorced fathers and their daughters: A review of recent research. *Journal of Divorce and Remarriage*, 52, 77-93.
15. Ahrons, C. R. and Tanner, J. L. (2003).
16. Doucet, J. and Aseltine, R. H. Jr. (2003). Childhood family adversity and the quality of marital relationships in young adulthood. *Journal of Social and Personal Relationships*, 20 (6), 818-842.
17. Heifetz, M., Connolly, J., Pepler, D. & Craig, W. (2010). Family divorce and romantic relationships in early adolescence. *Journal of Divorce and Remarriage*, 51, 366-378.
18. Staal, S. (2000).

19. Miles, N. J., Servaty-Seib, H. l. (2010). Parental marital status and young adult offspring's attitudes about marriage and divorce. *Journal of Marriage and Divorce,* 51, 209-220.
20. Collardeau, F. and Ehrenberg, M. (2016). Parental divorce and attitudes and feelings toward marriage and divorce in emerging adulthood: New insights from a multiway-frequency analysis. *Journal of European Psychology Students*, 7(1), 24-33.
21. Mullett, E. and Stolberg, A. L. (2002). Divorce and its impact on the intimate relationships of young adults. *Journal of Divorce and Remarriage,* 38(1-2), 39-59.

Acknowledgments

I have always had a love for working with adolescents and their families. Teens often come into therapy reluctantly even angrily, but once engaged their ability to share, search within themselves, and grow emotionally has always impressed me. My interest in sharing some of their stories and struggles helped to shape this book.

In 2011, I fulfilled a dream and goal of mine with the publication of my first book *The Parent Effect.* Writing a second book was always in the back of my mind but as everyone knows, life happens and some tasks take the back burner. In 2016, I retired and moved to beautiful Oregon. Then Covid hit and I found myself with the time needed to research and write this work. As with any book, this was not a solitary endeavor. Many family members and friends offered their support and input. Let me take a few minutes to share my appreciation.

First and always my encouragement came from my husband of almost 40 years, Pat. When I met Pat, he was a divorced man with a teenage son. I was a little apprehensive about becoming not only a wife but a stepmother. My stepson and even his mother made the transition easy and a newly formed family was created. I offer my thanks to David for making me feel welcome. During the writing of this book, Pat read every word, sometimes several times over, and corrected spelling, typos and strangely worded sentences. He offered a layman's view of what was of concern to families dealing with divorce. We have had a life filled with many memorable highlights, laughter, and easy everyday connection. I love you and look forward to more adventures with you.

To my beautiful daughter-in-law, Rachael Hyde, who offered editorial advice on my earlier chapters and helped develop my writing style with her well thought-out suggestions. Thank you, and I love you.

To my dearest friend, Lynne Watkins, MSW. You have always been there for me since we started graduate school together. Your encouragement meant a lot to me. To my new friend and neighbor, Lyn W., who read many of my rough drafts, offering helpful questions and suggestions.

To my friends, Barbara, Carolyn, Dianne, Julie, Pamela, and Tracy (my magnificent 7 support group). We started our support group in January Of 2020, making the Covid journey easier to bear and created lifelong friendships. Each of you shared your stories, offered editorial suggestions on my initial drafts, and celebrated the completion of this work. Thanks to all of you for being in my life.

No book moves forward without the work of a good editor. For me that person was Kimberly Lausten. Kimberly helped define my words so that they flowed easily, reworked sentences that were a little too long, and corrected any tense (past vs present) issues that may have arisen. Kim was gracious and patient throughout the whole process. Thanks Kim. It was a pleasure working with you.

I also extend my gratitude to Kathryn Galán at Wynnpix Productions for helping me get through the last hurdle (and my most frustrating stage), by formatting and indexing my manuscript. Kathryn untangled all my file formatting mistakes and then uploaded all of it so that an actual book could be produced. Your knowledge was there at a critical time and you were a lifesaver.

Finally, I express my appreciation to all the adolescents and their families that I worked with over the years. Many of you remain my heart. While your stories and names have been altered for privacy purposes, be assured that your struggles will now help others deal with the realities that divorce and change bring to a family.

About the Author

Joanne E. Carlson, MSW, is a psychotherapist with over 40 years of experience working with adults and adolescents. She had a special interest in treating adolescents, working with them in a variety of professional settings since 1977. Joanne often worked closely with family law attorneys providing therapy (including court-ordered) for teenagers and families dealing with difficult divorces and stepfamily issues.

Joanne graduated magna cum laude from the University of Texas at Austin with a B.A. in Psychology in 1976 and received her MSW from the University of Houston in 1980. Prior to starting her private practice in 1986, Joanne was a program director at an inpatient adolescent psychiatric hospital from 1980 to 1986. She was on the board of directors of the Houston Advocates for Mental Health in Children (now Child Advocates) from 1995 to 2000 and served as a consultant for the special education department of the Fort Bend Independent School District from 1991 to 1993. She has been a member of the National Association of Social Workers, Fort Bend Psychological Association, and the Houston Group Psychotherapy Society. Joanne is the author of *The Parent Effect: How Parenting Style Affects Adolescent Behavior and*

Personality Development (2011, NASW Press). She was the founder of the *Southwest Adolescent Treatment Alliance* and spearheaded the 2013, 2014, 2015, and 2016 Adolescent Treatment Conferences held in Houston, Texas. Joanne was active in providing community and professional workshops on a variety of topics throughout her career.

Joanne is now retired and living in Bend, Oregon with her husband of almost 40 years (plus a sweet dog and snarky cat). The couple have two adult children, a son, married and living in Portland and a special needs daughter who lives in Bend. The Carlsons are avid travelers (when feasible with the current situation). She currently volunteers at Healing Reins, an equine therapy program. Additionally, Joanne is actively involved in facilitating support groups for retired women. During the last year, she fulfilled her dream of writing a second book that allowed her to share her knowledge about the struggle adolescents face during family divorce and in their adjustment to parental remarriage.

Index

CPSIA information can be obtained
at www.ICGtesting.com
Printed in the USA
BVHW051951130722
641715BV00001B/31

9 780578 359175